A Labour History of Ireland
1824–1960

Emmet O'Connor

GILL AND MACMILLAN

Published in Ireland by
Gill and Macmillan Ltd
Goldenbridge
Dublin 8
with associated companies in
Auckland, Budapest, Gaborone, Harare, Hong Kong,
Kampala, Kuala Lumpur, Lagos, London, Madras,
Manzini, Melbourne, Mexico City, Nairobi,
New York, Singapore, Sydney, Tokyo, Windhoek
© Emmet O'Connor 1992
0 7171 1619 0 hardback
0 7171 2016 3 paperback
Print origination by
Seton Music Graphics Ltd, Bantry, Co. Cork
Printed by Colour Books Ltd, Dublin

A catalogue record is available for this book from the British Library.

Contents

Abbreviations and Notes
on Terms

1. ORGANIZATIONS, NAMES, PLACES, AND TITLES

ASE	Amalgamated Society of Engineers
ASRS	Amalgamated Society of Railway Servants
ATGWU	Amalgamated Transport and General Workers' Union
CIU	Congress of Irish Unions
CoIU	Council of Irish Unions
CP	Communist Party of Ireland
FUE	Federated Union of Employers
ICA	Irish Citizen Army
ICTU	Irish Congress of Trade Unions
ILLA	Irish Land and Labour Association
ILP	Independent Labour Party
ILP(I)	Independent Labour Party (of Ireland)
ILPTUC	Irish Labour Party and Trade Union Congress

IRA	Irish Republican Army
IRB	Irish Republican Brotherhood
IrLP	Irish Labour Party
ISRP	Irish Socialist Republican Party
ITGWU	Irish Transport and General Workers' Union
ITUC	Irish Trade Union Congress
ITUCLP	Irish Trade Union Congress and Labour Party
MP	Member of Parliament
NAUL	National Amalgamated Union of Labour
NIC	Northern Ireland Committee
NILP	Northern Ireland Labour Party
NUDL	National Union of Dock Labourers
NUGGL	National Union of Gasworkers and General Labourers
NUR	National Union of Railwaymen
OBU	One Big Union
PUO	Provisional United Trade Union Organization
RIC	Royal Irish Constabulary
RWG	Revolutionary Workers' Groups
SDF	Social Democratic Federation
TD	Teachta Dala

TUC	Trade Union Congress
UK	United Kingdom
UTA	United Trades' Association
WUI	Workers' Union of Ireland

2. SOURCES, ARCHIVES, AND LIBRARIES

BPP	British Parliamentary Papers
NA	National Archives
NLI	National Library of Ireland
PROL	Public Record Office, London
QUB	Queen's University, Belfast
TCD	Trinity College, Dublin
UCC	University College, Cork
UCD	University College, Dublin

NOTES ON TERMS

1. The Irish Trade Union Congress was founded in 1894, added 'and Labour Party' to its name in 1914, changed its title to the Irish Labour Party and Trade Union Congress in 1918, and reverted to the original in 1930. Throughout this period it was also known simply as Congress.
2. Unionists—that is, supporters of the political Union with Great Britain—whether members of the Unionist Party or not, have been capitalized to avoid confusion with trade unionists.
3. Regional descriptions like Ulster, the north, the south are used for pre-partition Ireland. Thereafter, the North is

capitalized or referred to as Northern Ireland, the six counties or Ulster as seems appropriate. The south or 26 counties is also referred to as the Free State or Saorstát Éireann from 1922 to 1937, Éire from 1937 to 1949, and then as the Republic.

A NOTE ON MONEY VALUES

In the period covered by this book, the Irish currency was either sterling or—in the case of the Free State/Republic after 1922—a sterling equivalent tied to the British pound and broken into exactly similar units.

The basic unit of currency was the pound (£1), which was composed of twenty shillings (20s.). Each shilling was, in turn, composed of twelve pence (12d.).

Wage rates in excess of £1 were conventionally expressed in shillings, so that it was more usual to write 25s. instead of £1. 5s. 0d., or 26s. 9d. instead of £1. 6s. 9d. I have followed that practice in the text when noting rates of pay. In other cases, however, I have set out monetary amounts in the more usual way for pre-decimal currency, using the £ s. d. symbols in full.

Preface

The first historians of Irish labour, Thomas Brady, James Connolly, J.M. McDonnell, and W.P. Ryan, emerged in the 1900s. They set out to offer a radical version of the people's past and, in the process, to re-interpret the evolution of the nation in a socialist way. Since the 1920s, that tradition has been continued by republican and Marxist pamphleteers and the modern reader is indebted to the Cork Workers' Club, *Historical Reprints Series* for making it accessible. Academic studies of Irish labour have appeared from J.D. Clarkson, *Labour and Nationalism in Ireland* (1926) onwards. Up to the 1970s however, publications came at lengthy intervals and the authors were almost all based abroad. Academics challenged the assumptions of the Connolly school, but underscored its fundamental approach in examining labour in the light of nationalism.

The founding of the Irish Labour History Society in 1973 and the annual publication of *Saothar* brought significant changes in the philosophy and content of scholarship. Radical history gave way to the narrower concept of labour history, understood as the study of labour organizations and movements and of the politics and consciousness produced by these forces. The bibliography now includes a substantial corpus of monographs, together with a few general surveys. Recent years have seen a commendable output of commissioned trade union and trades council histories. The effect of this flowering of interest has been to establish the integrity of the subject and disentangle labour from the seemingly all pervasive story of nationalism. At the same time, labour history has become detached from the wider picture, and monographic research, of its nature, has not been able to construct an overall framework or chart the course of events.

The book is intended as an introduction for the general reader and a synopsis for the specialist. The basic concern has been to outline the course of labour history, to illustrate the different phases of its chronology, and to determine the forces behind its development. Secondly, it has tried to unravel the puzzles on which there is contention in the published texts. Some of these are general questions. Why was labour marginalized in disaffected nineteenth-century Ireland? Why did nationalism present such a problem in the twentieth century? Why does Ireland have a strong trade union movement and a stunted political left? How have unions survived the divisions in Northern Ireland? Others are more specific. Why did labour not contest the 1918 election? Was the Trade Union Act (1941) motivated by nationalism? Why did Congress split in 1945? Finally, the book seeks to broaden the definition of labour—a focus on conventional trade unions is hopelessly inadequate for nineteenth-century history, for example—and to set it within the context of mainstream political and economic trends, partly in the hope that scholars in the field will edge away from their current compartmentalized outlook and re-integrate with Irish historical consciousness.

There are two themes in this book. The first, which needs no explanation, is the evolution and efficiency of labour structures, labour policy, and radical politics. The second is colonization. From the 1830s onwards, the trajectory of trade unions was determined by economic colonization; their mentality was dictated by reaction to economic and political colonization. During the 1890s, a more complex factor was added to the equation as trade union organization and values were themselves colonized. Attempts to iron out this legacy, sometimes visionary, sometimes neurotic, became inter-meshed with the class theme from 1908 to 1959.

University of Ulster,
Magee College,
July 1992

Acknowledgments

The research for this book is based largely on the work of others, and my greatest debt is to them, especially the late Professor Charles McCarthy, Professor John Boyle, and Dr Fergus D'Arcy. Colleagues in the Irish Labour History Society offered inspiration and advice, and I must thank Peter Collins, Francis Devine, Noirin Greene, Gerry Moran, and Sarah Ward-Perkins for help with sources. I am obliged to Donal Nevin for details on the origin of *Trade Union Information*, to Jim Mullen and Charlie Spillane for technical assistance, to Fergal Tobin and Gill and Macmillan for commissioning the book, and to the staffs of the National Archives, the National Library, Magee College Library, the University of Ulster at Coleraine Library, the Public Record Office, London, the British Library, and Waterford Municipal Library. Remaining mistakes are my own. The University of Ulster kindly granted sabbatical leave to expedite research and, as ever, I am grateful to staff and students at Magee for their encouragement. The book is dedicated to Bridgett O'Connor.

Prologue

After the partial conquest of Ireland in the late twelfth century, the royal charters granted to Anglo-Norman towns provided for trade representation in companies of guilds, which brought journeymen and masters together for the good of their common calling.[1] The guilds were built into the political system. After serving seven years indenture to a member of the guild, a journeyman would be made free on payment of levies to the guild and the Corporation. He might then petition for the freedom of the city and the right to vote. In their economic role, the guilds enjoyed powerful privileges. They could regulate working practices and apprenticeships. Through the Corporations and the assizes they could set wages and prices. Guilds also had a benefit function, and from their sundry incomes could assist needy brethren in distress. In theory, the arrangement offered a mutual accommodation to masters and men, while subordinating both to the common welfare. The guild protected the masters by controlling wages; it protected the employment and wages of journeymen by restricting apprenticeships and fixing prices; and it protected the consumer by maintaining standards of workmanship. Similarly, the Corporation and the courts could prevent any one guild from abusing its privileges, while guildsmen collectively as enfranchised citizens could ensure that adminstration served the interests of commerce. In practice, the system depended on a careful management of the labour supply to restrain either masters or men, on the journeymen's prospects of becoming masters, on medieval social values, and on an economy based on trade rather than industry, and geared to a sheltered local market.

During the seventeenth century control of the guilds passed back and forth between Catholics and Protestants. Protestants introduced the status of lay, or quarter brother—so called because their membership had to be renewed each quarter—for Catholic guilds-men, permitting them to carry on their trade under certain disadvantages. Catholics restored their liberties under the brief tenure of the Jacobite corporations. The Williamite settlement final-ly secured a Protestant ascendancy. As sectarianism intensified under the Penal Laws, the guilds became instruments of Protestant privilege and levied quarterage payments on Catholic merchants, shopkeepers, and artisans. Their lingering claim to serve the com-mon good of the trade was compromised too by the increasing exclusion of Protestant journeymen from guild membership and the municipal franchise. The guilds' traditional purpose was in any case in decline. With the emergence of capitalism, liberalism, mech-anization, and specialization, parliament began to dismantle or appropriate historic guild functions. Faced with the collapse of old mechanisms of trade regulation and the alienation of the masters, journeymen combined in defence of their working interests.

The process of combination was under way from the 1670s in Dublin, and the early eighteenth century in the provinces.[2] Gen-erally combinations were formed for specific purposes such as the defence of wages, hours, and conditions, the regulation of appren-ticeships, or the exclusion of 'colts'—men who had not served a proper apprenticeship—or strangers, and disbanded if the demands were met, though in Dublin, Belfast, and Cork some combinations evolved into societies. As traditional forms of control corroded, employers turned to parliament for help. From 1729 onwards, a series of acts was passed making combinations of masters or men illegal, though masters had little fear of prosecution. For the most part the acts had no greater effect than the battery of local statutory restrictions governing industrial relations, and depended in any case on local law enforcement. Demands for tougher acts mounted regardless. In 1780, the Irish Grand Committee for Trade concluded that combinations were becoming a threat to prosperity, and noted that 'committees of trade' among weavers, butchers, coopers, tailors, and shoemakers were spreading throughout Ireland. That same year, 20,000 artisans paraded in the Phoenix Park in protest at the introduction of legislation allowing masters to employ as many apprentices as they wished, and providing penalties for absence from work or for violence resulting from combination.

By the 1780s, regular combinations of Dublin artisans were func-tioning under the guise of mortality or friendly societies, and public meetings were lawful for purposes of petitioning parliament. At least three other aggregate assemblies of the Dublin trades occurred, in 1789, 1814, and 1824.[3] Dublin societies were certainly the best organized in Ireland and evidently secured a degree of toleration from the masters and magistrates. In Belfast, combination was most developed among cotton weavers, who were able to negotiate wages with their masters in 1792, 1810, and 1818.[4] Cork's Common Council had an act passed through parliament in 1764 'to prevent unlawful assemblies and combinations of artificers, journeymen, apprentices, labourers and manufacturers [which] have of late greatly increased in the said city . . .'[5] Waterford coopers were active in combination from the 1770s, though there is no evidence of a regular society behind them.[6] Generally speaking, provincial artisans were more likely to operate in clandestine conditions and face blacklisting, imprisonment or fines should they resort to combination. Records of strikes, or 'turn outs', appear with increasing frequency from the second half of the eighteenth century, and there were general turn outs in the early 1800s when wartime inflation spurred unskilled operatives to became more prominent in combination. Unable to enforce a scarcity of labour by regulating apprenticeships, these men processed their wage claims through anonymous, threatening letters. Aside from employer hostility, use of the law and social inequality, the routine brutality of living conditions gave industrial relations a jagged edge. Violence to property, and sometimes to masters or scabs, made turn outs notorious up to the 1840s.

Genealogically, it is valid to locate the origins of modern trade unionism in the continuum of guilds, combinations, journeymen's associations and latter-day craft unions. Yet trade unionism is not a tradition, but an idea; one which requires no antiquity or arcane ritual to be adopted at any time by any group of persons. The importance of craftsmen lay not in devising, or even sustaining, the concept, but in creating its most formative expression. The core tenet of its creed, collective action for defence of common interests, was familiar to peasant movements as much as to artisans. Tensions caused by economic expansion and massive demographic pressure on the land holding system produced various regional peasant movements between 1761 and the Great Famine, with discontent most persistent in the west midlands, the south, and south east. Some groups lasted for months, others for years, and the first such, the Whiteboys, gave its name as a generic term for subsequent agitations. Described by one contemporary as 'a vast trades' union for the protection of the Irish peasantry', White-boyism usually sprang up to challenge a specific grievance; it offered no programme of general reform.[7] But once in being, Whiteboys often addressed a wider range of issues, such as tithes, tolls, taxes, rent increases, the price of conacre, renewal of leases, land division, employment of strangers, and wages. Their support was equally eclectic and extended from small farmers, cottiers, and labourers to urban craftsmen. Operating in oath-bound secret gangs led by 'captains' with ominous pseudonyms like Slasher, Cutter, or Burnstack, Whiteboys sometimes acted openly to turn land from pasture to tillage, or make plots available for potato cultivation, but more frequently sought redress or protected their people through measured terror. Despite the 'Whiteboy Acts' and clerical condemnation, a new and quasi-political version of White-boyism, the Defenders, spread from Armagh after 1785. During the 1790s, as war with the French heightened political and economic unrest, popular protest erupted with greater frequency. The Defenders' vague political creed blurred into Catholic sectarianism in Ulster and republicanism in the south. To the extent that the 1798 rising constituted a culmination of Defenderism, it was in part a trade union revolt.

Whiteboy movements retained a broad social composition, but organized class conflict within the peasantry was not unknown. Faction fighting assumed an increasingly social dimension during the early nineteenth century. Competition for access to land and agricultural employment during the Napoleonic wars produced uniquely class-based forms of Whiteboyism in the rival Caravats and Seanavests. These factions operated in east Munster from 1806 until suppression by the military in 1811; the Caravats being 'a kind of primitive syndicalist movement whose aim was apparently to absorb as many of the poor as possible into a network of auto-nomous local gangs, each exercising thoroughgoing control over its local economy'; and the Seanavests recruiting counter-gangs among strong farmers, merchants, publicans, and migrant *spailpíní* who sought their protection or patronage.[8]

The dispute between the Caravats and Seanavests is interesting too for its ideological content. Whereas the former defined their message as unity of the poor against the 'middle class', the latter invoked the vestiges of '98 nationalism to legitimate their counter-terror. And so the story might have developed in Ireland generally, with politics evolving along the lines of contending appeals to class and nation, had it not been for the Act of Union and the economic decline that followed.

1

Into the Light, 1824–1850

Trade unions were decriminalized in June 1824 when Westminster revoked all Combination Acts.[1] Initially, the post-war recession had raised a clamour for more Draconian laws. However legislators, if not employers, could see that the acts were not effectual. Trade unionists said they merely encouraged violence. With the tide of history moving towards laissez faire, a radical utilitarian and staunch opponent of the acts, Francis Place, deftly manouevred a select committee on deregulation into slipping a repeal bill quietly through parliament. An immediate outbreak of strikes in Britain, due mainly to price rises in a time of good trade, led to another act being introduced in July 1825 which laid down stringent penalties for violence and intimidation. Legal combination was restricted to matters of wages and hours. However the act confirmed implicitly that trade unions were no longer unlawful. This was of immediate advantage to artisans, but offered nothing to labourers who continued to seek redress through secret societies.

The economic world of labour was governed by de-industrialization and a continuing crisis in agriculture. Being based on the traditional trades, craft unions were the first to suffer the economic palpitations caused by free trade with 'the workshop of the world'. A recession in manufacture followed the removal of the last tariff barriers between Ireland and Britain in 1824.[2] The recession had a ruinous impact on many branches of textile production, a sector which still engaged one in five employees in 1841. Though a few ventures of imperial stature, cotton spinning at Portlaw or iron shipbuilding at Cork and Waterford, were launched after 1824, exporters generally lost out to the more rapidly developing British manufactures while the introduction of steamships increased British penetration of Irish markets. The food processing and packing industries also contracted as better transport allowed safe, fast access to English abattoirs and bacon cellars, creating that cliché of Irish undevelopment, the shipment of cattle on the hoof. Agriculture remained dangerously dependent on British demand, with disastrous consequences after 1815.

The north coped more successfully with external competition. Domestic linen production enjoyed a large export trade by the late eighteenth century.[3] Mechanized cotton production, for the home market mainly, was also carried on in Ulster from the 1770s, and cotton remained the chief textile sector in Belfast until about 1825. When duty free competition from Lancashire drove the industry into terminal decline, the cotton factors switched to flax processing, using the new technique of wet-spinning to make a quantum leap to the forefront of the more promising linen trade. By 1850, there were twenty-six flax mills in Belfast alone, and linen weaving too would soon become mechanized. Mechanization in turn encouraged an engineering industry to meet local requirements. In the short term, the north's first industrial revolution brought little benefit to the masses. It destroyed the home-based linen industry across Ulster, and the workshop freedom that went with it, relocating employment in regimented factories to the east of the province. It broke the power of craft unionism in textiles, and created a largely unskilled, low-waged labour force. And Protestant dominance of the process at management and shopfloor levels marginalized the Catholic workforce, fostering a sectarian division of labour.

EARLY LABOUR ORGANIZATION

Textiles and food production engaged the great bulk of wage earners before the Great Famine. The 1841 census enumerated 2.2 million occupied males aged fifteen and upwards. Almost half that number were farm labourers. The clothing trades employed a further 212,500 men, nearly half of them weavers, and there were 158,000 men engaged with lodging, furniture, and machinery. The range of female employment was more restricted again. Of just over 1 million working women aged fifteen years or over, nearly two-thirds were in clothing, and two-thirds of these, 485,000, were spinners. Another 236,000 were in domestic service. Women lay beyond the ambit of any kind of labour organization. Unskilled unionism therefore operated among 1.2 million labourers, who to contemporary eyes were the poor; craft unionism accounted for 240,000 artisans in apprenticed trades. At one extremity of labour organization were 1.1 million agricultural workers; at the other were 26,000 Dublin artisans.

The most formal combinations existed among urban craftsmen, and these were stronger in the south than in the industrializing north. In the short term, undevelopment benefited the craft elite by reproducing a scarcity of skilled labour and an abundance of unskilled men. Wage differentials between skilled and unskilled were greater in Ireland than in Britain. Economic weakness also made industry vulnerable to protracted strikes. Employers occasionally imported British artisans to break strikes, but it was an expensive option which usually provoked an aggressive reaction. That combinations could operate at all indicates the relatively strong bargaining position of craftsmen *vis-à-vis* labourers. The craft unions profited from, rather than created, this situation. The employers' claim that combinations were pricing them out of the market is based on highly selective evidence. One case in point, commonly cited, was the decline of Dublin's shipbuilding industry, choked to death by restrictive practices.[4] Generally speaking, trade union attempts to restore the wage cuts introduced in the post-war recession met with fierce and successful resistance.

Average weekly wage levels in the Dublin building trades rose from 25s. in the 1810s to a little over 26s. for the next three decades. Allowing for deflation, Dublin printers and shipwrights maintained even better wage levels over this period. However, average skilled rates in textiles rates fell from 26s. 9d. per week in the 1810s to 21s. 6d. in the 1820s and then continued falling to 11s. 8d. by the 1840s. Outside Dublin, many textile operatives were reduced to penury after the 1820s. In the leather trades, a Dublin craftsman earned about 19s. 10d. in the 1820s, and 14s. by the 1840s. Average rates for other Dublin trades declined from 30s. 2d. in the 1820s to 24s. 6d. in the 1840s. Provincial wage levels were generally lower. Waterford artisans in good trades earned about 20s. per week in the 1830s. Weekly rates for carpenters in Derry fell from 20s. in 1821–22 to 16s. in 1831–34. Most urban general workers received 7s. to 8s. weekly, while a prized job in Guinness's paid about 12s. per week in 1824. Apart from domestic servants, the lowest paid male workers were agricultural labourers. Before the Great Famine, they formed three sub-classes: indoor servants receiving bed and board in return for a yearly wage; cottiers holding a cabin and an acre or so of land at fixed rent, payable in labour; and landless outdoor labourers, some of whom cultivated a plot on conacre. Most outdoor labourers and men engaged on public works schemes subsisted on 8*d*. to 10*d*. per day in the 1830s. If dieted, the labourer received 4*d*. to 6*d*. per day. During these decades, the better-off urban employees were compensated by the falling cost of bread and clothes. In Dublin, bread prices dropped by 44 per cent between 1816–20 and 1840–44; artisans' wages fell by 27 per cent between the same periods. But whereas the wage decline was fairly steady, bread prices fluctuated. And in some trades the wage decline was steeper.[5]

Craft unions understood their function to be benefit and protection. Depending on the peculiar requirements of the trade, the wealthier societies might provide benefit for unemployment, victimization, sickness, tramping, or emigration. But most unions maintained funds for mortality only, relying on loans in cases of emergency.[6] Friendly societies were more important with regard to benefit. Under the Friendly Societies Act (1829), which updated an original act of 1797, 281 such societies were registered. One hundred and nineteen existed in Dublin. The remainder were spread throughout the anglophone east of the country from Derry to Cork.[7] Other sources of help for thrifty artisans were the savings banks and loan companies which developed after 1815 to provide credit for small depositors. Protection meant the defence of wages, jobs, and working practices. In the canon of craft unionism, there were three 'acts of tyranny' committed by masters: the employment of too many apprentices or boys, the employment of cheap or non-union labour, and wage reductions. Ideally, craftsmen hoped to deal with the three by regulation, protection, and arbitration respectively. Their method in struggle was to be the public appeal or, failing all else, the turn out. In reality, the difficulties in applying peaceful methods of restraint led unions frequently to resort to violence. With a few exceptions, craftsmen alone had the bargaining strength to combine openly. That strength, they believed, rested ultimately on their ability to maintain a scarcity of labour; without it, the artisan would sink into the poverty that engulfed the labourer. Therefore, controlling entry to the trade was vital, and more useful than strikes.

Societies were mostly small, local, and based on a trade recognized traditionally by a guild. None the less, many unions maintained contact with colleagues in other cities of Ireland or Britain; in 1836, Dublin shoemakers claimed to be in touch with France and Germany.[8] The practice of 'tramping' in search of work bound far-flung societies together in a brotherhood of mutual hospitality, regulated by passes entitling the tramping artisan to a few days sustenance while he enquired about a job. Locally, societies frequently assisted each other in industrial disputes. Occasionally, they lent money to support colleagues on strike in other cities. During the 1830s in particular, some attempts were made to federate societies on a United Kingdom (UK) basis. Though federations tended to locate centrally in Liverpool or Manchester, the logistical problems ultimately defeated them, and many broke up or withdrew from Ireland in the 1840s.

Dublin was the only part of the UK where a preponderance of trades was in continuous association in the early nineteenth century, and the city acquired a reputation for being the strongest centre of trade unionism in the 1820s, with about 10,000 organized artisans. Quite exceptionally, the guilds remained important in Dublin.[9] If their industrial function had virtually disappeared, they none the less demonstrated a model of organization and regulation. Twenty unions are known to have been active locally in 1820, thirty-nine in 1840, and forty-five in 1850; some trades contained more than one society. Union density varied. Figures for 1836 show that about ten unions had recruited more than half their trade; the hatters, cabinetmakers, and paperstainers claimed 100 per cent recruitment. The largest societies were the tailors, with 1,000 members out of 2,500 men in the trade, and the carpenters, who represented 900 out of a possible 1,500 men in 1838. Building unions were the biggest and most active, with a reputation for violent militancy. Organization was also extensive in textiles. The legendary 'Board of Green Cloth' may have functioned as a joint committee of the largest section in clothing, the woollen weavers. Woollen weavers sustained some kind of organization between 1815 and 1824, though they never developed a recognized society. By 1850, nearly all trades were unionized to some degree.

In structure, style, and public expression, Dublin craft unions modelled themselves on the city's twenty-five guilds, often adopting guild ritual and symbols. It was common for guild and union alike to be called after the patron saint of the trade. However, this outward appearance has concealed, as it was intended to do, the comparisons between trade unionism and agrarian or Ribbon movements. In matters of conflict and solidarity, unions drew on Whiteboyism. Normally, the societies were run by a committee elected at an annual or quarterly general meeting. The committee usually met once a week in a public house, collected subscriptions, and dealt with routine business. Most societies also had executives and secretaries to handle emergency issues. By the 1840s, some maintained full-time secretaries. Unions engaged closely with the tramping system were more likely to belong to federations. Eight Dublin societies, and others in Belast and Cork, were linked to UK federations at some time or other between 1821 and 1835. One national federation formed in 1836, the Irish Typographical Union, became the Western District Board of the British National Typographical Association in 1845. Uniquely, the UK Federation of Bookbinders was centred in Dublin from 1843 to 1848. Federation usually involved obligations to curb colts, assist tramps, and subscribe to strike funds. Otherwise, branches made their own rules.

Membership of a branch or society was open to all who had served the required apprenticeship, though strangers might be denied entry in times of poor trade. Some unions included small masters; others excluded them deliberately. Entry fees were lower for the sons of members, while strangers would be admitted at the highest rate; the required sums varied from 2s. 6d. to two guineas, one guinea being about average. Weekly dues ranged from 2d. to 3s.; the smaller the membership, the higher the subscription. There were fines for drunkeness, strike-breaking, or disorderly conduct. When necessary, members were levied for political, legal, charitable, or strike purposes. In addition to benefit and protection, unions offered their members the status of being a recognized artisan, an opportunity to defend the wider interests of the trade, and a social comradeship.

Such was the intensity of unrest in the city in the 1820s, and the degree of co-operation between unions, that employers believed them to be in conspiracy, co-ordinated by the 'Board of Green Cloth'. The practice, common in Dublin and Cork at least, of members of one society carrying out acts of violence on behalf of another society to reduce the risk of recognition or conviction, lent credence to the myth. There is no certainty that the 'Board of Green Cloth' ever functioned outside the woollen trade, and it was not until August 1844 that unions in the city formed a trades council, the Associated Trades of Dublin, which was renamed the Regular Trades Association in October. By 1846, there were thirty-seven societies affiliated to the Association.

Ireland's first trades council had emerged in Cork about 1820, and was believed to represent all local crafts.[10] The Cork Union of Trades shared the same combative conception of industrial relations as its affiliates and aimed primarily to co-ordinate them in organization and conflict. Cork trade societies paraded publicly, probably for the first time, in June 1832 to inaugurate the more respectable Cork Trades Association, but the Union of Trades survived into the 1840s. At least nineteen craft unions existed in the city in 1845, some of them branches of British federations. Limerick societies mustered occasionally as the Congregated Trades from the late 1820s onwards.[11] Whilst no similar councils operated elsewhere at this time, combination was carried on to a considerable extent; especially among bakers, coopers, printers, the building trades, and weavers. The National Association for the Protection of Labour, formed in 1830 as a UK federation of trade unions by John Doherty and linked to the co-operative movement of Robert Owen, attracted strong support in Belfast.[12] The Association had collapsed by 1832, but in 1834 about 1,500 artisans in over a dozen trades, chiefly in construction, were affiliated to the Belfast branch of a successor body, the Grand National Consolidated Trades' Union. Craft societies in the provinces were broadly similar in style to their Dublin counterparts though, due to more implacable employer opposition, were less extensive, more intermittent in activity, and shadowy in form.

There is some evidence of organization among unskilled urban workers. The 'Billy Welters' and 'Billy Smiths' operated to defend the interests of Dublin coal porters. Unlike the craft societies, these quasi-secret brotherhoods could sustain a protective function only. The parliamentary enquiry into trade unionism in 1837–38 was told that Dublin draymen and coal porters 'would not allow any man to be dismissed from his employment or at least if they were put out no one else went in their place, and if they did go they were beaten'.[13] What enabled this limited bargaining power was the carter's effective control over his horse; 'one man was assigned to each horse, and while the proprietor kept that horse he was obliged to keep the man and could not dismiss the man without selling the horse'. A similar system obtained on the canals and inland waterways, where the enquiry noted powerful combinations of boatmen, with violence applied against offending captains or owners.[14] In 1842 the Tory *Dublin Evening Mail* detailed a range of restrictive practices maintained by the Carrick boatmen who handled the flyboats and barges that plied between Waterford and Clonmel. According to the *Mail*, only a set number of vessels were allowed on the river, each new barge built having part of the old craft worked into it.[15] Labourers without such *de facto* property rights did combine occasionally to demand higher wages, but were in no position to sustain trade union practices.

Whiteboyism remained the most extensive form of labour defence up to the Great Famine. Agrarian secret societies were most active in the midlands, south-west Leinster, and Munster, in areas of desperate competition for access to plots of land where marginal men lived one 'degree removed above the lowest level of poverty', and normally emerged in times of stress occasioned by exceptional prosperity or hardship.[16] Composed mainly of cottiers, labourers, and subsistence tenants they employed the traditional methods of threats and violence against landlords and farmers to prevent evictions, discourage grabbers, regulate rents and wages, prevent land being turned from tillage to grazing, and frustrate tithe proctors. Support levels varied. Agitation to restrain rent increases had a marked class composition, while the social base of unrest tended to broaden in times of falling prices. Societies operated within local economies; the Rockite agitation that spread across east and central Munster from 1819 to 1823 was one of the widest Whiteboy outbreaks before the Famine. These Rockites acquired a cohesion from the prophecies of Pastorini, which predicted the fall of Protestantism in 1825. However, their millenarianism was less a programme than a bonding ideology. A similar point may be made about the Defenderist type nationalism of the Ribbonmen, the most political of Whiteboy factions, who might toast 'the rights of man' or 'no king' as easily as 'the end of heresy'. After 1815, Ribbonism spread from the border counties to north Leinster and north Connacht. Through the Ancient Order of Hibernians and the Molly Maguires, its influence would reach to Glasgow, Manchester, Liverpool, and the United States. Quite exceptionally, Ribbonism became strong in the towns, especially

Dublin, where it extended to both artisans and transport workers. Initially a Catholic anti-Orange movement, Ribbonism gradually blended into popular agitation movements, and became as generic a term as Whiteboyism. Leinster lodges particularly operated as labour leagues, with benefit and protective functions.

Whiteboys achieved reasonable success in restricting the consolidation of farms and opposing evictions. But the chronic inequality of the agrarian economy and social structure, in which both production and poverty were increasing, demanded that agitation be a recurrent battle against the tide of economic forces.

INDUSTRIAL CONFLICT

Once the Combination Acts were repealed, trade unions immediately demanded higher wages to offset rising prices. Dublin police reports noted fifty-three incidents of violence relating to trade disputes between June 1824 and April 1825.[17] Thirty-two of them occurred in the building line, including the assassination of a jobber, bludgeoned for his refusal to dismiss non-body men. A meeting convened by the Lord Mayor in April 1825 to discuss the situation concluded by condemning the conspiracy 'for some time existing among the operative hands; not confined as hereto fore to any particular branch, but embracing all denominations of tradesmen, in a close confederacy . . . .'[18] It was agreed to establish a fund to reward informants of outrages. Some wished to go further and break trade unions. Master cabinetmakers, chairmakers and upholsterers proposed to employ 'country operatives', who would be given adequate protection. For their part, thirty-two trade societies met in August to reiterate their belief in arbitration as the best means of ending strikes with violence.

Unrest persisted in Dublin, but by the end of the year it was employers who were on the offensive, seeking wage cuts in conditions of deep recession. The recession in British industry in 1825–26 was novel in the degree of its impact on Irish manufacture. Deflation caused by the assimilation of the Irish currency into sterling in 1825 sharpened the exceptionally industrial character of the crisis. As the Mayor of Waterford reported to his Relief Committee in March 1826, local distress stemmed from dismissals from employment, not from food shortages or food prices.[19]

Perceptions of the resultant social problems had an industrial rather than pre-industrial aspect. Proposed solutions emphasised job creation more than food distribution. The recession became most severe in the summer of 1826, when widespread unemployment coincided with high food prices due to an exceptionally dry season. Adding to the distress, many migrant workers returned from England. In July, Dublin artisans toured workshops calling out men to demand wage payment in English currency. Masters met the strike wave by forming an Association of Trades 'to arrest the programme of intimidation and violence . . . which have characterized the proceedings of journeymen . . . .'[20] Yet some trade unions won their demands immediately.

It was in textiles that the slump caused a long-term crisis. Bounties granted by the linen board for coarse weaving had been withdrawn in 1823. With free trade and recession, imported British machine spun yarn undersold the native handspun product. English woollens and cottons too were dumped on the Irish market. Following an unsuccessful strike of Belfast cotton workers in 1825, the recession dealt a terminal blow to trade unionism in Ulster's textile sector. Northern cotton weavers earned up to 24s. per week in the early 1820s. In 1835, there were approximately 10,000 cotton weavers in the Belfast area living on 3s. 6d. to 8s. per week. The 'cotton famine' during the American Civil War finally destroyed the industry in the north.[21] Almost 20,000 textile operatives were idle in the Liberties of Dublin in 1826, causing an outbreak of 'famine fever' and bread riots. Cork's textile operatives marched from Blackpool into Patrick St behind a banner saying, 'We Want Employment—Ourselves and Our Families Are Starving'. Textiles engaged about 60,000 people in west Cork in 1822. Bandon supported over 1,500 cotton weavers up to 1829. Ten years later there were 150 weavers left in Bandon.[22] Some mills survived precariously. In Drogheda, 1,900 linen weavers remained in part-time employment in 1840, earning about 4s. per week. As Ulster adapted from cotton to linen, the south made a limited switch into cotton. Cotton mills continued to operate in Drogheda and Balbriggan, while Malcolmson's Portlaw Spinning Company, established in 1825, employed over 1,800 operatives in what was claimed to be the biggest factory in the world.[23]

The conflict generated by the recession confirmed employers in their opposition to trade unionism *per se*. Even in Dublin, masters no longer appealed for a harmony of common interests. Once trade began to recover, industrial relations became increasingly bitter. In two sensational incidents in Dublin, a master builder was attacked with acid and a sawyer was bludgeoned to death by a gang of over twenty combinators. Four men were hanged for the latter crime.[24] In 1827, Dublin masters had initiated a national petition for the re-enactment of the Combination Acts, inviting merchant bodies in Belfast, Cork, Limerick, and Waterford to lend support. Dublin trade unions replied with public meetings to refute employer allegations, arguing that violence was worse before 1824, and currently affected only five or six of the seventy trades in the city. Again, the trades called for arbitration. Strikers remained liable to prosecution under the Master and Servant Act, which made it a criminal offence for an employee to leave his work in breach of contract, and provincial employers still used the law to suppress strikes or attempts to maintain a scarcity of labour. In 1826, apprentices who struck at a calico printing works in Carrickfergus were promptly imprisoned. Two years later, a general turn out of mill labourers and storemen at Clonmel over wages and hours led to five men being sentenced to the treadmill in the local house of correction. One convict hulk out of Cove, the *Essex*, transported seven men sent down for combination offences between 1825 and 1834.[25]

Unrest intensified in the 1830s. The campaign for Catholic Emancipation had sharpened popular political awareness. Following the Emancipation act in 1829, expectations were raised among all social classes. When Catholics in Graiguenamanagh, Co. Kilkenny withheld tithe payments in 1830, similar resistance spread throughout the country, escalating into a 'tithe war'.[26] Opposition to tithes united all social classes but, at a time of falling prices, Whiteboy groups called the Whitefeet, the Terry Alts, and the Poleens emerged in south Leinster, Clare/Limerick, and Waterford to turn the war into a wider social struggle. Disillusion with Emancipation now acted as a spur. 'Mr O'Connell and the rich Catholics go to parliament', a Whitefoot leader told de Tocqueville, 'We die of starvation just the same.'[27] Rural unrest, in England as well as Ireland, the 1830 revolutions in Europe, and Daniel O'Connell's new campaign for Repeal, prompted the government to take strong measures to curb popular agitation. Rural disorder was met with insurrection acts and increasingly frequent use of troops and police. After the introduction of a particularly tough Coercion Act in 1833 rural protest diminished. The longstanding friction over tithes was finally resolved in 1838 by a Commutation Act, which converted tithe into a rent charge amounting to about 75 per cent of the old composition, effectively wrote off the arrears of 1834–37, and eliminated the hated tithe-proctors.

The law was also applied more pointedly against craft unionism after 1833. In addition to widespread convictions for attempts to restrict apprenticeships, intimidation, assault, conspiracy, and turning out in breach of contract, Cork magistrates sentenced eight men each to three months imprisonment for membership of a benefit society. In February 1834, twelve Dublin shoemakers were convicted of conspiring to reduce the livelihood of a colleague who had refused to join their society. The Belfast *Newsletter* noted with satisfaction that 'every individual who is obliged to leave his situation in consequence of the decrees of Trades' Unions [henceforth] has a valid action against the members of those Unions'.[28] George Kerr's *Exposition of Legislative Tyranny, and Defence of the Trades' Union* was a unique response to one such case of judicial browbeating. A leading figure in the Belfast Cabinetmakers' Club and an Owenite, Kerr was arrested while organizing in Derry, charged with administering illegal oaths, maltreated in prison, and interrogated about trade unionism by Mayor Gillespie. Kerr's pamphlet recalling his experience and offering a high minded, God-fearing defence of trade unionism contributed to his acquittal. In April 1834, Kerr chaired a meeting of the Belfast branch of the 'General Trade Union' to petition on behalf of the Tolpuddle Martyrs. Fifteen hundred members attended and they were joined by 'several thousand' sympathizers. The assembly coincided with an upsurge of craft militancy in Belfast involving action by bakers, printers, flaxdressers, coopers, coachmakers, cabinetmakers, shoemakers, and stonecutters. Notable too was the absence of sectarian animosity in labour proceedings; already the presence of Orange and Catholic trade unionists on the same platform had become an event worth congratulation in Belfast. However, before the year was out, employers had crushed the strike wave with law and lockouts, and then proceeded to establish an exchange for non-union labour in the city. No more was heard of the 'General Trade Union' in Belfast.

After years of relative tranquillity from 1830 to 1833, union violence in Dublin reached a crescendo in 1836–37, when the price of bread rose to its highest level since the famine year of 1817. Most violence occurred subsequent to the outbreak of attacks on bakeries and bread carts in the summer of 1837. On this occasion, union aggression generated relatively little public odium, while the extent of hunger protests overstretched the police. Constables were severely beaten in October when they intervened in a trade union assault, and in November police stood by as an employer was attacked by thirty carpenters. There were thirty-nine cases of assault in connection with combination in Dublin in 1836, and ninety-seven in 1837; some incidents involved the two unskilled gangs, the 'Billy Welters' and 'Billy Smiths'. All assaults aimed to maintain wage levels, limit the employment of apprentices, or prevent the employment of colts.

IN SEARCH OF CONSENSUS

When food prices declined in 1838 violence fell sharply. By the 1840s, unions were turning to public pressure and moral force as a means of seeking redress. A severe slump from 1839 to 1842 depressed trade union activity. Moreover, economic decline was now creating concern among all industrial classes in southern Ireland, and middle-class leaders began to join trade societies in appeals to promote native industry. In 1840, Fr Matthew Flanagan, a priest in the Dublin Liberties, set up the Operative Board of Trade to encourage self-help ventures in textile and footwear production. Renamed the Repeal Board of Trade following O'Connellite intervention, the board ran eighteen marts of local produce in Dublin in 1842, and had kindred bodies in Clonmel, Waterford, and Wexford. Lack of investment sent the board into abrupt decline in 1843. There were other, less elaborate, efforts along these lines too, involving Tories as well as Repealers.[29] A dawning realization that both masters and men were common victims of free trade induced a limited class collaboration. Also of significance in changing the social climate was the phenomenal success of Fr Mathew's temperance crusade, which emphasised material improvement through moral reform.

As unions recovered after the slump, they embarked on agitation that was more campaigning than combative. The 1840s were notable for three major trade struggles, unprecedented in extent or sophistication, involving bakers, tanners, and tailors.[30] In July 1842, Dublin bakers initiated a campaign to end night-work, offering to work from 6.00 a.m. to 8.00 p.m. six days a week instead. Within weeks, the demand was taken up by provincial colleagues. With a reputation for price fixing and adulteration, the master bakers were not popular men, and the operatives enjoyed broad public backing, including support from the *Freeman's Journal*. Temporary successes were recorded in securing the abolition of night-work in Derry, Belfast, Kilkenny, and Cork. After fruitless canvassing Dublin bakers issued a formal strike notice in November. But the campaign petered out in 1843, and night-work was re-introduced in the provinces. Agitation by Dublin tanners in 1844 to raise wage rates led to a prolonged strike and lockout that summer. Whilst the conflict centred on Dublin, support came from all categories of leather operatives throughout the country, as well as from tanners in Leeds and Liverpool. Sympathetic action extended beyond financial assistance to joint employer and employee boycott of goods produced by the offending masters. In Wexford, agents recruiting for the masters were run out of town. From this dispute emerged the Dublin Regular Trades Association, formed as a 'moral and peaceful union' to articulate grievances, co-ordinate activities, and defend the 'character of our tradesmen from the many wanton and unfounded charges of combination . . . .'[31] The tanners' campaign did not survive long beyond 1844, but the association remained active until 1847.

Unlike the earlier unions of trades, the Regular Trades sought no role in managing internal union affairs, exalted the 'moral force principle' above combination, and operated largely as a public lobby. Religious or political questions were excluded from its deliberations. Over 1846, the association sent forty-seven deputations to employers in dispute, and deemed only sixteen of them to have failed. During this year also, two labour papers were issued in Dublin, the *Argus* and the *Guardian and Tradesman's Advocate*. The *Guardian* especially reflected the trades' view that 'the interests of the employer and employed, when properly understood, are and ought to be identical . . . .'[32] In contemporary eyes, the logical extension of this scenario was the revival of the guilds, moribund since the Municipal Corporations Act (1840) had abolished their political privileges. Calls for guild regulation of trade were not new. As the guilds lost their role in industrial conflict, artisans came to see them as potential allies against economic liberalism. From the outset, the Regular Trades Association had been committed to the restoration of guild privileges.

In June 1845, the courts upheld a claim of Benjamin Pemberton, sometime bricklayer and master of his guild, that the 1840 Act had not affected the rights of guilds in regulating trade. Artisans and guildsmen combined to reassert these rights. The campaign coincided with the third major trade union agitation of the decade, that of the journeymen tailors against sweating. The tailors had commenced their fight in January. In October, the revived Guild of Tailors took up the cause, and subsequently warned that after 31 December no master could operate without a licence from the guild. Writs were then served on offending masters. During the early months of 1846, Dublin Chamber of Commerce and the Regular Trades Association fought a political battle over the issue of guild authority. The former prevailed, and in August a bill to abolish guild trading rights passed into law. Interest in the Regular Trades slackened in 'black '47', and the Association fell into abeyance.

INTO POLITICS

The struggle for Catholic Emancipation introduced the working class to electoral politics. If Emancipation brought no immediate benefit to the mass of the people, it gave an immense psychological boost to all Catholics, and raised hopes of further concessions. The Catholic Association was strong in the towns, where collectors for the Catholic Rent Committee could be drawn from any class to suit the occasion. Such social harmony would not be so easy to achieve in the Liberator's next campaign.

Dublin artisans greeted O'Connell's decision, in October 1830, to agitate for Repeal with relief.[33] The ill-effects of the Union were felt keenly in the ex-capital. Though Repeal generally commanded even less support from Protestants than Emancipation, inconclusive evidence suggests that Dublin's Protestant artisans, who comprised about 20 per cent of city tradesmen, favoured the cause. So too did some of the minor guilds. However, the Catholic hierarchy and Catholic middle class, on whose social leadership O'Connell relied, preferred to await the fruits of Emancipation or press for moderate reforms of administration, tithes, and policing. With their former enthusiasm for Emancipation turning to cynicism about its consequences, artisans expected little benefit from such palliatives. Repeal alone, they believed, would restore prosperity. The argument for Repeal assumed that an Irish government would make Dublin a centre of patronage, and protect and foster native industries, as the old College Green parliament had done through tariffs, development boards, and grants.[34] Repealers spoke constantly of the need to encourage indigenous industry, and by the 1840s tariff protection had become a standard nationalist demand. Young Irelanders went furthest in rejecting the free trade ideas of the Manchester school; the philosophically liberal O'Connell actually remained a free trader, though he indicated that he would be flexible on tariffs if need be. The politics of industrial revival could be double edged for tradesmen. Both Old and Young Ireland were sometimes critical of trade unionism as a disincentive to enterprise. Nonetheless, the strategic interests of labour lay with self-government. However unsatisfactory that government might be, artisans saw no future for themselves, their societies, or their jobs under London rule. And they were convinced that only O'Connell, the man who had blackmailed Westminster into granting Catholic Emancipation, could deliver.

By 1831, the provinces too were active. In January, bodies of trades in Cork and Tullamore, Co. Offaly held Repeal rallies, determined to generate a tempo that would prevent O'Connell from dropping or compromising on the demand for self-government. On 19 August, Dublin tradesmen reconstituted the Liberal Mechanics' and Trades' Association, founded in 1830, as the Dublin Trades Political Union to promote the cause. O'Connell then entered into discussions with the union to bring it under his control and dilute its class orientation. In return for the admission of recommended artisans to O'Connell's association, the National Political Union, and the promise to build a hall for trades' meetings, it was agreed to recast the Trades Political Union on a national basis and open membership to all. Primarily, the National Trades Political Union sought to win Repeal through political canvassing. It also agitated against tithes, petitioned for triennial parliaments and the secret ballot, and prepared reports on the decline of trade since 1800. Its own rules forbade it to interfere in industrial relations. Membership stood at about 1,000 initially, rising to about 5,000 by 1832, of whom

3,000 were electors. Though now largely middle class, the Union offered a platform for radical Repeal politics to the trades. Cork trade unionists formed a vociferous lobby in the 1833 general elections when the Hutchinson and Boyle families lost a seat to 'the democratic custody of a body of electors under the influence of the 'Trades Association".[35] The growing political importance of organized labour was reflected in an ephemeral reform press. The radical *Comet* (1831–33), *Plain Dealer* (1832), and *Press* (1833), were joined by the more labour oriented *Repealer and Tradesman's Journal* (1832), and the *People* (1833). The O'Connellite *Express* (1832) also accommodated radical opinion.[36]

O'Connell's failure to subsume trade union politics into his movement ensured a thorny relationship with labour. Friction hinged on tactical and class questions. O'Connell pursued a delicate political strategy in the 1830s. Though he believed, wrongly as it turned out, that Westminster would be more sympathetic to Ireland after the 1832 Reform Act, he knew that Repeal could not be won through parliamentary means alone. At the same time he supported the Whig administration; partly because he shared government concern about social unrest, partly to prevent his movement being suppressed, and partly in the hope of securing interim reforms. His supporters were less patient, and urged that Repeal be raised in the House of Commons. O'Connell eventually conceded to this pressure in April 1834, and proposed a House Committee of Enquiry into the effects of the Act of Union. Parliament dismissed the motion by 523 votes to 38. The first phase of Repeal agitation was over. When the English radical, William Cobbett, visited Dublin in September, the enthusiastic reception he received from artisans was taken to imply a censure of O'Connell. O'Connell's relations with trade unions deteriorated further when he entered into the Lichfield House compact with the Whigs in 1835: it confirmed that Repeal had been dropped.

Class interests created deeper tension between labour and the Repeal movement. As a liberal and a pacifist, O'Connell disliked unions for restraining trade and resorting to violence. In November 1837, after a crest of labour conflict in Dublin and a notoriously violent Glasgow spinners' strike, he departed from his policy of public neutrality on industrial relations and openly condemned trade unionism as practised in Ireland. Dublin trade union secretaries disputed O'Connell's charges, and in January 1838 the

Liberator met his critics face to face in two extraordinary debates at the Old Chapel, Ringsend. O'Connell echoed a common supposition in contending that Irish trade unions were more militant than those in Britain and were the cause of decline in Dublin's printing and shipbuilding industries. Spokesmen for the artisans made no attempt to justify violence, but defended restrictive practices as essential to the maintenance of employment and living standards. 'What advantage is it to the tradesmen of Ireland', they asked, carrying the attack into politics, 'that thirteen hundred situations have been thrown open by emancipation? . . . Has it given a loaf of bread to any of the thousand starving families of the poor operatives of this city?'[37] The artisans squared up to the great man in the first debate, where the atmosphere turned decidedly rancorous. In the second round, the seasoned counsellor got the upper hand. Evidently confirmed in his views, O'Connell then persuaded the House of Commons to appoint a Committee of Enquiry on trade unionism. The enquiry paid particular attention to Ireland, but neither of its reports made any recommendations.[38]

Although O'Connell had contrasted Ireland with the 'honest and praise worthy system of trade union' in Britain, the parliamentary enquiry alienated British labour from him. Relations were already strained by his support for the Whigs. In 1838, O'Connell openly denounced the People's Charter, completing his breach with British radicals. At home, he tried consistently to insulate Ireland from the British left. Ireland had featured on the agenda of British movements for democracy since 1815. Utopian socialist ideas spread across the channel in the 1820s. In response to near famine conditions in 1822–23, Captain Robert O'Brien invited Robert Owen to outline his plans for agriculture oriented philanthropy in Dublin.[39] On foot of Owen's lectures at the Rotunda in 1823, Lord Cloncurry led O'Brien and other socially concerned squires to found the Hibernian Philanthropic Society as a solution to the twin evils of distress and Whiteboyism. The Society presented a memorial to parliament but achieved nothing else. A circle of philanthropic landlords remained, and the most brilliant amongst them was William Thompson, whose writings on political economy were to influence Karl Marx.[40] Two practical experiments in Owenism were launched in 1830–31. In January 1830, the Belfast Co-operative Trading Association was founded by artisans with ambitions to set up factories, farms, schools, libraries, hospitals, and boarding houses on Owenite principles. The co-operative did establish a library, two schools, and the monthly *Belfast Co-operative Advocate*, but all had collapsed by March.[41] The internationally renowned Ralahine Agricultural and Manufacturing Co-operative Association, founded by John Scott Vandeleur in 1831 after an outbreak of disturbances on his estate, lasted two years. Vandeleur brought fifty-two tenants and their dependents into this commune to improve their moral and material welfare and keep them out of the local Whiteboys, the Lady Clares. All was going well when Vandeleur's gambling addiction led him to wager away the estate. Receiving no recognition or compensation from Vandeleur's creditors, the commune collapsed.[42]

Developing political consciousness in Ireland, emigration to Britain's burgeoning industrial cities, trade union contacts, and the influence in Britain of leaders like John Doherty, Feargus O'Connor and Bronterre O'Brien, offered widening opportunities for cross-channel co-operation in the 1830s.[43] Feargus O'Connor had begun his political career as a Repeal Member of Parliament (MP) for Cork in 1832. Personality and policy differences with O'Connell, including O'Connor's suggestions for an alliance of Irish peasants and English industrial workers, led to bitter enmity between the two men. O'Connor lost his seat in 1835, and went on to lead Chartism in Britain, but never lost interest in the land and Repeal questions. Chartism acquired support in Ireland in spite of O'Connell, and came under the leadership of another former O'Connellite, Patrick O'Higgins. O'Higgins' paper, the *Tribune* (1834–36) established close links with Cobbett's *Political Register* and enjoyed a large circulation among the Irish in Britain.[44] A Dublin Chartist group was formed in July 1839, only to have its first meetings smashed by the Trades Political Union, but Chartism recovered within the Irish Universal Suffrage Association, set up by O'Higgins in 1841. At its peak, the Suffrage Association claimed 1,000 members, the bulk of them in Dublin, Belfast, and Drogheda. Whilst small masters and tradesmen predominated at leadership level, Chartist activity in towns like Ballyragget, Cashel, and Loughrea reflected wider support from subsistence tenants and agricultural labourers. Irish Chartism took a more moderate line than its British counterpart. Its strategy was to maximize constitutional pressure on parliament. Physical force did not become an issue until 1848. The Universal Suffrage Association issued pamphlets, distributed newspapers, organized petitions on the charter,

Repeal, and emigration, and popularized these issues in Britain, where it attracted stronger interest than in Ireland. In the face of O'Connellite opposition, clerical denunciation and employer victimization it was rarely strong enough to mobilize publicly. By 1842, Chartist progress in the provinces had been checked.

When O'Connell revived the Repeal cause in April 1840, his relations with Dublin artisans improved immediately. The Repeal Association remained dominated by Dublin artisans and their grievances for the next two years. As in 1830, reforms diluted support from the two groups whose backing O'Connell prized; the Catholic middle class and Protestants. The Municipal Corporations Act (1840) gave the former limited control over urban administration in the south. By the same token, the erosion of privilege alienated Protestants. Membership of the Orange Order had swelled to over 100,000 by 1835, and working-class Protestants became active in Tory politics. Even Dublin Protestant tradesmen, while still hostile to free trade, gave scant support to Repeal in the 1840s. Orange operative associations were formed in Dublin, Cork, Bandon, Youghal, and Belfast during the decade; though Belfast Chartists collected 2,000 signatures for the second Chartist petition of 1842, which included a demand for Repeal.[45] Repeal agitation gathered pace in late 1842, spurred on by bad harvests, widespread social unrest, and Young Ireland's phenomenally popular paper, the *Nation*. More than forty monster meetings took place over the summer and autumn of 1843, labelled by the Liberator as 'the Repeal Year'. But there was no way that Westminster was going to grant Repeal without massive coercion. In October, the government banned the monster meeting planned for Clontarf on the northern outskirts of Dublin. O'Connell backed down, and the cause foundered. For the contemporary Dublin trades, Repeal was their last collective intervention in politics. They had long lost faith in the Trades Political Union and, for the moment, Chartism held little attraction. Even the Universal Suffrage Association suspended activities as a gesture of solidarity following O'Connell's arrest on a trumped up conspiracy charge. Significantly, the rules of the new Regular Trades Association forbade discussion of politics.

'48

Young Irelanders offered fresh prospects for radicalism. Founded in 1842, Young Ireland represented advanced nationalism but gave conditional support to the Repeal Association. Debate on response to the Great Famine strained relations with O'Connell. Young Ireland demanded an embargo on food exports. O'Connell demanded that members of the Repeal Association sign a pledge renouncing violence. Young Ireland demurred. Thomas Francis Meagher finally made the breach with his famous speech refusing to 'stigmatise the sword'. Starvation was in any case creating a sharp increase in agrarian crime, and popular disbelief in the logic of food ships leaving Ireland past relief ships sailing in eventually turned into violence.[46] Young Ireland's expulsion led to a large swing in working-class opinion away from O'Connell. Though trades societies still inclined towards the Repeal Association, 15,000 Dubliners, craftsmen and labourers in the main, signed the Remonstrance of October 1846 in protest.[47] The failure of the potato crop that winter and the inadequacy of Whig measures to deal with the catastrophe discredited Old Ireland.

In response to pressure from artisans and shopkeepers, Young Irelanders founded the Irish Confederation in January 1847 to unite all nationalists at odds with O'Connell. A Trades and Citizens Committee was set up contemporaneously by artisans under the auspices of the Confederation. The pull/push of support from urban workers and the imperative of separatism, propelled advanced nationalism steadily to the left.[48] Young Ireland had rejected appeals for an alliance with Chartism. Influenced by the Trades and Citizens Committee and radicals like James Fintan Lalor, who wanted to link nationalism with land agitation, some Confederate leaders took a more sympathetic view. On the British side, O'Connell's death in May facilitated a confluence of Repealers and Chartists. But the Confederation still baulked at the idea. Further confusion reigned over aims and methods. The Confederation demanded self-government but disavowed separatism or physical force. In February 1848, John Mitchel led a breakaway group to found the radical and separatist *United Irishman*, which gave extensive coverage to Chartism. With such internal dissent and no great support in the countryside, the movement appeared to be falling into disarray. Thomas Francis Meagher struck out independently to challenge Old Ireland in a by-election at Waterford. Though unsuccessful, he was elated with the popular response. The results were barely announced when news filtered through that Louis Philippe had been toppled and a republic declared in Paris. The fall of the last French king was hailed by workers and bourgeois liberals throughout Europe, and it revitalized the flagging Confederates.

Whiggish expectations that the revolution would be confined to a simple change of authority were to be disappointed. What began as a liberal challenge unleashed a rapid mobilization of popular power. Moreover, Paris set off a chain of revolt in European capitals, triggering speculation as to when Ireland would follow suit. Now came the reckoning for advanced nationalism. Conservatives like Smith O'Brien and Gavan Duffy argued initially for alliance with the Repeal Association to strengthen moderate opinion, but in March contacts with British Chartism developed quickly. Joint meetings of Confederates and Chartists were held in Manchester and Oldham. For the first time, the bulk of Irish emigrants in England's industrial north became involved with Chartism. On 22 March, the government tried to cripple this evolving union by arresting Mitchel, Smith O'Brien, and Meagher on a charge of seditious libel. After the great Chartist demonstration at London's Kennington Common on 10 April, in which Confederates were prominent, security legislation was rushed through the House of Commons. In May, Mitchel was sentenced to fourteen years transportation. But the crown failed to convict Meagher and Smith O'Brien, due to the dissent of the solitary Catholic on the jury. Meanwhile, Irish Chartism re-surfaced to strengthen the alliance with Confederates. From late April, the revived Universal Suffrage Association organized public meetings to swing the Confederation behind universal suffrage, and a Chartist newspaper, the *Irish National Guard*, was published. It was the zenith of Chartist influence.

On 22 July, as Confederate leaders prepared for insurrection, the government acted decisively. Parliament suspended habeas corpus, the Confederate Clubs were suppressed, and arrests were intensified. Chartism too was crushed. Patrick O'Higgins spent seven months in jail on a charge of concealing arms. In Meagher's Waterford, 700 hundred police and troops conducted searches in the city, scouring Ballybricken for weapons and felons.[49] Whilst urban workers awaited 'the word', Confederate leaders still at large had fled to the country, where support was weaker. Quixotically, Smith O'Brien toured south Tipperary to rouse the people into rebellion. Poor preparation, confused planning, clerical hostility, and popular debilitation after three years of famine combined to frustrate him; and the rising fizzled out ingloriously in the widow McCormack's cabbage patch at Ballingarry. Meagher had eluded arrest, and went to incite revolt in Co. Waterford. On 1 August, despairing of the popular will to fight, he set out for Thurles under cover of night, and ran into a police patrol. Some sporadic action continued, but '1848' was over.

Against the odds, Confederates attempted a recovery. Bertram Fullam founded the *Irishman* in January 1849 as a successor to Mitchel's *United Irishman*. Fintan Lalor meanwhile regrouped the remnants of the Confederate clubs to prepare another rising. Trades sentiment in Dublin had not changed. The 'Famine Queen's' visit to the city that year drew a protest from an aggregate meeting of craft unions. In nationalism's last appeal to insurrectionary spontaneity, Lalor made a vain effort to foment insurgency in the Waterford-Tipperary area. On 16 September, the appointed day for a general uprising, Cappoquin alone responded.[50] Lalor returned to Dublin, ill and disappointed, and died two days later. A further blow to radicalism came when Gavan Duffy revived the *Nation* and siphoned support away from Fullam's *Irishman*. Fullam set about building a separate and vaguely socialist organization. In January 1850, he launched the Irish Democratic Association to educate workers in nationally minded radicalism. With encouragement from Feargus O'Connor, branches of the Association were formed in Glasgow, Liverpool, Manchester, Wigan, and Barnsley as well as Dublin, Kilkenny, Limerick, Cork, and Carrick on Suir. Fullam claimed 2,000 members. In fact, there were only about fifty paid-up supporters. By May, the Association and the *Irishman* had folded.[51]

Working-class politics lost its revolutionary edge after 1848. Over the next generation, labour would turn to more conservative forms of organization and politics.

2

Atrophe, 1851–1888

Post-Famine Ireland was a land of paradox; of undevelopment and social progress. By exporting its surplus population and integrating into the UK economy, in a way that in turn accelerated depopulation, what had been one of Europe's poorest countries raised its income *per capita* to the point where it compared favourably with the continental average by the end of the century.[1] Rising incomes were paralleled by the emergence of modern state services. The national schools clipped the level of illiteracy from 53 per cent in 1841 to 18 per cent in 1891, and legislation for better housing finally took effect in the 1880s and 1890s following the Labourers (Ireland) Acts and the Housing of the Working Classes Act. Though public health, housing, and welfare provision remained pitifully inadequate at the turn of the century, the material quality of working-class life had advanced more in the past forty years than over the previous 400.[2]

Trade unionism similarly evinced a paradox of slow decline and incremental sophistication. Progress in organization raised the question of forming a national labour congress in the 1860s. It was a premature step in the short term; while in the long run, industrial trends threatened the very existence of an Irish labour movement. After the Famine, the railways intensified the process begun by the steamships, facilitating unprocessed exports and cheap imports. When the mid-Victorian prosperity gave way to slump in 1874, the vulnerability of Irish industry to free trade became ruthlessly exposed. The slump revealed a manufacturing base over-dependent on obsolescent minor crafts, and discouraged from modernizing by depopulation and the fall in gross agricultural purchasing power. A flood of cheap British goods undercut native manufacture on the home market, while the international recession threatened exports, sending the more advanced industrial sectors to join the obsolescent trades in terminal decay. The composition of the working class changed. Already decimated by the Famine, agricultural labourers continued to suffer a reduction in numbers. Their marginal role in the land war reflected the eclipse of Whiteboyism by tenant right. In the towns, the demise of traditional handicrafts was compensated for partly by the growth in housing provisions trades. By the end of the century, building would rival manufacture as a source of craft jobs, and therefore the core of trade unionism. Conveyance employment shifted from carriage and sail to steam and rail. Together with the growing number of general labourers, transport would become of strategic importance to the resurgence of the labour movement in the twentieth century. Job opportunities for women contracted with the decline of employment in agriculture and a steady reduction in the number of fishmongers, egg dealers, fruiterers, dairy keepers, and hucksters. Their staple occupations however, domestic service and textiles, remained buoyant. Attitudes towards women in work changed. As the century wore on, heavy manual labour became less acceptable as suitable employment and the view that, where possible, wives ought not to leave the home became prevalent.

Against the trend, the north east experienced a second industrial revolution as mechanized linen production primed an expansion of engineering in the 1850s, which complemented the development of shipbuilding in the 1860s, which in turn generated a marine engineering industry in the 1890s.[3] Unlike textiles, shipbuilding and engineering employed a sizeable skilled artisanate, self-confident, highly paid and able to command an effective bargaining power through maintaining a scarcity of labour. Whereas Ulster's first industrial revolution generated no major differences in wage levels or the agenda of trade unionism north and south, the second produced a deviant industrial relations environment in the Lagan valley. As the century wore on, the prospect of Belfast being incorporated into an Irish labour movement receded. Which way the rest of Ulster would lean was not to be decided until the First World War.

ATTEMPTS AT RECOVERY

Labour protest by urban workers during the 1850s kept within the bounds of 'moral force' trade unionism, and concerned itself mainly with reductions of hours. The length of the working day became an issue of general and persistent concern in the latter half of the nineteenth century. 'Nine hours' movements developed in Britain during the 1850s, and by the end of the next decade the 60 hour week was not uncommon.[4] Dublin drapers' assistants combined briefly to win 6.00 p.m. closing in 1855, but needed to address the question again within four years.[5] The greatest wave of agitation involved bakers. Dublin journeymen took up their old grievance against nightwork and Sunday work in 1859, and the cry was echoed in the provinces in 1860, leading to a national campaign the following year. The agitation achieved immediate successes but, as in the 1840s, bakers could not prevent masters reintroducing old hours in many areas. One permanent gain was the Bakehouses (Regulation) Act (1863), which outlawed nightwork for journeymen under the age of eighteen and empowered inspectors to visit bakeries. Movements to reduce work time, often involving grocers', drapers', or shop assistants, persisted through the 1860s. Usually they were concerned with seeking holidays on particular calendar days, such as church fêtes, and agitation took the form of annual appeals for public sympathy.[6] Unskilled workers too were caught up in the mood of militancy. Dublin paviors formed a union in 1860, as did Limerick dockers in 1863, and Dublin builders' labourers in 1864. Over 1,100 copper miners and face workers at Bun Machan, Co. Waterford struck for wage increases in July 1860. After six weeks, the unorganized miners were starved back to work. A similar fate awaited 200 Waterford dockers when they turned out in October 1862.[7]

Contemporary labour confidence extended to ambitions to restructure the movement. Dublin craft unions resolved in October 1862 to form a new trades council, the United Trades Association (UTA). By 1865 there were twenty-five societies affiliated, and the Association later claimed 10,000 members. The UTA lobbied employers on behalf of workers, defended affiliates in dispute by mobilizing popular opinion and in 1871 set up a committee to mediate in inter-union disputes. Not infrequently, it disbursed strike pay. A constant concern was the promotion of native products and the discouragement of imports. It was a measure of the straits to which the southern economy was being reduced that where foreign goods were concerned no item was too petty to be overlooked by the UTA, or indeed any other assembly of Irish craftsmen. Yet though strictly a body of artisans, the UTA assisted the formation of unions for general and semi-skilled operatives. Nor was their generosity confined to Dublin. Lurgan Damask Weavers, on strike against wage cuts, received a hearty reception from the UTA in 1874.[8] A number of trades councils were formed or re-formed in the early 1860s, and the laying of the foundation stone of the O'Connell monument in Dublin in August 1864 provided an opportunity for the trades to meet and take stock. It was, too, an occasion to remember a man who once clashed bitterly with trade unionists, and yet promised them the thing they wanted most: a huge procession of the trades dominated the proceedings. To refresh the provincial delegates, the UTA provided a dejeuner at the Mechanics' Institute. On returning home, the delegates were quick to canvass trades unity. Cork trades formed their own, ephemeral, UTA shortly afterwards. Waterford Trades Guardians Association, founded in January 1862, wrote to Dublin suggesting an amalgamation of all trades to promote organization, foster native manufacture, and develop a benevolent society. The UTA then urged that trades councils 'knowing neither politics nor religion, but trade and protection of tradesmen's rights alone' be formed locally, each federated to the UTA. In November, the UTA noted favourable responses from the Cork UTA, Limerick Congregated Trades, and the Waterford Guardians, to a call for a general union of trade unions. Galway, Ennis, Enniskillen, and Wexford were reportedly taking steps to form trades councils with a view to affiliating to the new confederation. However, the proposal never came to fruition. After 1868, labour notionally accepted the British Trades Union Congress (TUC) as its spokesman. Although the TUC met in Dublin in 1880 and Belfast in 1893, Irish concerns were swallowed up in its agenda and a limited Irish involvement denied it any effective representative role.[9] The question of forming a national trade union centre therefore remained open.

A glimpse of the dimensions to the real challenge confronting trade unionists, that of sustaining an effective general unionism, emerged in Cork in 1870.[10] Three societies catering for unskilled men appeared in the city in 1868-69; two of them, the Cork Working Men's Association and the Labourers' Society, were general unions in effect. In 1869, a Working Men's Society was formed at Mallow, and a Labour Club at Kanturk. A decade of fermenting unrest in

Cork came to the boil in May 1870, when tailors struck for an upward revision of wages. Tailors also opposed the introduction of sewing machines. The dispute evolved quickly into a general strike and lockout of 240 tailors in the city. Cork's craft unions rallied behind the Tailors' Society and 22–27 June saw consecutive nights of rioting and streetfighting against the Royal Irish Constabulary (RIC) and military. During the second week of June, porters on the Cork and Bandon Railway had turned out for a wage rise. On 22 June, a series of wage demands appeared from unskilled workers in the city. Over the next five days, wage demands flooded in from dockers, railway porters, flour millers, and timberyardmen; the rate requested soon settled on 15s. per week. On Monday 27th, the gathering strike wave culminated in a general strike of unskilled operatives. Pickets toured factories and workshops calling out those still at work. Women and boys also joined the protest, textile girls striking on their own accord. Membership of the Cork Labourers' Society swelled to 1,400, whilst many others belonged to the Working Men's Society. This was a revolt of the unskilled. Shoemakers were the only trade to join the Tailors in striking for higher wages and restriction of machinery. The unrest spread rapidly to the county, extending as far as agricultural labourers at Killarney, and navvies on the Waterford and Lismore Railway. Queenstown boatmen came out on 27 June, Glanmire bleachworkers and Mallow dairymen on 28th; by 30 June, the agitation had reached farm labourers, railwaymen, and artisans in north and east Cork. Groups combined on a sectional basis, though in Charleville all classes united in a general local strike. Parity with city wage rates emerged as a common demand; but artisans also sought curbs on machinery or an end to the use of imported goods, and farm workers began campaigns of systematic machine breaking.

After a hectic week of workers' parades and military policing in Cork city, the atmosphere relaxed on Thursday 30th. In most cases, workers' demands were granted, though sailors' and coalporters' disputes lasted into mid July and were less successful. Unrest in the county ended in the first week of July. Here too, employers had normally acceded to the men's pay demands. While agricultural machine breaking had been stopped by RIC intervention, there is some evidence that labourers were compensated with wage rises. A Labourers' Club was inaugurated at Glounthane on 31 July, and north Cork sustained a fragile 'club movement' over the next decade. The tailors' strike dragged on until 3 August, when a settlement was reached through the mediation of George Druitt, secretary of the London Operative Tailors' Association. A big increase in living costs sparked renewed unrest in Cork and Dublin in 1871, and the Cork Nine Hours League, initiated by the local branch of the Amalgamated Society of Engineers (ASE), achieved significant success in various industries the following year.

The recurrence of opposition to machinery in the Cork disputes illustrates the pressures facing obsolescent handicrafts at this time. After the international slump in 1874, these pressures became overwhelming. Within a context of general decline, labour organiz-ation enjoyed minor recoveries towards the end of the decade, and continued to mature during the 1880s. Following legal reverses in 1871, two acts of 1875 legalized peaceful picketing, and repealed the Master and Servant Act which had made employee breach of contract a criminal offence. The Trades Union Amendment Act (1876) finally confirmed some of the legal benefits recommended by the minority report of the Royal Commission on Trades Unions appointed in 1867. Unions now found it safer to register under the law, which gave protection to their funds.[11] Trade union membership increased slowly in fresh local societies or branches of British-based bodies. New trades councils were formed in Waterford in 1879 and Cork in 1880; Belfast trades council was established in 1881, with an affiliation of 4,000 members, following a meeting to support linen tenters on strike against a pay cut. Some major disputes occurred, notably that of 1,100 milesmen on the Great Southern and Western Railway in September 1877 over wages and conditions.[12] However, small unsuccessful selective strikes were more common. The deep pessimism that pervaded southern cities after 1874 reduced trade union policy to a pathetic dependency. Significantly, the establishment of Dublin United Trades Council in 1886 stemmed immediately from a deputation to the new Lord Lieutenant requesting that His Excellency provision the Viceregal household from native goods and services.[13]

'AN ELYSIUM FOR WORKING MEN'

As the south slipped into despond, northern capitalists broad-ened their economic base. The 1860s was a decade of tremendous growth in Belfast, when the city's population rose from 119,000 to 174,000. By 1911 Belfast had burgeoned to 387,000 souls, making it the biggest city in Ireland; with 8.8 per cent of the total population, it contained 21.0 per cent of all industrial workers. Like Dublin, the city enjoyed a sizeable trade in food, drink, and tobacco, but its near monopoly of other sectors gave it an exceptional importance. In 1907, the Belfast region accounted for £19.1 million of the total £20.9 million worth of manufactured exports, excluding food and drink. This performance was based mainly on textiles, engineering, marine engineering, and shipbuilding, the last being the locomotive of progress. Belfast's two shipyards were employing a staff of 12,000 by 1900 and 20,000 by 1914. Working-class conditions were by no means easy, but compared favourably with those in the main British cities. Fifty thousand new houses were built between 1880 and 1900, as many as were completed throughout the six counties from 1919 to 1939. This was the stuff of Lord Mayor Henderson's celebrated boast to the 1898 Irish Trade Union Congress that here was 'an elysium for working men'. With lesser centres of manufacture scattered across the province, Ulster accounted for almost half of the industrial workforce in 1911.[14]

The cotton famine during the American Civil War decimated what remained of the Belfast cotton trade, leaving some 20,000 handloom weavers unemployed or slaving sixteen hours for a daily wage of 8*d*.[15] However, the linen industry survived the hiccups caused by the Crimean War, the American financial crisis of 1857–58, and the potentially disastrous loss of the American market in the 1860s, to profit from the substitution of linen for cotton after 1862. Boom times continued up to the international slump in 1874. Thereafter, technical innovation and cheap wages allowed Ulster to maintain its position in a contracting market by consolidating its share of UK production. Employment in Irish linen rose from 62,000 to 65,000 between 1885 and 1904. Spin-off industries also developed, chiefly handkerchief-making in Lurgan-Portadown and shirt production in Derry. By 1896 there were twenty shirt factories in Derry employing 10,000 people.[16] Both linen and shirt making supported considerable outwork employment in dressmaking and 'making up'.

Mechanization of linen had accelerated in the 1840s and with the demise of domestic production it turned weaving and spinning, overwhelmingly, into women's work. A small male workforce performed skilled tasks, tended machinery, and did the more physical, semi-skilled work. Working conditions were poor due to the climate required for each process. Weavers·suffered bronchitis from the humidity caused by steam jets. Male hacklers and roughers worked in a constant cloud of fibre dust, which caused fits of coughing each morning. Spinners new to the job commonly experienced 'mill fever' until accustomed to the noise and poor ventilation. Occupational health problems were accentuated by overcrowded housing, bad sanitation, and a staple diet for women of bread and stewed, sweet tea four times daily.[17] The difficulties in unionizing a low-paid, largely unskilled, easily replaced workforce, 60–70 per cent of whom were female or juvenile, were compounded by pronounced caste distinctions of sex, grade, and religion. Skilled men earned 30s. per week or over; weekly rates for the semi-skilled flax roughers and dressers averaged about 21s; while most women earned 7–8s. per week, less fines for indiscipline or damage to goods. Even among women grade consciousness was strong. Weavers were 'swanks'; the lower-paid spinners were 'down'. And weavers were predominantly Protestant, while spinners were disproportionately Catholic. Underlying sectarian tensions erupted during the home rule crises. A further disincentive to militancy was employer paternalism, which extended to the construction of model industrial villages. Employees did enjoy one advantage; the solidarity encouraged by their aggregation in the mills. A government inspector wrote during the prosperous 1860s:

> the workers consequently now are very independent of their employers. Small strikes for wages are often occurring, the girls sometimes appearing, in consequence, in the police courts, where they are lectured from the bench, and let off on contritely promising to return to work and fulfil their 'notice'. Occasionally they assemble in groups in the mill-yard, shouting and cheering, but determinedly refusing to enter the factory 'till prices go up' . . . The masters naturally refuse to be driven into concessions, but, in the long run, they have generally given way.[18]

Wage rates in linen rose by 15–20 per cent in the 1860s, and the cost of living fell. At the same time, many mill owners responded to the boom by stretching the working day from twelve to fourteen hours. In Derry, shirt factories stayed open as late as 10.00 p.m.[19]

The increase in living costs in 1871–72, and the subsequent long-term stabilization of wage levels, prompted male workers to turn to trade unionism. A Flaxdressers' Union was formed in 1872, and demanded an extra 4s. per week. The employers offered 2s. On 13 May Belfast flaxdressers came out, and within a week the strike had spread beyond the union to 2,500 workers, including flax roughers. Masters replied with a lockout on 31 May, closing the mills one by one. Support came from Belfast trade societies, and popular feeling ran high. At one point a crowd of about 250 workers attacked a mill owners' residence. But the strikers were ill-prepared for a long struggle. On 17 June, they accepted the employers' original offer and went back. A second total lock-out of linen workers in Belfast occured in 1874. The Flaxdressers' Union survived, organizing about 1,300 members in the 1880s. Two small societies, the Power-Loom Tenters and the Power-Loom Yarn-Dressers, were founded in 1877, and a tiny Hackle and Gill Makers' Union opened its books three years later.[20]

Though textiles remained the largest employment sector, the shipbuilding and engineering trades, with their higher quota of skilled men, came to dominate local trade unionism. By the 1850s, most engineering grades had assumed their modern form of patternmakers, moulders, turners, and fitters; though smiths carried on their traditional skills, and sheetmetalworkers continued the work formerly done by tinkers and braziers. Marine engineering later created a strong demand for boilermakers. This organization and strength, together with immigration of craftsmen from England and Scotland, stimulated pull/push forces for the growth of British-based craft societies. The Ironmakers' had a branch in Belfast from 1826, the Boilermakers' from 1841, and the ASE from its inception in 1851. By the end of the century, the proportion of unionized men in the northern shipbuilding and engineering trades exceeded the UK average. Industrial relations in the trades were fairly harmonious. Unlike their British colleagues, Belfast engineering employers made no attempt to break trade unions in the 1860s and 1870s. As early as 1872, the Belfast Employers' Association negotiated directly with unions on conditions and hours. Between 1860 and 1900, skilled rates in Belfast rose faster than in Britain, though actual earnings tended to be lower due to the absence of piecework. Due to the scarcity of artisans and abundance of unskilled men, the differential between skilled and unskilled rates in the north exceeded the UK average, sometimes reaching a 3:1 ratio.[21] The ASE submission to the Royal Commission on Labour in 1893 claimed rates of 34s.-39s. for a 53- or 54-hour week in engine shops, and a 56½ week in the mills and factories. Non members usually worked for 2s. to 6s. less. The union complained of poor safety practices, lighting, and sanitation in the shipyards, but otherwise it was happy: 'Disputes in Belfast are very rare, as the employers generally meet their employees in a fair manner, and again the trade has never been the first to demand advance of wages, nor has the Society pushed demands to extremes'. Over the preceding twenty-six years the ASE had been involved in just one general dispute in the city, when 500 members struck in 1880 against a 10 per cent pay cut. The boilermakers' agent told the commission: 'We are getting on very nicely . . . with our employers'.[22] Where disputes did occur they were largely sectional, and reflected the deep craft exclusiveness of the unions.[23]

Urban and industrial growth intensified the sectarian divisions in Ulster. As Catholics migrated to Belfast in search of work, their proportion of the city's population rose from less than one-tenth to a peak of about one-third in the mid century. Craft unionism, with its emphasis on controlling access to the trade, functioned ideally to exclude the newcomers or their offspring from the plum jobs, but sectarian inequality was reproduced ultimately by an institutionalized intimidation, nowadays called the 'chill factor', which drove the minority to seek safety in numbers. Competition for jobs against a backcloth of declining ascendancy privilege and rising nationalism sparked intermittent sectarian riots from the 1830s onwards. As early as 1835, one witness informed a select committee on handloom weavers that there was 'so much political difference between the men, that they cannot permanently co-operate together'.[24] Being poorer, fewer, and less well connected, Catholics gravitated to unskilled occupations and the building trades. In 1901, when they accounted for 24 per cent of Belfast's population, Catholics constituted half the number of female linen spinners, one-third of general labourers, 41 per cent of dockers, and 27 per cent of bricklayers. By contrast, the proportion of Catholics in the shipyards fell from 28 per cent in 1861 to eight per cent in 1911. Shipyardmen were prominent in sectarian riots in 1857, and in attempts to expel Catholic workers in 1864, 1886, 1893, 1912, and 1920.[25]

With a maturing confidence, Protestant artisans became more prominent in conservative politics. In 1868, a body of Belfast tradesmen met to endorse the parliamentary candidature of 'the indomitable' William Johnston, an Orange leader of unorthodox views. Johnston was subsequently returned as an Independent Conservative MP for Belfast. When, in 1871, the Belfast Grand Lodge opposed Johnston's re-election as Grand Master, his supporters launched the Belfast Orange and Protestant Workingmen's Association to protect 'the political rights of the Protestant workingmen'. If evangelical and anti-elitist in attitude, the association's democratic spirit did not extend to labourers. Nominally restricted to Orange artisans, it was led by small businessmen and professionals. Johnston's reconciliation with the Conservative party in 1873 undermined the association, though it recovered somewhat to play a minor role in Orange politics from 1876 to 1878.[26] After 1881, Belfast trades council tiptoed between local Conservatism and the Liberal politics of its British mentors. The council forbade political discussion at its meetings from the outset. Individual members were politically engaged however, including the council's secretary, Alexander Bowman, an official of the Flaxdressers'. Bowman stood as a Liberal candidate for North Belfast in 1885, the first such trade unionist to contest Westminster. The 1886 home rule crisis destroyed this embryonic Liberal Labourism. On 30 April, large numbers of workers attended a rally in the Ulster Hall at which Belfast Liberals rejected Gladstone's Bill. Arrangements were made too for workers' deputations to lobby British Lib-Labs, and working-class opposition to home rule would later feature in Unionist claims for the democratic and progressive nature of its case. Belfast trades council avoided comment on the home rule crisis, but its real sympathies were no secret. Bowman's attempt to swing local Liberals behind Gladstone provoked a storm of reaction, compelling him to resign as secretary. The council did call on trade unionists to keep out of the subsequent sectarian violence in the shipyards, but it was powerless to prevent conflict and unable to sustain an enduring labourism in the face of Conservative and Unionist sentiment.[27]

RURAL LABOUR

In the transformation of the rural social structure initiated by the Great Famine, the tenant farmer benefited at the expense of the landlord and the labourer. Between 1845 and 1851, the number of agricultural labourers declined from 700,000 to 500,000. Over the same period, the cottier class dwindled from 300,000 to 88,000.[28] Unemployment and underemployment, low wages and bad housing conditions ensured continuing high rates of emigration for labourers. The 1881 census recorded 336,127 labourers; by 1911 the figure had fallen to 199,901, still a significant fraction of the country's wage earners but less impressive as a proportion of the agricultural community. In 1841, there were 2.71 labourers to each farmer. In 1911, the ratio stood at 1.31 to 1; and where the waged labour force was greatest, in the tillage counties of Munster and Leinster, only Waterford, Dublin, Meath, and Kildare contained more than two labourers to each farmer.[29]

Labourers' conditions improved little in the 1840s and 1850s as low prices for wheat and barley caused a switch from tillage to pasture.[30] The replacement of the sickle by the scythe and the introduction of machinery in the 1850s brought further threats to the labourers, who relied on harvest bonuses for spare cash. Reports of Irish migrant harvesters to England and Scotland in 1862 remarked on their youth in comparison with the mature or middle-aged migrants of the 1840s. The bulk of these migrants hailed from west Ulster and Connacht, and about two-thirds were landless. Less is known of internal migration, which was more significant in Munster and Leinster. A rise in grain prices following the Crimean War drew additional *spailpiní* into the tillage counties. The harvest of 1858 saw protests against mechanization in the south-east. Threshing and hay-tedding machines were smashed and scythes broken in Waterford, Tipperary, and Kilkenny. Hundreds rioted at the hiring fair of Callan, Co. Kilkenny, in demand of 3s. rather than 2s. per day.[31]

Agricultural wage levels rose considerably in the late 1860s. In 1870, average weekly rates for outdoor men varied from 10s. to 12s. around Dublin and Belfast to 6s. in the poorer areas. Resident farm servants, normally engaged by small farmers, were paid from £8 to £14 per annum.[32] However, these increases did nothing to diminish the almost universal discontent amongst farm workers, and it was to staunch the flow of cheap or scab labour to Britain that the first attempt was made to extend conventional trade unionism to the land. In August 1873, Joseph Arch and Henry Taylor, President and General Secretary of the English National Agricultural

Labourers' Union, inaugurated the Irish Agricultural Labourers' Union at Kanturk, where a Labour Club had been formed in 1869.[33] Prompted by the 1870 Land Act, the Kanturk Labour Club had aimed to secure legislative improvement of labourers' conditions; it played no part in encouraging the 1870 strike wave. Arch hoped that the new union would concentrate on pushing rates up to English levels; branches formed in Munster and south Leinster and achieved some success. But if a union could complete the patient task of building membership and maintaining subscriptions among such scattered, isolated, subsistence waged men, its bargaining position was made vulnerable by unemployment, the seasonal nature of the work, the low ratio of employees to employers, and the 'living in' system. The Agricultural Labourers' Union soon reverted to a strategy that would inform agricultural labour organization up to 1918: alliance with the national movement and emphasis on legislative reform. Isaac Butt had been a patron from the outset. The union finally disintegrated in 1879 at a time of harvest failures and rising unemployment. A few cognate labour clubs which had emerged during the decade also collapsed.

The land war created a fresh opportunity for advancement. Whilst labourers gave little active backing to the Land League, their refusal to work as 'emergencymen' for boycotted landlords was vital to the farmers' success. Landlords tried to sow dissent between labourers and farmers. They were particularly scathing about the fact that while farmers shouted about injustice, their own record as employers was abysmal. Parnell appreciated that the labourer had got nothing out of the land war. Calling on masters and men to stand together, he promised to lead a labourers' movement if the farmers did not give them fair treatment, and spoke vaguely about settling men on reclaimed land. Labourers themselves were becoming restless. Workers around Kanturk struck for higher rates during the harvest of 1880. A Labour League was established at a convention in Limerick in 1881, where speakers advocated wage strikes after the manner of Joseph Arch's union in England. Over the coming months, north Cork experienced another spontaneous strike wave, with gangs of labourers touring farms calling out those still at work.[34] Internal nationalist politics also dictated Parnell's labour policy. Among a number of rural labour bodies to emerge in the 1880s was the County of Waterford and South of Ireland Labour League under the patronage of Villiers

Stuart MP. In 1884, Stuart funded a rally of over 400 League delegates from west Waterford, east Cork, and Limerick on his estate at Dromana, where he denounced the Parnellite home rulers to a respectful audience.[35] In October 1882 a list of labourers' demands was incorporated into the National League programme. With the scope for appeasing both labourers and farmers so restricted, Parnell focused on housing. The Dwellings for the Labouring Classes (Ireland) Act (1860) had encouraged landlords to obtain loans for the construction of labourers' cottages. However by the 1880s, most farm labourers still lived in one-roomed mud cabins with thatched roofs. The 'Parnell cottages' built under the Labourers (Ireland) Acts from 1883 onwards did nothing to tackle underemployment, low wages, or the persistence of the demeaning hiring fairs, but they offered rural labour a better return for its nationalism than urban workers received. And they provided in turn a focal grievance for organization. Housing was thus the one area where the rural worker acquired an advantage over his urban counterpart. Sixteen thousand cottages were built or authorized by 1900. By 1921, 54,000 cottages had been completed. Structurally, the dwellings set a standard for this class of housing, being generally superior to accommodation for unskilled urban workers, and occasionally better than neighbouring farm houses.[36]

TOWARDS A NEW MODEL

Revolutionary politics revived after 1860. Workers were heavily implicated in the Fenian conspiracy. A series of raids and detentions between 1865 and 1867 netted a variety of occupations, ranging from labourers and carpenters to publicans and law clerks.[37] Irish Republican Brotherhood (IRB) membership was drawn largely from the working class, with middle-class radicals providing the leadership. Yet, despite many and deep connections with Fenianism, and allowing for its secretive nature, trade unionists did not display the same revolutionary fervour in 1867 as in 1848. Workers were no longer as aggressively class conscious, or as brutalized by social conditions. Their unions were becoming concerned with distinct organizational interests, separate from politics, and were being drawn into the values of social consensus and moderation. Furthermore, the closing decades of the nineteenth century saw a growing specialism in popular mobilization. By the 1870s, the unprecedented wealth created by capitalism was finally percolating to the people through improvements in housing, services, and leisure. As organizations catering for social activities, sports, and party politics emerged, trade unions began to hive off these functions, restricting their ambit to industrial issues.

The Fenian movement had ever been favourable to labour organization, and after the fiasco of 1867 some IRB elements re-directed their energies into trade unionism. Cork's Working Men's Association, Labourers' Society, and Grocers' and Wine Merchants' Working Men's Society, all formed in 1868–69, were Fenian dens.[38] The post-rising amnesty campaign, which allowed bodies to express Fenian sympathies without preaching sedition, drew open trade union backing. Cork trades passed a resolution for amnesty in 1868, followed by Dublin, and the campaign continued into 1869, with the trades of most towns heavily involved. On 10 October 1869, forty-five Dublin unions paraded at an amnesty rally which reputedly attracted a crowd of 300,000 people. It was through a Fenian journalist, J.P. MacDonnell, that the International Working Men's Association made a brief foray into Ireland in 1872. The treatment of Fenian detainees had first aroused the International's interest in Ireland, though Karl Marx and Friedrich Engels had long regarded Ireland as the Achilles' heel of the British ruling class. In July 1871, Marx proposed MacDonnell as the International's Irish secretary. MacDonnell first organized Irish emigrants in London and in late February 1872 the International set foot in Cork, then the most promising of Irish cities for the propagation of socialism. With pledges of financial aid, the Cork Internationalists recruited large numbers of coachmakers on strike for a nine-hour day. Reports that ten other unions were considering association with the International sent panic signals through the Cork bourgeoisie. Within three months the International had sunk beneath a clerically induced red scare. Branches in Dublin, Belfast, and Cootehill suffered a similar fate. Well might Engels remark with disdain: 'Ireland still remains the *sacra insula* whose aspirations must on no account be mixed up with the profane class struggles of the rest of the sinful world'.[39]

Fenian echoes persisted in trade unionism. Many trades or trades councils commemorated the Manchester Martyrs until well into the new century. Parnell's efforts to incorporate labour within the home rule alliance might have extended to urban workers the same tactical opportunities it afforded their rural colleagues. In 1881, Parnell restyled the Land League as the Irish National Land League and Labour and Industrial Movement; in 1882 he founded the Irish Labour and Industrial Union, and called for legislation to improve workers' conditions.[40] Workers remained convinced of the necessity of home rule to economic regeneration, but labour's capacity for independent political mobilization was nearing exhaustion, and trade unions could no more than limp along with the national movement. The root cause of political debility lay in organizational atrophe. Like the economy, labour organization entered a tailspin of undevelopment after the Great Famine. And as with the economy, the most obvious symptom of decline lay in increasing dependence on Britain. In 1851 the ASE introduced a 'new model' of organiz-ation to British trade unionism. The Engineers set out to create a big, relatively centralized society, through a cautious policy of consolidation. Entrance fees and benefits were high. Strikes were discouraged, the tactical emphasis falling overwhelmingly on maintaining demand for labour through control of apprenticeships and enforcement of restrictive practices. Gradually other societies emerged, roughly similar in style to the Engineers. New model unionism, as it came to be called, restricted itself to craftsmen. Politically, it sought to win public acceptance and legal toleration of trade unionism by advertising its responsibility and respectability. In social values it reflected the growing conservatism of the British craft elite, the 'labour aristocracy', during the era of mid-Victorian prosperity. The importance of British craft unionism was reflected in its spreading influence throughout the English speaking world. Dublin and Belfast branches took part in the initiation of the ASE, and by 1891 the Engineers had fourteen Irish branches with 2,228 members; 1,515 of them in Belfast. Other British engineering unions, notably the Ironfounders, the Boilermakers, and the United Pattern-makers, also established a strong base in the north-east. The British Amalgamated Society of Tailors and Tailoresses included a Dublin branch on its formation in 1866, and spent considerable sums to surmount the difficulties of organizing sweated employment in the main towns over the next twenty years. British printing unions absorbed local societies in Dublin, Belfast, and Cork after 1877. By now, Ireland was firmly on the British takeover list, and local unions came to resent what they regarded as unfair competition from the amalgamateds. The strongest resistance to assimilation came in the building trade. Bricklayers, plasterers, stonecutters and slaters generally remained in local unions. The Dublin Regular Carpenters and the Ancient Corporation of Carpenters of Cork rebuffed the entreaties of the Amalgamated Society of Carpenters and Joiners until the 1890s.[41] The still important benefit function of trade unions gave the amalgamateds a major advantage over their smaller Irish rivals. As benefit societies, they were well run and reliable. Should a craftsman need to seek work in Britain, an amalgamated society offered him a recognized card.

Outside the north-east, new model unionism had a very limited application. To the mass of workers in unskilled or declining skilled trades it offered no effective means of achieving a bargaining power. Yet limited though it could be, the spread of the amalgamateds was sufficient to establish them as the paradigm of trade unionism. These unions had the backing of the mighty British labour movement behind them; like a drop of ink in a glass of water, they tinted the values and outlook of urban labour, preparing the way for an accelerated anglicization of trade unionism during the 1890s. The moderation of rural labour protest and the anglicization of urban society after the Great Famine reinforced this orientation towards the British model. The view that unions should address internal affairs alone dovetailed neatly with the new model unionist conception of responsibility. Thus, renewed labour endorsement of nationalist politics in the 1880s was followed by a rapid disengagement after the fall of Parnell.

3

New Unionism and Old, 1889–1906

As the American and European economies pulled out of recession in 1887, an unprecedented burgeoning of trade unionism culminated in a great spasm of unrest that shook the industrial world between 1889 and 1891. This militancy challenged existing conceptions of labour organization. In France it laid the seedbed of syndicalism. More moderately, British workers adopted a 'new unionism'. From the mid 1880s, unions catering for unskilled workers had been active in the English provinces, notably Tyneside and the Black Country. By 1889 the spirit had spread to the capital; the London dock strike that summer marked its arrival as a force. With an alacrity encouraged by the prominence of Irish emigrés amongst them, British new unions commenced operations in Ireland almost simultaneously.

New unions were distinguished by their focus on the unskilled; some recruited on a general basis. Unlike their craft counterparts, they offered low subscription rates and gave priority to winning improvements in wages and conditions rather than providing friendly benefits; and they aimed to defend their members' living standards through strike action, or the threat of it, rather than the old craft union device of maintaining a scarcity of labour through control of apprenticeships. During the first flush of militancy they used tough strike tactics, including violence and blacking. New unionists believed also that labour interests should go beyond purely industrial matters to campaigns for legislative reform and political representation. The demand for an eight-hour day especially, which labour was raising throughout the world, gave contemporary unrest a universal appeal and an exhilarating sense of internationalism. Most workers, skilled or not, clocked up over seventy hours on the job each week. By 1890, there was a widespread determination to reduce this to under sixty hours.

New unionism, therefore, offered something for everyone but it appealed to unskilled men mainly, and its recruitment strategy targetted employees in transport and essential services, sectors where strikes of unskilled workers were most likely to succeed. With little manufacture outside the north-east, and a relatively high import-export trade, Ireland relied heavily on commerce. At the turn of the century, 'transport and general' not alone summed up the Irish working class but defined the alliance vital to trade union success. Being located at the hinge of infrastructure, disputes in transport had an extensive impact, and from 1889 to 1913 transport constituted potentially a 'leading sector' in the evolution of trade unionism. Moreover, the weakness of the craft echelon made plain the imperative of organizing unskilled workers if labour as a whole was to win effective bargaining power, so that new unionism acquired an exceptionally inclusive nature in Ireland. In the smaller towns, artisans were often to the fore in replacing trades clubs with 'trades and labour' councils. Socialist ideas enjoyed an ephemeral vogue. And the option of forming a national labour centre reappeared.

The strength of new unionism depended absolutely on two external factors: the trade cycle and British support. The years from 1889 to 1906 were intersected by the recessions of 1891–94 and 1900–04. With the first of these, new unionism faded. Whilst British labour retained something of its vigour and made slow progress throughout this period, the Irish movement lost its expansionist dynamic. Old unionism reclaimed its ascendancy until the advent of Larkinism.

NEW UNIONISM

New unionism represented the first serious attempt to modernize the labour movement and it set the questions later taken up by Larkinite and syndicalist militancy: how to organize the unskilled, how to develop political consciousness, and whether the path of progress lay in building an indigenous movement or joining with the big battalions of Britain? Contemporary answers were ambivalent. Thirty Irish unions, many of them catering for unskilled and semiskilled workers, were founded between 1889 and 1891. Dublin United Labourers' Society mushroomed to 2,300 members by 1890, when it restyled itself the United Labourers of Ireland. Some older bodies like the Bakers, the Brick and Stone Layers, and the United Corporation Workmen of Dublin were placed on a regular footing. Yet membership of native general unions did not exceed 4,000 at maximum.[1] British unions played the key role, and new unionism accelerated Irish assimilation into the British movement. The vintage phase of advance lasted from early 1889 to mid 1891; the most remarkable year of unrest being 1890, with sixty-nine strikes compared with thirty in 1889 and thirty-nine in 1891. The sudden growth of conflict reflected the diffusion of militancy beyond traditionally unionized sectors like engineering and construction to a range of employees as diverse as Jewish tailors in Sligo and grave-diggers in Dublin. Newly recruited sectors continued to dominate unrest in 1891, but the high attrition rate—roughly two-thirds of all strikes were lost that year—took its toll. Official records log just eighteen disputes the following year, only five involving new sectors. Yet the new unionism never quite disappeared, and there were ripples of recovery in 1894–95, 1897 and 1900.[2]

Together with transport and essential services, general employment, the Belfast shipyards, textiles, and agriculture comprised the theatre of new unionism.[3] As with Larkinism a generation later, waterside workers were in the van. In January and February 1889 the Tyneside-based National Amalgamated Sailors' and Firemen's Union struck with near complete success in Dublin, Belfast, Cork, and Derry, and extended its operations during 1890. As seamen's strikes frequently involved sympathetic action by dockers or carters, a close association developed between the Sailors' and Firemen's Union and the Liverpool-based National Union of Dock Labourers (NUDL). Commonly known in England as 'the Irish union', the NUDL followed the Sailors' and Firemen's Union to Ireland, spreading south from Belfast in late 1889. By mid 1891 it organized in fifteen ports and claimed 2,000 members. The tide was on the turn however. The railway and shipping companies, widely regarded as the most obdurate employers, had given a lead to their fellows by granting concessions initially. Now they set another example by weeding out activists and replacing them with 'nons', the polite term for non-unionists. Protest stoppages were then met with 'free labour'. Strikes were broken in Derry, Sligo, Dundalk, and Waterford, and a heavy defeat followed in Belfast in 1892 after four months of struggle. In this dispute the Unionist press had exploited the nationalist politics of the NUDL's Belfast organizer,

Michael McKeown, to divide the men. These tactics killed the crippled Belfast branch during the second home rule crisis when Protestant dockers withdrew. Decline continued over the next decade, and by 1905 the NUDL had dwindled to feeble outposts in Derry and Drogheda. Where and when possible, local societies or unorganized movements tried to carry on. In 1900, over 1,000 quaysidemen in Dublin, Limerick, and Newry struck for higher wages. But in this, as in many similar stoppages of unskilled grades, they were not successful.

A second growth area in transport was the railways. Like many longstanding unions the Amalgamated Society of Railway Servants (ASRS) espoused new unionism with enthusiasm. The ASRS had opened its first Irish branch in Belfast in 1885, and then commenced an all-grades recruitment drive. In December 1889, as Great Northern Railwaymen agitated for better conditions, a series of wage strikes broke out on the Great Southern and Western Railway and continued throughout the following year, spreading to the smaller systems. The biggest stoppage began in March when 1,500 Great Southern and Western Railwaymen struck in sympathy with two colleagues dismissed for blacking goods. Once the dispute became general, questions of wages and conditions were raised. On 5 May the strike ended with a promise to consider the men's grievances. Membership of the ASRS, which stood at 163 in 1889, had now soared to 3,659, giving the union about one-third of its potential establishment. With the employers' counter-attack in late 1890, the ASRS lost ground in the south. When men on the Dublin, Wicklow, and Wexford Railway struck in protest at victimization, they were replaced. Similar troubles befell Waterford and Limerick railwaymen. A stronger presence on Great Northern lines largely accounts for the union's 2,893 members in 1893. Three years later, in step with a related drive in Britain, the ASRS hazarded a comeback, boosting membership to 6,203 by 1897. Strike notices followed for a 'national programme' demanding recognition, better conditions, and higher wages. But when the railway companies applied their standard threat of dismissal and replacement with scabs, the ASRS backed down. It was a crushing blow. The next year brought plummeting membership and defeat in a violent strike on the Cork, Bandon, and South Coast Railway, leaving the union with 1,100 members by 1900.[4]

Societies catering for unskilled men existed in most cities by 1890. Almost all such groups were local and sectional, representing builders', brewery, municipal, or quayside labourers. An exotic exception were the Knights of Labour assemblies. The Philadelphia-based Knights were a truly general union, operating 'mixed locals' in a masonic type brotherhood which preached temperance and thrift. In September 1888, they spread to Belfast from the English Black Country. Erin's First Assembly was instituted formally in Belfast the following March by organizer R.H. Feagan, a nationalist and later secretary of the local Fabians. Erin's First recruited about 300 shipyardmen and bootmakers. It was soon joined by a second Belfast assembly, of ropemakers, and in August 1889, Alpha Assembly 1601 was inaugurated in Derry. Then disaster struck in Belfast. Loyalist opposition forced Feagan's resignation, and the ropemakers blundered into an ill-prepared strike. After fourteen weeks, the strike was crushed, and the Knights with it. In contrast, Alpha Assembly flourished, reaching 800 members by 1891.[5] The greatest successes among general workers fell to the National Union of Gasworkers and General Labourers (NUGGL), launched in 1889 by a Birmingham Irishman, Will Thorne. With assistance from Eleanor Marx and others of the leading British Marxist group, the Social Democratic Federation (SDF), Thorne recruited 20,000 members in England within four months, and prised the eight-hour day from a number of employers. Towards the end of the year the NUGGL was active in Belfast and Dublin, where its organizers, Michael Canty, Adolphus Shields and William Graham, were all socialists. Belfast Corporation quickly conceded the principle of eight-hour shifts in its municipal gasworks. When Alliance Gas of Dublin followed suit in January, the union's reputation was made. It now turned its attention to general workers. A signal victory came in March, when 1,500 bricklayers' labourers in Dublin struck twenty-five firms to win a wage increase. Dublin coal merchants reacted by forming an employers' association and one of the biggest coal factors, McCormick's, dismissed two union activists. On 1 July the NUGGL struck the entire trade for their reinstatement. Two thousand members were affected. McCormick's brought in scabs to keep business going. Pickets massed to halt coal transports, carts were overturned, and scabs assaulted. Dockers in Dublin and Belfast blacked colliers bound for McCormick's and there were strikes at firms which accepted black coal. After two weeks of struggle the men agreed to resume work in return for an employers' assurance that all future disputes would be referred to arbitration. But before August had ended, strike notice in pursuit of a wage demand was met with a lockout. On 10 September, the NUGGL recommended an unconditional return to work.[6]

Outside Belfast, general unionism was undermined fatally by the reverses suffered in 1891. The year began with a series of wage strikes involving 1,400 railway navvies in the west and south-west, all of which were quickly defeated. In June, Dublin cornporters struck thirty-nine firms to compel ship owners to employ more tallymen. Lightermen, draymen, warehousemen, brewers, millers, and bakers came out in sympathy, bringing the total number on strike to 3,000. By mid August the strike had been broken with scabs supplied through the Shipping Federation. Of eighteen disputes involving unskilled workers that year, just two minor actions did not end in defeat; by contrast, roughly half of craftsmen's strikes succeeded, about the average rate for this era. Over one-quarter of disputes in 1891 resulted in some or all of the strikers being dismissed.[7] For those without a recognized trade or union benefit to fall back on the price of failure could be very high. By August 1891, the Knights of Labour in Derry had shrunk to 100 members. In 1892, the NUGGL's twelve Dublin branches disintegrated amidst persistent problems of keeping members in benefit and recriminations over strike pay; Michael Canty fled from unpaid bills to work for the new Irish National Labourers' Union. This Dublin body, bolstered with stragglers from the Gasworkers', rose to a peak of 1,200 members in 1891, falling back to 600 by 1897. The NUGGL enjoyed a slightly longer tenure in the less militant north. In Belfast it had expanded to eight branches, representing 1,400 workers in municipal, building, and general employment. Four branches operated in Derry, and others in Lurgan, Newry, Armagh and Portadown. Decay set in in 1893, and the Gasworkers' had vanished from Ireland with two years. Of general unions, only the Tyneside-based National Amalgamated Union of Labour (NAUL) established a strong enduring presence in Ireland. Founded in 1890, the NAUL's Belfast branch numbered 204 members by 1891. Its core support lay in the shipyards, where it organized labourers and semi-skilled men. Absorbing remnants of the NUGGL, the NAUL embraced builders' labourers, mineral water and other general workers in 1893. Membership peaked in 1897, with 2,856 members in twelve branches, including one in Dublin.[8]

Only where transport or essential services inter-connected with general work were unskilled operatives able to make full benefit of the new unions. In no respect was this more evident than in the two largest employment sections, textiles and agriculture. As male operatives seized the prevailing climate, the four existing craft and semi-skilled textile societies were supplemented by four more unions between 1889 and 1894. With little over 3,000 members on aggregate, they lacked muscle. When, in 1892, the Linen Lappers' Union demanded that weekly rates be raised from 15–20s per week to a minimum of 25s, the employers replied with a general lockout. Belfast trades council rallied 12,000 workers in a support march. To enhance the sense of solidarity, Catholic and Protestant bands were invited along and stewards sported orange and green rosettes. The linen lappers lost their fight, being replaced with machines and female labour.[9] Attempts were made too to tackle the more for-midable challenge of organizing women, who made up 70 per cent of the workforce in textiles. Female mill hands could sustain brief protest stoppages, usually lasting a day or two. In the circum-stances, these were remarkable feats of solidarity. Three thousand girls in Lurgan struck against a wage cut in 1889. The Truck Act (1896), which compelled employers to list rules regarding fines and work penalties, provoked a series of stoppages by over 14,000 flax and linen operatives in 1897. Smaller protests for wage improve-ment had became more common after 1889.[10] Backed by Belfast trades council, the London-based Women's Trade Union Provident League set up three unions in the mills in 1890, but all fell apart within a year. Eleanor Marx inspected conditions in the Derry shirt factories in 1891, probably at the prompting of the NUGGL who had opened a branch for female shirt operatives prior to the visit. Derry trades council gave the Gasworkers' its full backing. The most enduring initiative followed the British TUC meeting in Belfast in 1893 when the Textile Operatives' Society was launched. This union enrolled about 1,000 members and was to be long identified with Miss Mary Galway, a tenacious but none too radical lady who concentrated on signing up the better-paid weavers.[11]

Efforts at rural labour organization took a more political direc-tion. Kanturk again led the field with the formation of a local Trade and Labour Association in 1889. Similar bodies sprung up through-out central Munster. Michael Davitt acted to coordinate this energy in January 1890, when he launched the Irish Democratic Trade and Labour Federation to reassert the claims of labour within the national movement. Davitt's programme demanded universal suffrage, free education, shorter working hours, and the provision of land and cottages. The Federation attracted agricultural and small town labourers mainly, extending to about thirty branches in and around Co. Cork.[12] The complications created by the Parnell split reduced it to total inefficacy. Davitt was the first to call for the Chief's resignation, whilst organized labour generally took the Parnellite side. But the split also politicized labour as rival factions competed for popular support. Backed by Davitt on the one hand, and powered by ubiquitous Fenian intervention on the other, several groups attempted to continue the work. The Federated Trade and Labour Union recruited widely in Munster, while a more ephemeral Labour League mushroomed in the south-east in 1891, forming thirty-three branches with 3,880 members, of whom 1,334 were in agriculture. In towns throughout the south, trade or workingmen's associations emerged, many of them under IRB control. Later, the Athy based Knights of the Plough became active in Leinster, under the patronage of Labour-Parnellite MP William Field. To the north, Richard McGhee, a founder of the NUDL and later a Nationalist MP, set up the Ulster Labourers' Union. The NUDL itself recruited a handful of farm workers in Wexford.[13]

None of these groups could hope to meet the challenge of agricultural trade unionism. As ever, the labourer remained notoriously underpaid. In 1902 the Wilson Fox report estimated the cash value of weekly emoluments (including allowances in kind and extra payments) for male labourers in Ireland as 10s.11d. compared with 17s.3d in Wales, 18s.3d in England, and 19s.3d in Scotland. A man dieted by a farmer might receive as little as 4s. per week.[14] None the less, new rural unionism showed that it was possible to agitate for cottages, for rent abatements, and for employment on road works. An increase in the statutory allotment with each cottage in 1892 from half to one acre added a further incentive to agitation. Labour pressure on the Boards of Guardians increased, sometimes spilling over into direct action. On 15 August 1894, the Irish Land and Labour Association (ILLA) was formed at Limerick Junction to pursue grievances such as these. Run by Nationalist politicians D.D. Sheehan and J.J. O'Shee as a labour lobby within the national movement, it would prove to be the most enduring of rural labour groups.[15]

With the ebb of new unionism, the more widely organized trades alone could strike with prospect of victory. During 1892, general stoppages of building tradesmen in Belfast and of tailors and printers in Dublin were successful. In 1896, 4,500 building workers in Dublin stayed out for four months to win pay rises and a cut in the working week from fifty-seven to fifty-four hours. In 1900, almost 1,000 woodworkers struck seventy firms in Belfast to reduce their standard week to 52½ hours.[16] However, the skilled sector in the south was too small to exert a leading influence on working-class morale, whilst the numerically significant artisanate in Belfast was too sectional. Of the forty recorded strikes involving shipbuilding and engineering workers between 1888 and 1913, fourteen emerged from demarcation disputes.[17] New unionism raised expectations of breaking down Belfast's parochialism. In 1892, the NAUL won pay parity with Tyneside for its platers in Harland and Wolff and tried to end the system whereby plater's helpers were paid directly by the platers rather than by the company. But a recession the following year brought wage and staff cuts, for which the crafty trades council refused to condemn Mr Harland or Mr Wolff. As trade recovered in 1895, a fresh opportunity arose to promote labour unity. Hardened by new unionism, Belfast shipbuilders took the unusual step of joining with colleagues on Clydeside in a common front against wage demands. In a move deeply resented by craftsmen as a breach of the city's harmonious tradition of industrial relations, a strike in one area was to be met by layoffs in the other. In October, 1,100 ASE men struck to restore a cut of 2s. per week; 190 ironfounders also came out for the same demand. Trade slumped, and by December 10,000 workers had been made idle, many of them labourers with no benefit to fall back on. In January the engineers accepted an extra 1s. per week. The ironfounders held out a week longer and won the full 2s. Despite the efforts of radicals to mobilize a class-based response, the sectionalist mentality of local trade unionism survived, and it was to be reinforced in 1897 by the British engineering trades agreement. This, the first such UK arrangement to include Belfast, still left wages to be decided on a district basis, and it soon embroiled Belfast in another upheaval; the general lockout of ASE men from July 1897 to February 1898. Yet, it proved a stabilizing influence in the long term and did not, as militants hoped, bring Belfast into the current of British labour politics.[18]

NEW POLITICS

Just as the new militancy spread from the unskilled to permeate mainstream trade unionism and become diluted within it in turn, so a new politics sprang from the socialists to fizzle and fade within labour. The impact of militancy on class consciousness is evident in the introduction of Mayday parades, the growth of trades councils, and the publication of papers like the new unionist *Irish Labour Advocate*, the more moderate *Irish Worker*, and Michael Davitt's *Labour World*. Responding to the designation of 1 May as a labour holiday by the Second International, Dublin celebrated on the first Sunday of May from 1890 to 1896. Thousands marched each year, with 20,000 taking part in 1893. The initial parade, organized by the NUGGL, was largely confined to new unionists, but subsequent Maydays were convened by Dublin trades council and assembled a confluence of new and old unionists, Parnellites, Fenians, and socialists. Parades were held also at Belfast, Cork, Dundalk, Drogheda, Newry, Derry, and Waterford during these years. Speakers usually appealed for the eight-hour day, legislative reform, and labour representation in politics. Trades councils provided a more mundane but enduring platform for radicals. Only Dublin, Belfast, and Cork boasted councils in 1886. Over the next ten years trades councils were formed in Drogheda, Derry, Kilkenny, and Newry, while those in Limerick, Sligo, and Waterford were revived or revamped.[19] Though still dominated by artisans, the councils now indicated a concern to unite 'trade and spade', and to speak for labour collectively. The very weakness of trade unionism gave the councils a direct role in promoting organization for the unskilled.

In the course of successive attempts to build a national centre for the movement, labour hovered between two contending conceptions of progress; its eventual choice would define the future framework of trade union political action. Labour nationalists and nationally minded radicals aimed to develop a congress which would be geared primarily towards legislative reform, inclusive in its definition of labour organization, and open to tactical engagement with the national movement. The second option, one with no rationale other than the English example, was to replicate the British TUC, concentrate on building industrial strength in a congress confined to orthodox trade unions, and nurture a strictly trade union based politics detached from nationalism. There were radical and conservative dimensions to both options; the essential difference between their protagonists was one of cultural orientation and strategic emphasis rather than ideology. At rank and file level and in the provinces the historic inclination towards labour nationalism remained vibrant. Crucially however, Dublin trades council took a more anglocentric view of things and, as the premier trade union forum, the ball kept coming back to its court. When the British TUC established a Labour Electoral Association in 1888, Dublin trades council kept in regular contact with the association through its long-serving secretary, John Simmons. Though a nationalist himself, Simmons consistently championed the British model and its assumed dichotomy between labour and nationalism.[20]

The first of four contemporary attempts at forming a congress was floated in 1888 by Dublin trades council. Trades council and other delegates from Dublin, Belfast, Clonmel, Cork, Derry, Dublin, Limerick, and Waterford assembled on 4 May 1889 to found the Irish Federated Trade and Labour Union. The Federated Union adopted a pragmatic programme, concerned chiefly with legislative improvement of working conditions, labour organization, unions for women workers, native manufacture, technical education, and political representation. The real clue to its potential lay in its broad appeal to all labour bodies and the inspiration of the Parnellite constituency machine, the National League. High hopes were soon dashed however. Belfast trades council involvement lapsed after a row over Sabbath breaking and Dublin's commitment was not sufficient to get the project operational.[21]

Differences on the merits of the options facing labour were brought to the fore by the Parnell split. Like most advanced nationalists, from the United Irishmen to the Provisionals, Parnell turned to the men of no property when abandoned by the rich. Moderates saw only problems in the schism; though the urban working class went Parnellite in the main, Dublin trades council declared its neutrality. Radicals grasped the opportunity for powerful allies. In February 1891, Michael Canty and Adolphus Shields announced a conference with Parnell on the labour question. On 14 March, a convention of urban and rural labourers met in Dublin to constitute the Irish Labour League. The adopted programme indicated a gray eminence of socialists behind the league; points included free education, nationalization of land and transport, taxation of land values, and the removal of tax on food. Parnell addressed the afternoon session. It was all too advanced for most. Dublin trades council, the craft unions, even the NUDL held aloof. The radical nationalist Labour League died the death.[22]

Still the matter would not go away. In July 1891, Dublin trades council convened a national conference of craft, labour, and trades council delegates to establish the nucleus of an annual trades congress. Three political resolutions were adopted, demanding direct labour representation in parliament, payment of MPs, and assimilation of the franchises. The conference accommodated an ambiguity on strategy. Its moving spirit, John Martin, president of Dublin trades council, believed that labour candidates should be independent of political parties, and wished to involve the absent Ulster trades councils—a sure-fire recipe for reducing political debate to the lowest common denominator. At the same time the conference included delegates from Davitt's Democratic Labour Federation and the labour-nationalist Michael Austin was elected vice-president. However, Martin's death in August caused the project to go the way of its predecessors. Davitt continued to assert a place for labour within the national movement, recommending seven candidates in the 1892 general election. Four Labour Nationalist MPs were returned: Austin, Davitt, Eugene Crean, and the Parnellite William Field.[23] Labour none the less ignored the growing recognition of the 'Lab-Nat' option in home rule circles.

BUILDING AN ILLUSION

When Dublin trades council convened the Irish Trade Union Congress (ITUC) in April 1894, following consultation with other trades councils, the departure took a more conservative and apolitical form than any of its forerunners. Ironically, the break with the TUC came at a time when the British were making belated efforts to ease the Irish sense of neglect. Just a year previously, the TUC had met in Belfast and agreed to reserve an Irish seat on its parliamentary committee.[24] In a further irony, the secessionists proceeded to replicate the style and structures that had made the TUC so irrelevant to the Irish working class. If Congress was a consequence of new unionism, it evolved into a talking shop with no political or

mobilizing functions; one which fostered a regression to old unionism. To avoid antagonizing pro-British feeling. Congress justified
itself on pragmatic grounds. Subventing delegates to the TUC was
expensive and offered little in return. Ireland still had lower wage
rates, worse working conditions, and fewer factory inspectors.
British labour could be generous in good times, but put its own welfare first when things got tough. With unconscious anticipation of
the later interplay between nationalism and trade union development, the first Congress declared, 'Like the Imperial Parliament, the
Congressional machine has become overladen . . . they cannot be
expected to understand the wants of a community largely agricultural . . . be expected to help revive Irish manufacture. . .'.[25] Yet,
as George Leahy said in his presidential address to the seventh
annual Congress: 'We are not ashamed to admit that we took as our
model the procedure and methods which resulted in bringing about
material benefits for the workers of England during the past quarter
of a century'.[26]

Implicit in this strategy lay an error so blatantly obvious that
it can be rationalized only through the mental colonization of
contemporary labour; emphasis on strength through industrial
organization, where labour was weak, rather than through political
intervention where labour was, potentially, quite influential. True,
the ITUC executive was called the parliamentary committee, as its
purpose was to make representations to MPs. But here again the
title was a straightforward copy from Britain and carried no direct
political implications.

The small, skilled societies dominated Congress up to 1909;
printers, carpenters, and tailors featuring prominently on the
parliamentary committee. Food and drink, transport and services,
construction and textiles were the main sectors represented; but
nowhere outside the building line could Congress claim a strong
presence. General labourers remained largely unorganized. Land
and labour bodies did not bother to attend after 1898. One of their
spokesmen, William Field, had his delegate status terminated in
1896 for not belonging to a recognized trade union or trades
council; the ITUC could not appreciate a politics or a form of labour
organization that did not conform to the British model. Not that
this impressed Ulster Unionists; the ineffectual textile societies
welcomed whatever moral comfort they might accrue from participation, but the engineering and shipbuilding unions kept their

distance. Belfast trades council had intended to keep a foot in both Congresses until, in 1895, in a move designed to clip the socialist presence within it, the British TUC terminated trades council representation. Belfast protested, but the TUC was too peeved about its Irish breakaway to appreciate the finer points of Ulster politics. Down to the turn of the century, northern officials of amalgamated unions regarded co-operation with the ITUC as disloyal and northern delegations to Congress rarely reached full strength.[27] Despite a growing Belfast participation after 1900, Congress retained a southern orientation and implicitly nationalist proclivities. Throughout these years, affiliation fluctuated between 40,000 and 70,000 members. These figures included overlapping trades council and trade union membership: a more accurate measure of Congress strength is provided by aggregate trades council membership, which stood at 37,150 in 1894. This level dipped and recovered over the next five years and then fell sharply from 37,345 in 1899 to 27,271 in 1901. Thus, the ITUC spoke for little over 5 per cent of waged labour. So small a pool had many minnows. Of the thirty-eight unions who sat in the 1901 Congress, the largest of them, the Federal Bakers, mustered 3,200 members.[28]

Did Congress make a difference? Issues like the eight-hour day, manhood suffrage, technical education, fair wages, and working conditions formed the staple of its debate. A few socialist voices achieved rare rhetorical success. Motions calling for the nationalization of the means of production, distribution, and exchange were defeated by reformist amendments in 1895 and 1896, but passed comfortably in 1898. The parliamentary committee played a useful role in monitoring labour legislation, but it lacked any means of giving weight to its expression. In the first flush of enthusiasm, there were calls for action. Motions passed in 1895 and 1896 urged the parliamentary committee to establish a political fund and draw up schemes to unionize unskilled and rural labour. Nothing was done to implement them. Congress was hopelessly ill-equipped for the task. It employed no secretariat. Finances were limited and uncertain. Over one-quarter of the annual budget came from voluntary subscriptions. In 1906, when a small levy on affiliates was introduced, the annual income amounted to £190.10s.1d. As the years rolled by, delegates became a little more philosophical about all these resolutions that were never implemented. They sat back and enjoyed the occasion; the mock parliamentary pomp and circumstance, the patronizing addresses of welcome from mayors, clerics, and other dignatories, and the hospitality of local employers. What really interested the brothers were dealings that affected their trades. Many delegates worked in declining skilled occupations threatened increasingly by British mass production. Protection of native industry and custom was of immediate concern. Unions kept an eagle eye on the distribution of patronage in their trades and no grievance was too petty to come before Congress. Dublin coach-makers frequently tabled motions condemning lord mayors who held successive terms of office as it deprived them of new orders.[29] The irrelevance of Congress to its founding philosophy of self-reliance is most evident in its failure to arrest the retreat of trade unionism into the British movement. Thirteen craft unions dissolved themselves into amalgamated societies in 1896, and six more between 1898 and 1900. New native unions kept popping up but, with the exception of the Drapers' Assistants' Association, none achieved significance and few survived.[30] Yet Congress was worse than useless. It was a treacherous illusion. In the vain assumption that British TUC strategy could be duplicated in Ireland, a delusion that blithely ignored the vast differences in economy, employment structure, and politics between both countries, it split the urban from the rural labour movement, widened the breach between artisans and labourers, and denied trade unionists the political apprentice-ship of a genuine labour nationalism.

The colonized condition of the ITUC mindset is clearest in its stance on politics. Reality compelled the parliamentary committee to cultivate relations with Nationalist MPs for lobby purposes; J.P. Nannetti, MP, a former secretary and later president of Dublin trades council, acted virtually as liaison officer between the ITUC and the Irish party. No equivalent rapport developed with Union-ism. A balancing approach to the Ulster Unionist leader, Colonel Saunderson, in 1902 brought no response. None the less Congress deemed a formal labour nationalism to be illegitimate. From 1901 to 1911, with the solitary exception of 1906, and that as a gesture of respect to an address from Nannetti, Congress approved Belfast resolutions calling for 'non-political' labour representation or for affiliates to set up branches of the British Labour Party; even though British Labour MPs had no intention of organizing Ireland and regarded the Nationalists as their 'natural allies' at Westminster.[31] Each year the motions were passed and each year nothing happened;

because most trade unionists practised in private what they abjured in public.

LABOUR AND SOCIALIST POLITICS

Closer to the base, the social interests of trades councils drew labour into the electoral arena. Even the self-consciously non-political Dublin trades council made frequent use of William Field MP in lobbies on fair wages in government contracts, pensions, and protection of native industry.[32] As trades councils went, Belfast now boasted the biggest and best. In 1897, it had fifty-six affiliates and 17,500 members; by comparison, Dublin had 12,000 members, and Cork 2,000. Conservative control of the council declined after 1894 when the president and vice-president, Samuel Monro and Joseph Mitchell, resigned in a protest over the selection of delegates to the British TUC and alleged over-representation of labourers on the council. The council returned six members to Belfast Corporation in 1897, and subsequently published a short-lived paper, *Belfast Citizen*. The elections of John Murphy and William Walker as president and assistant secretary in 1899 signalled an era of labourite dominance; both had come to prominence in new unionist agitation.[33] It seemed as if the Local Government Act (1898) would generalize this shift to the left. The act assimilated the local and parliamentary franchises and gave women who met the franchise qualification the right to vote at local elections. Dublin's municipal electorate, for example, swelled from 8,000 to 38,000. Amidst much sunburstry about the new age of the people, trades councils and cognate bodies throughout Munster and Leinster launched electoral associations. The 1899 local elections whisked a candy floss of popular power. 'Labour' candidates recorded spectacular success in the major towns. Limerick returned a labour majority; nine labour men were elected in Cork; seven in Dublin; two in Waterford. But outside Belfast, where the trades council funded its candidates, the hustings brought disillusion in their train. In September 1899, Dublin trades council was demanding an enquiry into charges of bribery against its city councillors. Later attempts to reform Dublin labour representation met with repeated frustration.[34] 'You can buy a labour vote for a pint of beer' summed up a common view of labour representation over the next decade.

Rural workers were quick to grasp the potential of local democracy for agitation for plots, cottages, and direct labour on council
roadworks. Branches of the ILLA grew to sixty-six by 1899 and
ninety-eight by 1900, the bulk of them in Cork, Limerick, and
Tipperary. In recognition of its enhanced importance, the association was admitted to the National Convention that re-united the
home rule factions in 1900. Due largely to the Local Government
Act, the United Irish League made provision for greater rank and
file representation at constituency level. Both Sheehan and O'Shee
were elected subsequently as MPs, the former largely on an ILLA
ticket. After the Wyndham Land Act had met demands of tenant
farmers, pressure mounted for comparable treatment for labourers.
Labourers' Acts of 1906 and 1911 facilitated housing construction
considerably. Though labour had now become entangled in the
factionalism of the Parliamentary Party—there were two Land
and Labour Associations after the 1906 general election, and three
after that of 1910—the work went on: 30,000 cottages were built
between 1900 and 1916, compared with 15,000 over the previous
sixteen years.[35]

Meanwhile, for the first time since the International Working
Men's Association had been hounded out of Ireland, socialist
politics had re-appeared. In 1885 branches of the SDF and its
splinter, the Socialist League, were launched in Dublin. Neither
lasted more than a year, but Dublin socialists remained active in a
variety of debating clubs. Intervention in large demonstrations of
unemployed workers in the spring of 1887 secured leftist control of
the National Labour League, an agitational body with ambitions to
organize all workers. By November, the League had lapsed, and
socialists returned to their clubs, the most enduring of which was
the Dublin Socialist Union, founded in 1890. Through new unionism, and especially the NUGGL, the socialists came into positions
of influence within mainstream labour. The Gasworkers' were
instrumental in Dublin's early Mayday festivities. Two weeks after
the 1891 parade, Will Thorne, Pete Curran, Edward Aveling, and
Eleanor Marx spoke at a Gasworkers' demonstration in the capital.
On the heels of the new unionism Fabian Societies appeared in
Belfast and Dublin, and branches of the British Independent
Labour Party (ILP) emerged in Belfast, Dublin, and Waterford. The
Belfast ILP had been inaugurated in September 1892, one of a
number established before the formal launch of the party. If Dublin

had become a little more tolerant of socialists, the climate in Belfast could be aggressively hostile. The trades council dissociated itself from the branch and there were frequent disruptions of its public meetings by Arthur Trew and his Orange henchmen. When the engineering disputes of 1895–96 failed to generate the militant class response urged by the ILP, the branch sank into decline, to be replaced by an eclectic leftist forum, the Belfast Ethical Society. A Belfast Socialist Society was formed in 1898 and a Clarion Society in 1900. Both the Dublin and Waterford ILP branches began more promisingly, with support from local trades councils and prominent labour-nationalists. Within two years, each had contracted to middle-class debating societies. Dublin ILPers then re-formed as the Dublin Socialist Society and invited James Connolly to become their full-time organizer. Taking the comrades by storm, Connolly dissolved their society and formed a new party to prosecute his views; one whose energy, policies, and significance derived entirely from himself.[36]

Connolly was born of Irish parents in Cowgate, the worst of Edinburgh's slums, in 1868. Leaving school aged ten or eleven, he went through a succession of menial jobs until 1882 when he joined the British army. Army days had a radical effect on his thinking, and imprinted a passionate hatred of British imperialism. After military desertion in 1889, he returned to Edinburgh and immersed himself in Marxist politics. Within a few years he had surmounted the drawbacks of limited schooling and a speech impediment to win a reputation as a promising thinker and agitator. Connolly took his Marxism from the SDF. In 1892 he became secretary of its Scottish wing, the Scottish Socialist Federation, but in one respect a Scots comrade, John Leslie, sowed the seeds of a very distinctive perspective. Leslie's *The Present Position of the Irish Question*, published in 1894, argued that the home rulers had betrayed the Irish people and advocated an Irish party of workers and peasants. The pamphlet inspired Connolly to urge the British left to develop a rootedly Irish socialist party, an approach at variance with the left's prevailing 'internationalism'. Meanwhile, material prospects for Connolly and his bairns were bleak in the extreme. He was considering emigration to Chile when, through an appeal from Leslie in the SDF paper *Justice*, Dublin offered him a precarious living.

The Irish Socialist Republican Party (ISRP), it was said, had more syllables than members. Though Connolly represented the

United Labourers on Dublin trades council, contacts with mainstream labour were few. A Cork branch materialized in 1899, but collapsed in 1900 following intense clerical and conservative opposition. Otherwise, the party remained confined to Dublin with pockets of support in Belfast, Dundalk, Limerick, Portadown, and Waterford. Programmatically, the ISRP drew on the SDF: and was no less sectarian than its mentor. Philosophically, it sought to reconcile internationalist socialism with Irish anti-imperialism. Commune Day, 18 March, featured as a leading commemoration in its calendar. The ISRP also affiliated to the Second International, sponsoring three delegates to the 1900 Paris congress, where it opposed the Kautsky compromise in the 'Millerand controversy'. Complementing this vigorous internationalism, Connolly sharpened his theses on the social and national questions. By 1896 Connolly had sketched his view of Irish history as a popular struggle against imperialism which the working class alone could complete. The ISRP paper, the *Workers' Republic*, stood firm on this point despite accusations of chauvinism from the British left. Party members, like many trade unionists, joined in the '98 centenary commemorations, condemned the Boer War, and demonstrated against the royal visits to Ireland. Connolly also collaborated with Maud Gonne on 'The Rights of Life and the Rights of Property', a manifesto urging direct action to prevent starvation in famine-stricken areas of Kerry and Mayo.

Curiously, given his determination to grapple with reality rather than ideological abstractions, Connolly had little to say on the land question. Stranger still were his writings on socialism and nationalism. His assumption that the labour and national struggles in Ireland needed to be brought together overlooked the fact that they had but recently been divorced, and, as yet, most workers had little conception of a tension between the two. Philosophically, Connolly's critique stemmed from thinking on the British left rather than Irish experience. Its colonized character is seen precisely in the recurrence of the nationality theme, its depiction of nationalism as problematic, and its predilection for ethnology rather than political economy in 'Hibernicizing' socialism. In starting from a presumed dichotomy between socialism and nationalism, albeit to reconcile them, Connolly confirmed the duality of the two in the popular mind, bequeathing a conundrum whose terms of reference inherently alienated socialists from the nation by treating it as an object rather than a subject. Compounding this legacy, Connolly exaggerated the conservatism of the constitutional nationalists, who have since received an undeserved bad press on the left. Socialists remember that Connolly turned the British SDF view of the Irish question inside out; they forget that it was a British view.

In 1902, a new edition of Connolly's writings, *Erin's Hope*, indicated a transition from British Marxism to the American syndicalism of Daniel De Leon. Connolly helped to found a British section of the De Leonist Socialist Labor Party that year and undertook a lecture tour of America for De Leon. In his absence, the ISRP slid into financial chaos. Political funds had been used to subvent a licensed bar. The teetotal Connolly berated the comrades on his return. Bitterness welled up on both sides and Connolly broke with the party. In vain he cast about for similar employment. With his family reduced to desperate conditions, Connolly took the emigrant ship for America in September 1903. The Dublin comrades regrouped as the Socialist Party of Ireland the following year, keeping in touch with American developments, but remaining ineffectual at home.

As winter set in for the hard left in Dublin, it was springtime for social democrats in Belfast. The birth of the Labour Representation Committee, in effect the British Labour Party, in 1900 had aroused little interest, but in July 1901 came the Taff Vale judgment in which the Law Lords made trade unions liable for financial damages caused by strikes. Their Lordship's bombshell boomeranged by nudging a scared trade union movement closer to the Labour Party. In the north itself, the sectarian tensions inflamed by the Boer War were dissipating. Even Orangeism developed a left wing. Orange dissident T.H. Sloan captured South Belfast from the Unionist Party in 1902 to become the city's first working-class MP.[37] Sloan subsequently launched the idiosyncratic Independent Orange Order, which was founded to combat Conservative appeasement of nationalists and 'Romanization' in the Anglican Church, but evolved into a vaguely liberal vehicle of working-class resentment against the 'fur coat' brigade. Labourism too acquired a leader of note in William Walker. Walker had risen through the ranks to become a full-time official of the Amalgamated Society of Carpenters and Joiners. After 1899 he emerged as the most prominent figure on Belfast trades council, and acquired some national importance in ITUC circles. In 1903 Belfast trades council formed a branch of the

Labour Representation Committee, to which local sections of the ILP, the Co-operative Society, the Ruskin Hall Education League, the Clarion Fellowship, and the Ethical Society affiliated. Both the strength and the weakness of Belfast labourism derived from Unionism. Gladstone's conversion to home rule had left the trades council with the stark alternatives of Conservative or Independent Labour politics. Under Walker's guidance the council was sufficiently strident to opt for the latter, but always vulnerable on the constitutional question. To protect that flank, it clung to the British connection, oblivious to British Labour's well-known support for home rule. Unable to confront sectarian problems at home, Belfast labourites looked outward to an ideal world. Where reality intruded, they inclined towards social imperialism. The trades council consistently advertized its Protestant orientation. Electorally, it appealed to the Protestant craftsman, opposing home rule on grounds of 'internationalism'. Not until 1905 did Labour field a candidate in the Falls ward. The *Belfast Labour Chronicle*, published jointly by the trades council and the Labour Representation Committee from 1904 to 1906, indicated a preoccupation in its Irish coverage with condemnations of home rule and Catholic clerical influence.

Walker himself crossed the thin line between social imperialism and sectarianism during his campaign for the North Belfast by-election in 1905. Backed by the British Labour Representation Committee, who offered Ramsay MacDonald as election agent, Walker's prospects of success looked good. In his anxiety to confirm his pro-Union *bona fides* however, Walker endorsed the Belfast Protestant Association's demands for the maintenance of the Protestant ascendancy. The gaffe lost him Catholic votes and probably cost him the seat. Walker edged closer to winning North Belfast in the 1906 general election, but yielded ground in a by-election the following year. He never recovered from this third failure. Though Belfast received a fillip from hosting the British Labour Party's annual conference in 1907, and three ILP branches were formed in the city that September, local Labourism had peaked. Despite Labour's biggest effort since 1897, all of its seven candidates for municipal honours were defeated in 1907, including Walker himself. With the Liberals back in power, the home rule question was again on the agenda and the scope for pro-Union Labourism already contracting.

4

Larkinism and Easter Week, 1907–1916

After four years of gathering momentum, a second wave of new unionism broke in 1907. Though beset by unemployment and falling wages over the next two years, labour continued a leftward drift into what employers called 'Larkinism'. Larkinism was part of an international acceleration of militancy, and represented, in particular, an Irish variant on syndicalism. Originating in France (*syndicat* is the French for trade union) in response to the failure of existing socialist politics—reformist, Marxist, and anarchist alike—syndicalism surfaced in most advanced countries between 1890 and 1914. It was never a uniform movement, more a pervasive mentality. Syndicalists argued that party politics created an elite, which would always betray the base. In any case, political power merely reflected economic power. So the best means of struggle was directly, in workers' organizations. Thus, they sought to graft revolutionary ideas onto trade union practice. Strategy could be of two kinds. Revealing its anarchist genes, French syndicalism emphasised the promotion of class consciousness through sabotage and strikes, culminating in a general strike, when workers would seize control of industry. Critical of Marxist rationalism, it stressed the mobilizing power of irrational forces such as faith, intuition, will, morality, and myth. American syndicalism on the other hand, was more rational and influenced by general unionism. After all, general unionism *was* the American radical tradition. The Knights of Labor had identified it with class thinking, militancy, social-ism, and opposition to the moderate, a-political craft unionism of Samuel Gompers and the American Federation of Labor. For strat-egy, the Americans turned to industrial unionism. All grades of worker in each industry should be united in the same union. An injury to one should be the concern of all, and each industrial union should be federated, resulting ideally in One Big Union (OBU).

Ultimately, the OBU would be able to control each industry from the shopfloor, and at that point smash the shell of the bourgeois state and take political power. The prototype OBU was the Industrial Workers of the World, founded in Chicago in 1905.

Both French and American syndicalism were to exert an important indirect influence on Ireland through Larkin and Connolly, respectively. The impact of French syndicalism on British militancy, still a guiding example for Irish workers up to 1911, became increasingly evident after 1908. In this golden age of the agitator, organizer Larkin came to share syndicalism's aversion to politicians and bureaucrats, its hope for a state run by the workers themselves, its belief in the power of the irrational, and its conviction in an alternative proletarian morality. For Larkin, like many socialists of the *fin de siècle*, was essentially a moralist. An antique sense of virtue, of duty towards women and family, informed his rhetoric. Representing himself as the embodiment of moral resurrection he associated the people with his heroic style, elevating the routine grind of trade unionism with a moral grandeur. Although Larkin's career was to be strewn with the wreckage of lost strikes, law suits, and personal in-fighting, he is remembered not for this disunity, or even for his considerable practical achievements, but revered in legend.

Larkinism encompassed a strategy, a method, a morality, and a politics. Initially, Larkin pursued the vintage new unionist strategy of targetting workers in transport and essential services. However his method in struggle, with its emphasis on solidarity through sympathetic action, led to a spillover from transport to general, notably after the outbreak of major unrest in England in 1911. Whereas transport men dominated Larkin's early battles, in Belfast (1907), Dublin (1908), and Cork (1909), subsequent disputes assumed a wider and wider character, culminating in the general local strikes of 1913 in Galway, Sligo, and Dublin. The notoriety of sympathetic action stemmed in part from the values on which it was based. By ennobling solidarity to a moral duty, Larkin revolutionized the ethics of industrial conflict. With this transformation went a politics of self-reliance and socialism. The formation of the Irish Transport and General Workers' Union (ITGWU) laid the cornerstone of an Irish labour movement. Making a virtue of necessity, the ITGWU set out explicitly to decolonize labour consciousness, arguing that Irish workers should rely on their own resources and build a movement geared to tackling native conditions. In the process, Liberty Hall would use nationalism repeatedly as an enabling ideology. Yet nationalism alone could never suffice; people join unions to improve their wages and conditions, not to express an ethnicity. Fundamentally, the ITGWU's future rested on its ability to surmount the obstacles to achieving an effective bargaining power for the mass of workers in an undeveloped economy.

As ITGWU ambitions broadened, it looked to Connolly's industrial unionism for direction. Profoundly influenced by syndicalism during his American years, Connolly put its practicalities in a nutshell in 1908 in *Socialism Made Easy*. Part II of this beautifully clear pamphlet gave Liberty Hall a project to modernize the entire labour movement. Industrial unionism became the most original and coherent idea ever developed by Irish trade unionists. It would exert a formative impact on labour from 1909 to 1923, and might have played an even more decisive role in the 1930s. The dimensions of the project were awesome. According to the 1911 census, out of 900,000 employees, 350,000 were classed as agricultural or general labourers, 170,000 were in domestic or related service, and 200,000 worked in textiles or dressmaking. Thus, over seven out of every nine employees were to be found in largely unorganized, subsistence waged employment. Old unionism ignored all but a handful. Craft societies stuck to the shipbuilding and metal trades, which engaged 30,000 in 1911, the building line, which included 50,000 craftsmen, the tiny skilled grades in textiles and clothing, and the constellation of butchers, bakers, and candlestickmakers who held such a high profile in the pre-Larkinite ITUC. All told, the constituency of old unionism amounted to about 10 per cent of the waged workforce. It was a measure of the weakness of old unionism, and the limits of British-based unionism, that the young, radical, and even reckless ITGWU could attain a guiding influence over ITUC policy so quickly.

Where syndicalists pursued a 'dual union' strategy, creating specifically syndicalist unions rather than trying to convert the established movement, they were forced to operate in sectors regarded by the established unions as too hard to organize. The Industrial Workers of the World was most successful in the western states of the America, among miners, migrant labourers, and timber workers; farm labourers made up half of the *Unione Sindicale Italiana's* pre-1914 membership; and in Canada a clear division emerged in the post-war struggle between craft unions, based in the industrial heartland of the eastern provinces, and the Canadian OBU movement, which had originated among newly industrialized workers in British Columbia. As a fringe area of trade unionism, nominally a part of the British labour movement, but in practice neglected by it; as an economically marginal region with a heavy reliance on primary production; and as an area where effective industrial tactics had to be militant, Ireland was a fairly typical centre of syndicalism.

LIMBERING UP

James Larkin was born in Liverpool in 1874 of Irish parents.[1] Having left school at eleven, he eventually rose to be a dock foreman. During a convalescence from a quayside accident he took time to listen to socialist orators at open-air meetings. Larkin's early socialism centred on the ILP and drew its idealism from the Clarion Fellowship. When in 1905, a dock strike chanced to bring his talents to light, Larkin was appointed temporary organizer with the NUDL, whose general secretary, James Sexton, acknowledged his protege's abilities with rapid promotion. But Sexton soon detected a threat to his own job. When the British Labour Party convened its 1907 annual conference in Belfast, Sexton seized the occasion to re-organize the Irish ports and rusticate his rival.

Larkin disembarked at Belfast on 20 January 1907. By April, he had set up branches in Belfast and Derry.[2] The Belfast branch represented almost 3,000 dockers, including the Protestant cross-channel and the Catholic deep-sea sections, and soon extended to carters and coalmen; these three groups were to make the first Larkinite revolt. Larkin's work had two factors in its favour. Since 1906, the upturn in the trade cycle had been generating a resurgence of militancy, especially in Belfast. In May of that year, 17,000 spinners, weavers and others had struck for wage increases. Thirty-four strikes hit the city in 1907, beginning with a series of stoppages by textile operatives in February, and subsequently affecting engineering, the service trades, navvies and other labourers.[3] Secondly, Larkin's presence coincided with a low ebb of sectarianism, and he enlisted support from the Independent Orange Order. Larkin also took care to recommend himself to the local labour establishment. He affiliated the Belfast NUDL to the trades council on 4 April and campaigned for William Walker in the North Belfast by-election that month. In June and July, Larkin gave further proof of his loyalty in canvassing for the British Labour Party against an Irish Nationalist during a by-election at Jarrow.

By April the NUDL appeared to have secured recognition from employers, and Larkin was happy to consolidate before risking industrial action. Though often portrayed as a maverick, this was not to be the last time that membership spontaneity or employer militancy forced his hand. On 26 April, a request by men at Kelly's coal quay that carters join the NUDL was met with dismissals. Forty coalfillers stopped work in protest. On 6 May, 144 dockers with the Belfast Steamship Company struck against the employment of two nons. On Larkin's advice the dockers returned to work, only to find that the Shipping Federation had replaced them with scabs. Days later, the NUDL won a settlement at Kelly's but Thomas Gallaher, chairman of the Belfast Steamship Company, tobacco factor and shareholder in the Belfast Ropeworks, scented the wider implications of the struggle, and determined to quash the emerging insurgence of unskilled labour. Gallaher would meet union representatives, but not Jim Larkin. Already, the personalization of the revolt had begun and, for his part, Larkin grew to revel in it. Typically, he took the fight to the doorstep of Gallaher's tobacco factory. When Gallaher dismissed seven girls for attending Larkin's lunchtime meeting, 1,000 colleagues walked out in protest. The stonethrowing that followed their strike meeting was a portent. Larkin himself was arrested for assaulting a scab on 31 May. Gallaher crushed the tobacco dispute quickly, but the dock strike dragged on. Adding to the atmosphere, 350 ironmoulders began a seven-week stoppage on 1 June which affected a further 2,000 engineers indirectly. With no end in sight Larkin called out all dockers on 26 June for better pay and union recognition, and the conflict escalated suddenly the next day when 1,000 carters struck in sympathy and for their own wage claim. Larkin intensified the pressure in appealing to other carters not to handle goods of companies in dispute. Eighteen coal merchants retaliated with an ultimatum: no union members would be employed after 15 July; 880 porters and carters rejected the diktat and joined the struggle. By now, about 3,000 men were reliant on sustenance funds raised by Belfast trades council and trade unions. Sexton's executive did not sanction strike pay until 19 July.

Belfast revealed the combustible quality of Larkinism, and its familiar pattern of worker militancy, employer over-reaction, escalation, and violence. In developing into a trial of strength on the question of unskilled trade unionism, the conflict crystallized the supreme issue confronting the labour movement. It showed too that Larkin had the will, the ability, and the method to tackle that question in its widest form. Unlike other union officials, Larkin did not try to contain unrest; he marshalled the numerical advantage of his class to stretch its enemies to the limit, and celebrated that mobilization with flair. Thousands filed along to mass meetings to hear him fulminate against the employers and preach class unity. Hailing from Liverpool, Larkin was alive to the sectarian problem, and at one point offered to hand over leadership of the strike to Councillor Alex Boyd, an Orangeman. During 'the strangest twelfth', public opinion destroyed hopes that Orange feeling might be whipped up to divide and conquer. If his claim to have buried shopfloor sectarianism proved to be standard Larkin hyperbole, and there is no truth in the yarn that he led Catholics and Protestants in a 12 July parade, Larkin did forge a brief, triumphant solidarity across the religious divide. He also exposed the class nature of the state. Troops sealed off the quays, and cavalry escorted goods traffic. Even the navy was alerted to anchor warships in Belfast Lough. Overworked, the RIC buckled. Larkin had unsettled the authorities on 16 July with a speech alleging discontent in the ranks. Sure enough, on 24 July the Belfast police protested for better pay and conditions. By 6 August the mutiny was crushed. Some 200 RIC were transferred from the city and a further 2,500 troops drafted in. As unrest spread to west Belfast, the authorities reinforced the suspicion that Larkinism masked an attempt by Catholics to organize. An exceptionally heavy security presence triggered serious rioting in Divis St on 11 August when workers attacked two vans. Soldiers killed two rioters and wounded many others in the Falls area the following day.

Solidarity now began to crumble. If the disturbances convinced the government and employers to accept Larkin's appeal for arbitration, the weakening position of the strikers enabled James Sexton to marginalize him in negotiations. Intervention by the British General Federation of Trade Unions had ended the coal merchants' lockout on 25 July; the men went back without securing the closed shop. Through Board of Trade conciliation, Sexton pursued a similar compromise. Carters and dockers won wage increases and union recognition but at the expense of working with nons. The original dispute with the Belfast Steamship Company collapsed on 4 September. Employers moved quickly to reassert sectarianism by sponsoring an exclusively Protestant union, the Belfast Coalporters' and Carters' Benevolent Society. The initiative was frustrated by a rash of strikes and sympathetic action extending to Derry, Newry, Warrenpoint, Dundalk, and Drogheda. But Sexton's determination to clip Larkin's wings had disastrous consequences. On 26 November he instructed NUDL members to return to work with an assurance that 'no advantage would be taken of any man'. Next day, the majority were informed that their jobs had been filled.

Above and beyond the personal friction between Larkin and Sexton, Belfast demonstrated that British unions lacked the will to cope with Irish industrial relations, much less to address the wider problem of unskilled unionism. The NUDL spent less than £5,000 on the Belfast disputes. The British General Federation of Trade Unions contributed under £1,700. And cross-channel intervention seemed ever intent on damage limitation. Sexton was quite happy to restrict his union to dockers. He saw no reason for Larkin to recruit carters or anyone else. In Liverpool, the carters had their own body. By subverting the credibility of the British connection, and redirecting Larkin to the south, where the constraints of craft consciousness, politics, and sectarianism were considerably weaker, the dockers' and carters' strike had a major bearing on the course of labour history.

During the summer Larkin had visited Dublin to raise financial support, and availed of the opportunity to expand the NUDL. A Dublin branch was formed on 4 August.[4] Within a year it had 2,700 members. As in Belfast, Larkin aimed to avoid confrontation initially, concentrating on recognition rather than the closed shop. But in July 1908 the Dublin Coal Masters' Association paid off 250 dockers for wearing their union badges. No one wanted another Belfast and Board of Trade intervention secured temporarily the *status quo ante*. Larkin was claiming victory when Sexton took the negotiations out of his hands. Sexton accepted employer demands that they not have to deal with Larkin and that members not sport the button at work, contrary to NUDL rules. Having embarrassed Larkin in Belfast and belittled him in Dublin, Sexton told him to organize Cork.

In April, painters in the building line had struck eighteen firms in Cork to win improvements in pay and conditions. Prospects here seemed bright. Larkin despatched James Fearon, a former secretary of the NUDL's ill-fated Newry branch whose rough and ready methods would later cause trouble for the ITGWU. Both Larkin and Fearon travelled to Waterford in October to address a meeting in the City Hall. Despite the disruptive tactics of henchmen engaged by a local stevedore, a branch based on cross-channel coalfillers was formed. November brought a series of strikes which confirmed the irrepressible spirit of new unionism and raised Larkin's standing. On 9 November, 179 dockers struck the City of Cork Steam Packet Company. A small dock strike a month previously had given forewarning, and the Shipping Federation was prepared. Scabs were imported, but the carters then refused to handle 'tainted goods'. Clashes with the RIC ensued. Larkin arrived in Cork on 11 November to arrange a truce which led to a favourable settlement. Shortly after this success 150 carters struck for recognition and better pay in Dublin, to be joined by dockers, labourers, canalmen, and maltsters. By the end of the month 2,000 men were out. As in Cork, the conflict was marked by strike-breaking and violence. Sexton disowned the dispute, withheld funds, and suspended Larkin from his job on 7 December. Larkin none the less won a series of satisfactory settlements in early December.

It had not been a good year for the working class. With high unemployment and falling wage rates the level of industrial conflict fell sharply. Ten of the twenty-two strikes that year were unsuccessful. Widespread pay cuts were introduced in the textiles and clothing trades. In Derry, 1,000 shirt workers were locked out for five days to enforce a reduction.[5] In these circumstances, Larkin had done well and the spirit of unskilled workers indicated a great potential for general unionism. Joseph Harris had tried to develop the Workers' Union in Dublin during the spring. Given the heavy amalgamated presence at this time it seems scarcely plausible that Harris failed because the Workers' Union was British.[6] But failure did bring Harris, William O'Brien, and Larkin to discuss the option of an Irish general union. Larkin rejected the move as an unwarranted intrusion of nationalism into the labour struggle. However, when relations with Sexton snapped, Larkin became convinced that only Irish unions could address Irish problems. On 28 December, NUDL delegates from Belfast, Cork, Dublin,

Dundalk, and Waterford agreed to secede as an Irish general union. Derry stayed with Sexton, whilst in Belfast Alex Boyd, acting for Sexton, quickly played the Orange card to win the Protestant cross-channel dockers back to the NUDL. The ITGWU was born in haste and confusion. Larkin championed the move as a radical departure. At the same time he was anxious for legal, financial, and organizational reasons to represent the union as a successor to the NUDL. Equally, although it was to be a union for all workers, the 'Transport' tag showed that new unionism still dictated strategy; in particular, Larkin wanted to win over the railwaymen. The preface to union rules defined its objective as an 'industrial commonwealth', a term with syndicalist echoes, but gave no clue as to the means of attainment. Quite pragmatically, the preface also supported compulsory arbitration and defined the union as a medium to adjust wages and conditions.

The ITGWU had a stormy infancy. Labour discord offered a new weapon against Larkin. With passive assistance from the NUDL, Belfast employers introduced a system of victimization that gutted the local branch. Dundalk and Waterford branches dwindled to a paper existence. On 14 June, the Cork coalporters' section refused to work with members of the Workers' Union, which Joseph Harris allowed a stevedore to use as a 'yellow' union. Other quaysidemen came out in sympathy and railway porters blacked 'tainted goods'. A rebel spirit had survived in Cork. Tramwaymen had struck for a pay rise in April, and in May builders' labourers, supported by craftsmen, won an extra shilling a week in a general stoppage. The city's first Labour day demonstration for years took place on 16 May. Not content to rely on the inevitable Shipping Federation scabs, a Cork Employers' Federation was formed to blacklist anyone taking sympathetic action. By this means the dock dispute spread to 2,000 employees, including mineral water operatives, railwaymen, flour millers, building workers, and bacon factory hands. Violent clashes with the RIC became a regular occurrence. In the face of obdurate employer opposition to compromise, a return to work began in July and resistance collapsed in August. It was a serious reverse. The ITGWU's Cork branch disintegrated, and Cork trades council split on 12 August when tradesmen withdrew, tired of strikes and Larkinism. Another twist of the knife came the following week when Larkin, Fearon, and two others of the Cork branch were arrested and charged with 'conspiracy to defraud'. Larkin had spent NUDL dues collected in Cork on struggles elsewhere. On 17 June 1910, the court gave him twelve months hard labour. So harsh a sentence, widely regarded as a piece of class vindictiveness, won Larkin some badly needed sympathy. Public opinion compelled his release on 1 October.

On the political front, the ITGWU accentuated the transition of consciousness being wrought by employer militancy, fluctuating unemployment, and state intervention in disputes. The 1908 ITUC elected John Murphy of Belfast trades council as President.[7] Murphy, an ILPer, was the first in that post to advocate socialism. Speaking from the floor, Larkin challenged the hardy annuals of the agenda with uncompromising socialism. Though in a minority, he won election to the Parliamentary Committee. Those who had formerly been on the left of Congress now found themselves outflanked, and James Sexton's challenge to the ITGWU's credentials in 1909 threatened to pitch the right and old left against the new. After two days of debate, William Walker urged delegates not to make a martyr of Larkin and moved his immediate admission. The proposal passed by forty votes to ten. Walker's intervention isolated the old guard, and the congress marked their eclipse. These changes were underpinned at trade council level.[8] Dublin revived the annual Mayday parade in 1908, inviting socialist and advanced nationalist groups to attend. Larkinites fared well in the council's 1909 executive elections, and co-operation with advanced nationalists like Michael O'Lehane and P.T. Daly produced a radical majority on the executive in 1910. Thereafter, the Larkinites went from strength to strength. Having mushroomed and decayed in 1907, Belfast socialism enjoyed a slow recovery. D.R. Campbell, a leading light in the Belfast Socialist Society, was elected President of Belfast trades council in 1909. As Campbell's supporters gradually gained control of the council, Unionist delegates withdrew in disgust, weakening in turn the position of labourites like William Walker and antinationalists like John Murphy. Under Campbell's influence the council approved ITGWU admission to Congress, endorsed the establishment of an Irish Labour Party, and opposed partition. In the process however, it became steadily less representative of Protestant working-class opinion. Cork trades council had a chequered career. In the spring of 1908 it was sufficiently sanguine to publish the *Cork Trade and Labour Journal*, which inspired a similar effort in Dublin the following year. The 1909 dock strike smashed this spirit. Elsewhere that year, Drogheda trades council was dissolved, but new councils appeared in Dundalk and Waterford.

Realignments on the Dublin left culminated in June 1909 in the formation of *Cumannacht na hÉireann*. Over the following winter William O'Brien and other members canvassed James Connolly's return from the United States to work as party organizer.[9] Tired of America's sectarian far left, Connolly himself yearned for a politics more homely and more mainstream. In January 1910, he transferred his ethno-socialist paper *The Harp* to Dublin with Larkin as editor. He also penned *Labour, Nationality, and Religion* as *Cumannacht na hÉireann*'s reply to the Jesuit preacher Fr Kane, whose lenten lectures had denounced socialism. The same year also saw the publication of *Labour in Irish History*, the first critical analysis of the subject. This classic of scholarly empathy and originality was to have a seminal impact on agitational writing in labour history. With Thomas Brady's *The Historical Basis of Socialism in Ireland* it marked the birth of the tradition. Connolly debarked at Derry on 26 July 1910 and set about organizing for *An Cumannacht* at once. That autumn the party issued a manifesto which confirmed Connolly's drift to the centre. Although Connolly remained heavily influenced by American syndicalism, it was broadly social democratic in philosophy and remarkably open-ended on method and aims. With home rule in the air, and politics ready for the melting pot, Connolly wished to concentrate on his work for *An Cumannacht*. However, though the party was making strides, it could barely afford Connolly's weekly stipend of £2. O'Brien advised him to seek work with the ITGWU. Neither Larkin nor Connolly were the easiest men to get along with; and each made a shrewd reading of the other. But with a sudden outbreak of unrest in June 1911, Larkin needed an experienced agent in Belfast. Reluctantly, Connolly accepted the offer.

GATHERING PACE

Trade had improved in 1909, to reverse two years of high unemployment, falling wages, and falling union membership. Legislative reform also bolstered labour morale. Congress lobbying helped to ensure Ireland's inclusion in the Trade Boards Act (1909), which provided for the appointment of committees to enforce wages in 'sweated' occupations. Five trade boards were in operation by May 1916, catering for workers in clothing, textiles, and food preparation.[10] Labour exchanges were introduced in 1910, and health and unemployment insurance schemes followed in 1911. To avoid displacing the benefit provision of unions and friendly societies, it was made possible for these bodies to become 'approved societies' under the state system. This acted as an incentive to join unions and was the major factor behind the 60 per cent surge in British TUC affiliation over the next two years.[11] Of consequence too in Britain was the Osborne Judgment of 1909, in which the Law Lords found that unions could not lawfully use their funds for political purposes. Like the Taff Vale judgment before it, so blatantly partisan a decision proved counter-productive. It was repealed partially by the Trade Union Act (1913), which allowed unions to maintain a political fund if approved by members and provided members were allowed to 'contract out' of the political levy if they so desired. However, the urgent problem in 1910 was employer militancy, which kept wages lagging behind rising prices; most notoriously so through the Shipping Federation's scabbing. In November the British Transport Workers' Federation was formed to create a network of direct action sufficiently extensive to make scabbing ineffective. First to move in this new round of class warfare were seamen who refused to sail the S.S. *Olympic*, the largest liner then afloat, as she lay at Southampton. On 14 June, the National Sailors' and Firemen's Union took up the general clamour for wage movements with a strike at all ports for a uniform pay scale. Unrest then spread to dockers and carters. Sectional stoppages on the railways led to a national strike on 18–19 August. Although the spasm had passed in Britain by the end of August, the greatest outbreak of social disaffection since 1889 surged on to the brink of World War I and contained revolutionary stirrings within it. Permeating from France and America, syndicalism inspired a fervent interest in industrial unionism, culminating in the foundation in 1914 of the Triple Alliance by the National Union of Railwaymen (NUR), the Miners' Federation, and the Transport Workers' Federation.[12]

English unrest rapidly generated an extraordinary climate of militancy in Ireland. The eighteen strikes which occurred in the traditional industries of the north east in 1911 are distributed evenly throughout the year. By contrast, thirty-two of the thirty-six disputes in other sectors took place after mid June.[13] Notwith-standing the British impulse, Larkin justly emerged as the focal point of discontent. It was thanks to him that, unlike 1889, there existed a union which was on the spot and committed to do or die at home, and the ITGWU contributed to the spirit, and the speed in diffusion, of militancy; the large number of 'miscellaneous' mili-tants included paperboys and golf caddies, sandwichmen and bill posters. Agitation spread to the smaller towns and in Wexford, scene of a tough, six-month, cast-iron fight of foundrymen, brushed farm labourers with its wingtip.[14] With consummate timing, the *Irish Worker and People's Advocate* had hit the streets on 27 May. This outrageous paper gave Larkin, for he was the editorial board, access to virtually the entire Dublin working class. To the people it gave news about themselves, scandal about others, and a voice that spoke their seething anger at the grossness of social inequality. The ITGWU's waterside base brought it into direct contact with the forefront of events in Britain. The National Sailors' and Firemen's Union requested Liberty Hall to co-ordinate its Irish operations in June, and ITGWU members soon went on to press their own claims. Larkin finally recovered the recognition withheld by Dublin employers since his humiliation under Sexton in 1908. The most powerful and contentious demonstration of class solidarity took place on the railways. During the UK rail strike ITGWU members refused to handle 'tainted goods'. Dublin timber merchants retali-ated with a lockout. When the rail strike ended the timbermen would not go back without a pay rise. On 15 September the timber merchants tendered a 'black' consignment at Kingsbridge. Two Great Southern and Western Railway porters refused to touch it and were dismissed. As the dispute extended through the sympathetic principle, 3,500 railwaymen came out for their re-instatement. Although Irish members had supported the UK rail stoppage, the ASRS would not now call out its members in Britain. After 28 September the ASRS admitted defeat and addressed itself to getting the men back their jobs and pension rights. Larkin offered a further round of sympathetic action to prevent victim-ization but the railway directors would not be denied their revenge.

The high proportion of strikes over trade unionism *per se* con-firmed that labour was still struggling for recognition. It remained an unequal contest. Fifty-five per cent of those who took industrial action in 1911 encountered complete defeat.[15] Yet morale did not flag. Aggregate trades council membership jumped from 31,000 in 1910 to a pre-war peak of 41,000 in 1912[16] As the prestige of amalgamated trade unionism dipped even lower, the ITGWU marched on, rebuilding branches in the towns and boosting membership from 5,000 to 18,000.[17] Horizontal diffusion induced a significant advance in Larkinist technique. The sympathetic principle could intensify pressure or combat scabbing, but it did not meet the needs of workers in small-scale, non-essential employment. The Dublin timber strike, for example, pitted 350 men against 51 masters.[18] In these circumstances unity in offence, not solidarity in defence, mattered most; sympathy tactics evolved into generalized action, which would later mature as the leitmotiv of the post-war wages movement. Where strikes of dockers and carters at the smaller ports spread to general operatives, united action could become so extensive as to take on the flavour of a general local strike. This was true of disputes in Dundalk in 1911, Galway in 1912, and Galway and Sligo in 1913.[19] Herein lay the efficient contradiction of Irish syndicalism: the less aggregated the employment structure, the more class conscious the agitation.

Employers too prepared for general conflict. In June 1911, Dublin bosses formed an Employers' Federation modelled on the Cork namesake that had smashed the 1909 dock strike. In October, Chambers of Commerce met to consider forming an association 'which shall advise its members on labour troubles as they may arise and make effective preparation to protect the trade and commerce of the company'. A reluctance to exacerbate the situation prevailed, but within weeks employers' federations were springing on a local basis.[20] The rail strike especially carried Larkinism deep into the provinces and challenged the labour proclivities of nationalists. In hitherto quiet backwaters, where the middle class had customarily cast a benign regard on honest toilers, the strike drew a torrent of criticism, and popularized the employers' distinction between *bona fide* and Larkinite disputes. Conversely, advanced nationalists gave scattered support to the strike movements and edged closer to Larkin, whose *Irish Worker* displayed an evident Gaelic-nationalist orientation.[21]

The militant upsurge of 1911–13 stimulated a revival of labour representation in local government. Dublin trades council formed a Labour Representation Committee in January 1911. Sinn Féin had withdrawn from electoral politics in 1910 to concentrate on propaganda work, and the resultant vacuum both helped Labour and strengthened the overlap between radicals and advanced nationalists. Six of the thirteen Dublin Labour councillors elected between 1912 and 1915 were former Sinn Fein candidates. Dublin Labour, like the cognate initiatives that emerged in Cork, Castlebar, Sligo, Tullamore, Waterford, and Wexford, met with limited success.[22] The politicization of senior and middle-level trade unionism had yet to impress the masses. To the north, the conservative retreat from Belfast trades council undermined the pro-Union labourism associated with William Walker. Against calls for a Congress party, Walker upheld the traditional endorsement of the British Labour Party in 1911; but it turned out to be his swansong. Connolly attacked his position in the Glasgow socialist paper *Forward*, contending that Walker's 'internationalism' ignored Ireland's right to self-determination, as endorsed by Marx and Engels, and amounted to an *apologia* for imperialism. Walker responded by denouncing nationalism as parochial, and then spoiled the broth with a parochial eulogy of Belfast's 'gas and water' socialism. In the endless debate on socialism and nationalism, the 'Connolly-Walker controversy' acquired some weight retrospectively for seeming to confirm the correlation between unionism and conservatism. At the time however, the apparent immediacy of home rule was more important in bringing northern socialists, and the ITUC, round to Connolly's argument for an Irish Labour Party.[23] Preparatory to that departure, Connolly formed the Independent Labour Party (of Ireland) (ILP(I)) on Easter Monday 1912 as a ginger group, analogous to its British namesake.[24] The ILP(I) united *Cumannacht na hÉireann* with the Belfast branch of the British Socialist Party and four of Belfast's five ILP branches—Walker's old comrades stayed out, though Walker himself had since retired from politics.

Socialist unity meant little on the shopfloor. When a parade of Hibernians assaulted a Presbyterian Sunday school outing at Castledawson on 29 June, Belfast loyalists retaliated brutally; 3,000 workers were forced out of their jobs, by shipyard labourers and craftsmen's assistants for the most part, organized in Unionist Clubs or Orange Lodges. About 600 of the expelled men were Protestants, victimized for their Labour or Liberal sympathies. The expulsions were condemned by employers, trade unions, and the authorities, but no one would take effective counter-action. Unionists of course blamed it all on Castledawson. Efforts by the ILP(I) and the ITGWU to generate mass protest attracted no wider support. Already damned by the Unionist press as a 'home rule clique', Belfast trades council found itself hopelessly isolated. Trade unions largely confined their assistance to relief payments and lobbies. Some of the expelled men eventually returned to work; hundreds of others migrated.[25] With home rule, Labour hoped, the nightmare would end.

At the 1912 congress in Clonmel, Connolly's resolution 'that the independent representation of Labour upon all public boards be and is hereby included among the objectives of this Congress' was passed by 49–19 votes, with nineteen delegates not recorded.[26] The decision caused no immediate stir. As chairman of the ITUC executive, Larkin displayed slight enthusiasm. Industrial agitation remained his consuming passion. But Connolly, William O'Brien, Tom Johnson, and D.R. Campbell pressed ahead. A constitution was framed in 1913 and adopted at the 1914 congress. The new Irish Trade Union Congress and Labour Party (ITUCLP) did not formally endorse socialism until November 1918, but its constitution confirmed the syndicalist influence of Connolly. Connolly's first aim was to politicize the movement without encouraging electoralism. Thus, the party and Congress were to be coterminous. Congress rejected a Belfast proposal that socialist groups and co-operatives be allowed to affiliate. Replying for the executive, Tom Johnson stated that the true function of the party 'was propagandist merely—to educate, not to form a political party'. So the ITUCLP would contest elections without forgetting Connolly's dictum that politics was no more than the 'echo' of industrial warfare. By confining membership to trade unionists Connolly intended to exclude 'the professional politician who was doing as much harm as good' in the British Labour Party. The British TUC's failure to authorise sympathy strikes during the 1913 lockout had reinforced Connolly's abiding aversion to 'fakirism'. Whilst ever committed to industrial unionism, he rejected the introduction of block voting into Congress on the ground that the smaller unions were often the more militant. Connolly's second objective illustrates a concern of his 'mature' years; to link revolutionaries with mainstream labour without compromise. Thus, he opposed renaming Congress 'the Labour Party' for fear of provoking a breakaway, envisaging instead a dual arena of left agitation, in the catch-all ITUCLP and the vanguard ILP(I); a duality which paralleled the intended relation between unions and the OBU. It did not take long for the scenario to come unstuck. In the frenzied atmosphere of 1912–14, Belfast members of the ILP(I) regressed to Walkerism, and the branch generally retreated into the Catholic ghetto; whilst in Dublin, industrial conflict soon overshadowed all else.

'THE HIGHEST POINT OF MORAL GRANDEUR'

The upheaval of 1911 did not resolve the problem of keeping wages in line with escalating living costs. Nineteen twelve brought a mild recession and unemployed protests onto the streets. Exceptionally favourable economic conditions the following year enabled an unprecedented level of wage militancy, but early results were mixed. During the first six months of the year, employers in the north's staple industries recorded considerable success against these movements. In Belfast, the Flax Roughers' lost a two-month stoppage against dilution. At Derry, 1,200 shirt factory workers were locked out for three weeks to enforce a pay cut.[27] Other sectors fared better however. A succession of disputes in construction over the summer secured pay increases for craftsmen and labourers. Transport workers too won modest advances. By the summer of 1913 the ITGWU stood at the summit of its pre-war strength, numbering about 30,000 men, unskilled Dubliners in the main. Provincial outposts were making slow progress. Shipping companies had crushed Waterford's embryonic Larkinism with ease in 1912. Limerick dockers and carters lost a dispute over 'nons' in the new year. But in May the ITGWU won a favourable settlement to a violent generalized strike in Sligo. A recruitment drive amongst Dublin farm labourers commenced the following month. As always, Larkin's attention lay in the capital, and he was keen to push into steady employment areas like Guinness's and the trams. On 26 May, he concluded an agreement with six Dublin shipping companies conceding the sympathetic strike in return for union recognition and pay increases. It provided the basis of a new equilibrium in industrial relations, and in July Larkin called for a national conciliation board.[28] But some employers were still opposed to any form of general unionism, and they found their champion in William Martin Murphy.

Murphy, alas, represented Ireland's best example of a nationally-minded entrepreneur.[29] After inheriting the family building business it was in commerce, not manufacture, that he made his fortune. From England to west Africa to Buenos Aires, Murphy's money was there, building railways and tram tracks. As befitted a some-time Nationalist MP his primary interests lay at home where he owned the *Irish Independent*, the Imperial Hotel, Clery's department store, and was chairman of the Dublin United Tramway Company. If Murphy's uncompromising employment regime demanded no more of his staff than he did of himself, the rewards were hardly comparable. Trade unions offended the measured paternalism on which he believed economic efficiency must be based.

Throughout July the ITGWU consolidated within Murphy's empire.[30] In Independent Newspapers, Murphy countered with cajolery and threats, telling employees that they were able enough to form their own union but should they side with Larkin or withdraw their labour then starvation awaited. Still the men continued to join up. On 15 August, the dismissals commenced. Independent Newspapers were blacked immediately, and approaching 10.00 a.m. on 26 August, the start of Horse Show week, ITGWU men left the trams where they stood. Special constables and RIC were quickly deployed to supplement the Dublin Metropolitan Police. On 28 and 29 August, Larkin, Connolly, and Dublin trades council officers were arrested for sedition. Sunday 31 August, 'Bloody Sunday', is framed in labour memory as an identikit of class brutality. Police had banned a demonstration due to be held in Sackville Street. Larkin promised to be there 'dead or alive'. All morning crowds hung about the street not knowing what would happen. At midday, a bearded figure appeared on the balcony of the Imperial, Murphy's hotel, and began to address the people. It was Larkin, disguised to avoid arrest. Within minutes he was taken into custody. Down below, the police waded into the crowd, swinging their batons at will. Many who fled were chased into the tenements, where homes were invaded and ransacked. The rioting continued the following day. Two workers were killed. About 200 police and at least twice as many civilians were injured. Hundreds more were arrested. In September the conflict expanded to its full proportions. On 3 September, more than 400 employers weighed in behind Murphy with a pledge to lock out any employee who refused to sign 'the document' denying or renouncing ITGWU membership. In the country, where the union had recently won a harvest strike, the Farmers' Association followed suit. So too did the Master Builders, although building workers were not connected with the ITGWU. In other instances men were locked out for refusing to handle 'tainted goods'. By 22 September over 20,000 workers were affected.

While '1913' was fundamentally about the right to organize, and it has gone down in labour legend as such, contemporaries were more conscious of its syndicalist significance. Arnold Wright, the 'employers' historian' of the dispute, pinpointed his patrons' problem when he wrote, 'It is the essence of Larkinism, as of the Syndicalism of which it is the child, that there shall be no isolation of a quarrel'. Yet if Wright was honest in suggesting that employers would not be averse to 'an ordinary trade union of the English type', history had shown that ordinary unions could not secure a bargaining power for general workers.[31] Rising to the challenge, Liberty Hall made sympathetic action the hinge of union strategy and the sheer scale of suffering for the principle of solidarity lent itself to an enduring epic imagery. The class dimension was popularized, in typically Larkinite fashion, by the personalization of the conflict. Since 1907 Larkin had been villified mercilessly by employers, the clergy, and the press. For its part the *Irish Worker*, never known for understatement, pilloried Murphy as the epitome of hardfaced, sweating, capitalism. State intervention reinforced class consciousness, notoriously so in the case of the police. Middle-class opinion divided on the lockout. Though most blamed Larkin, the blatant assault on trade unionism, the aggressive policing, and the seeming indifference of employers to the misery of tenement life rallied the literati round labour. Sinn Fein and the IRB stood aside; Arthur Griffith consistently opposed Larkinism, but many advanced nationalists supported the workers. The lockout accelerated the labour-republican *rapprochement* consummated in Easter Week.

As the masters put their trust in starvation, labour cast about for allies before time ran out. The rhythm of unrest in 1911–12 had shown that militancy remained dependent on Britain, despite the ITGWU's philosophy of self-reliance. An integrated national labour movement was still in the future. Being little more than a talking shop, the ITUC played no part in events. Apart from Co. Dublin, the Belfast docks, and Sligo, provincial workers confined their solidarity to finance; and in some instances the clerical criticism of Larkin made public backing extremely tentative. So Liberty Hall's battle for support focused on Britain, where 'Bloody Sunday' had generated enormous sympathy for Dublin, and the *Daily Herald*, champion of the 'rebels' on the British left, would give regular coverage to events. Larkin appealed for sympathetic action. In early September three Liverpool railwaymen blacked Dublin-bound goods. Dismissals led to a snowball of unofficial action involving over 2,000 railwaymen in Liverpool and central England. British TUC leaders desperately wanted to avoid the lockout becoming a radical issue within British labour politics. Since 1910, the growth of syndicalism in Britain had stimulated direct actionist rank and file movements hostile to what they regarded as the class collaboration of union officialdom. Seen as part of the wider UK revolt, Dublin threatened the trade union leadership. The NUR general secretary, J.H. Thomas, a resolute opponent of the 'tainted goods' doctrine, quickly effected a return to work. Instead, the TUC and some trade unions opened 'fighting funds', while the Co-operative Wholesale Society helped to provision a series of relief ships to burst the boom of starvation.

On 29 September a Board of Trade enquiry embarked on the patient task of seeking the compromise which British Labour and Liberal opinion earnestly desired. The ITGWU offered to limit the sympathetic strike in return for union recognition, and to consider a conciliation scheme. Within days, and contrary to their claim that sympathy action was the bone of contention, the employers replied that the locked out workers would not be reinstated. Public attitudes shifted. AE expressed the indignation of intellectuals in his famous open letter 'To the masters of Dublin'. However, the detachment of middle-class sensibility from working-class reality was soon to be demonstrated. As the pressure on Liberty Hall's soup kitchens tightened, Mrs Dora Montefiore proposed a 'Save the Kiddies' scheme to board the children of distressed parents with families in England for the duration. This was a veteran syndicalist tactic, but insensitive to Irish susceptibilities. On 20 October, Archbishop Walsh condemned this 'most mischievous development' which would put Catholic children in the care of, presumably, Protestant homes. Hysterical scenes ensued when priests and zealots physically frustrated their evacuation. It was all very embarrassing and Connolly, deputising for the absent Larkin, was happy to scuttle the scheme. He then suspended free dinners at Liberty Hall for a week to bring the magnitude of the problem home to the archbishop.

With the rejection of Board of Trade proposals the struggle entered its critical, middle phase. Amidst expectations that the

'Save the Kiddies' blunder would crack the ITGWU, employers began importing scabs from England on 29 October. Connolly retaliated with mass pickets. When this failed he closed the port, invoking a higher moral duty to justify this breach of the 26 May agreement with the shipping companies. Connolly also assented to Captain Jack White's proposal for a workers' defence force. From the outset, Larkin had suggested that workers should take their cue from Edward Carson's Ulster Volunteer Force to arm themselves against the police. White formulated a plan in October, and on 23 November two companies of the Irish Citizen Army (ICA) paraded at Croydon Park, Fairview. If the ICA saw little action during the lockout, it boosted morale with dramatic symbolism. Meanwhile, Larkin continued to spend as much time as possible in England whipping up support for sympathetic action. On 27 October he was sentenced to seven months imprisonment for sedition, but released on 13 November. Immediately, he returned to England to raise the 'Fiery Cross', a campaign of torch-lit meetings. The reception was enthusiastic; popular pressure for action mounted, especially following the importation of scab labour to Dublin. But making Dublin part of the battle between 'rebels' and officialdom was a dangerous gamble. On 9 December, the TUC summoned a conference of full-time officials to consider its response. Larkin had already alienated the TUC Parliamentary Committee with personal attacks on trade union leaders. He now infuriated the conference with an intemperate speech. The meeting rejected overwhelmingly a 'rebel' motion calling for the blacking of all Dublin goods until the locked out workers were reinstated. Instead, it condemned Larkin's attacks, and expressed confidence in the Parliamentary Committee's ability to secure a settlement if supported by all parties.

Any informed observer would have known this to be a forlorn hope. Just three days beforehand Archbishop Walsh had brought the protagonists together for the first time only to have the employers again refuse to guarantee reinstatement. On 18 December a British Labour delegation to Dublin met the same response. In effect, the TUC special conference signalled the beginning of the end. There was no compulsion on employers to bargain any more. It remained simply to get as many back to work as possible. On 14 December the ITGWU executive advised members to return without signing 'the document'. Larkin overruled the decision but finally agreed to make it known publicly on 18 January. The British relief fund closed on 10 February. A week later there were still 5,000 workers locked out. The defeat was a severe set back for trade unionism in Dublin and for general unionism throughout Ireland. Labour candidates performed poorly in the municipal elections of January 1914. Nonetheless, the attempt to break general unionism had not succeeded. Murphy's paternalism was the first casualty of the wreckage. There had been no split in the ITGWU, no rejection of Larkinism; there would be no acceptance of 'yellow unions'. Unlike the 1890s, unlike Belfast in 1907, the clock had not been put back.

In the long term the lockout fattened labour's skeletal syndicalism. Briefly, it brought Dublin into the swirl of British syndicalist and guild socialist ideas. The *Daily Herald's* assistant editor, W.P. Ryan, a former member of *Cumannacht na hÉireann*, linked Larkinism with the co-operative commonwealth ideal; hoping that Larkinism, with the co-operative movement of Horace Plunkett and AE, and politico-cultural forces like Sinn Féin and Conradh na Gaeilge, marked a resurgence of the Gaelic primitive communism romanticized by Connolly in *Labour in Irish History*.[32] Larkin had always been attracted to the syndicalist idea of underpinning the socialist struggle with a working-class counter-culture based on collectivist values like sharing and solidarity, and standing in opposition to the bourgeois ethic of possessive individualism. The grounds acquired in 1913 at Croydon Park served as a social, sports, and educational centre for union members and their wives. As Larkin put, 'We make our family life focus around the union . . . .'[33] At the height of the lockout he spoke of extending this counter-culture into commerce through producers' co-operatives, and later he toured England raising funds for a programme of practical co-operation. Delia Larkin subsequently launched a small shirt manufacturing co-operative to employ girls victimized after the dispute.[34] Larkin's grand schemes bore little fruit, but within a few years Congress would turn to co-operation as a policy option and adopt the commonwealth as a goal. Connolly too was prompted to reassert the fundamentals of syndicalism. Provoked by the breakdown of trade union solidarity in 1913, he wrote *Old Wine in New Bottles* to emphasise that restructuring labour along industrial unionist lines was totally inadequate without an OBU philosophy. By aiming only at a rationalization of structures, non-revolutionary industrial unionism merely strengthened bureaucratic control over the rank and file. 'Fighting spirit', he warned, 'is of more importance than the creation of a theoretically perfect organization.'

TO THE GPO

In the immediate aftermath of the lockout however, Connolly's greatest concern lay with the spectre of partition, soon to be made real by the Curragh mutiny and Tory footwork at Westminster.[35] By now the mutual alienation of labourites and Unionism was virtually complete, the more so since the 1912 expulsions had given a foretaste of life under Orange rule. In the circumstances, few dissented from Connolly's critique of partition as an overriding evil which would subordinate a bifurcated movement to its bourgeois masters and lead to a 'carnival of reaction both North and South'. Congress sponsored an anti-partition meeting in Dublin on 5 April and in June condemned partition by eighty-four votes to two.[36] In strenghtening contacts with advanced nationalists, Connolly's anti-partition initiatives were complemented by reform of the ICA. In March Sean O'Casey, with Captain Jack White and Countess Markievicz, had changed the ICA from a picket-militia to a pocket army. As an ardent Irish-Irelander, O'Casey used his developing literary talent to nurture labour-republican solidarity; the annual Wolfe Tone commemoration in June saw ICA units parading alongside the Volunteers.[37] The outbreak of world war in August acted as a major catalyst in the process. Connolly determined on a military insurrection before the war was out, and co-founded the ephemeral Irish Neutrality League to rally all opponents of the war. But his situation was frustrating. Due possibly to the friction between them, Larkin left him to nurse union affairs in Belfast. Though Larkin took an anti-war stand, and spoke of expanding the ICA into a workers' army, with all unions contributing a company, he lacked Connolly's sense of purpose. There were difficulties too with the cantankerous O'Casey as ICA secretary, for in his persona of the hard-bitten lad from the slums, he could not resist attacking the middle-class people on whom a labour-separatist alliance depended. O'Casey gradually became hostile to any association with the Volunteers, and would later denounce Connolly's strategy in his purple prosed *Story of the Irish Citizen Army*. Then fortune intervened to bring Connolly back to the centre stage. In trying to have Markievicz expelled from the ICA because of her republican connections, O'Casey overreached himself. With no alternative but a loss of face, he resigned. Within a few weeks, Larkin too would be gone, leaving Connolly in control.

Throughout 1914, Larkin showed flashes of his old brilliance. Following on from his programme of co-operative reconstruction he pursued the development of Croydon Park. His presidential address to the ITUCLP that year made a powerful appeal for industrial unionism. But the strain of the lockout told on his health, and it is difficult to avoid the conclusion that his judgment and balance never recovered from the ordeal. Repeatedly he toyed with resignation from the union. Finally, in October, it was agreed that he spend a year in the United States raising funds for the ITGWU. Larkin wanted P.T. Daly to take over in Dublin until William O'Brien and Thomas Foran prevailed on him to choose Connolly instead.[38] Although anxious for the job, Connolly had mixed feelings. Only Larkin could build the workers' army he planned to lead into rebellion; but would so flamboyant a character work in tandem for a cause like that? Almost certainly Larkin's departure was a prerequisite of ICA involvement in Easter Week. Connolly promptly, and unsuccessfully, offered to affiliate the ICA to the Irish Volunteers.

From 1914 to 1916 Connolly's thought was conditioned by revolutionary pessimism. No sooner had the British Liberal government caved in to army insubordination and Carson's threats than Europe's workers marched off to kill each other with scarce protest from their socialist parties. Connolly was appalled equally at Irish acquiescence in the British war effort which, he believed, compromised the historic anti-imperialist character of the Irish people; something he enthused about in his latest pamphlet, *The Reconquest of Ireland*. This was not merely the anguish of a fervent nationalist. War service and war pensions were sealing bonds of blood and welfare between working-class families and the British state. In consequence, Connolly became near fatalist, believing that wartime labour regulations presaged the displacement of liberal capitalism by a new servility that would enslave the proletariat in the shackles of statism. The urgency of a political response to the crisis led to a recontextualization of struggle within the framework of nationalism. Although seen ever since as a new departure, and it was certainly original for a contemporary socialist, this view of politics had been the standard labour outlook from the Defenders to the fall of Parnell. The alliance of 1916 continued the tradition of 1798, 1803, 1848, and 1867.

Connolly tried desperately to bring labour round to this political perspective, the hinge of which was opposition to the war. When the College Green constituency fell vacant in May 1915 following the death of Nannetti he pressed the ITUCLP to fight this traditionally 'labour' seat, partly to stress the breach with the old labour nationalism represented by Nannetti, and drafted a strong anti-war manifesto for its candidate Tom Farren. Farren polled a creditable 1,846 votes to 2,445 votes for the Nationalist John D. Nugent. It was to be the only parliamentary election contested by Congress up to 1922. When a vacancy arose in Harbour constituency in September, Connolly advised against entering the lists. It would be a distraction, he argued, presumably from the coming insurrection.[39] His impatience with the pedestrian pace of labour's evolution and its bread and butter concerns was mounting. With about 340 members, the ICA failed to draw widespread trade union interest. By contrast about half of the ITGWU's 1914 membership had joined the British army by 1916.[40] Increasingly, Connolly turned to Fenianism for a purer spirit of revolt. The shift in emphasis was underlined in May when the *Irish Worker* was replaced with the *Workers' Republic*. Already, comments of a racial, chauvinistic, or anglophobic nature had begun to pepper his writings, while his public stance on the war seemed blindly pro-German; though this exaggerated nationalism reflected less Connolly's sober analysis than disgust at the prevailing pro-war sentiment and a pointed rejection of the British world view. Still the Irish Volunteers refused to ally formally with the ICA, leaving Connolly to conclude that under Eoin MacNeill's leadership they would never seize the moment. It was only to forestall unilateral ICA action that, in January 1916, Connolly was informed of IRB plans and the union of Easter Week was sealed.

Pessimism caused Connolly to underrate emergent trends. Inflation and food shortages were beginning to generate resentment against the farmers, employers, and shopkeepers who seemed to be doing well out of the war. Trade union membership underwent a slow recovery. If strike action remained largely within the craft sector, movements of transport workers gathered pace from late 1914 onwards.[41] In August 1915 Connolly felt sanguine enough to propose a unity conference of unskilled unions. After September, the ITGWU won a series of pay increases for Dublin dockers. During a strike with the Burns Laird line, ICA arms were lent, quite exceptionally, to pickets. Indeed, Connolly's difficulty lay in keeping dockland militancy within the resources of his financially crippled union. Spontaneous organization of ITGWU members in the provinces commenced in early 1916.[42] Connolly regarded these developments as no more than a limited response to improved market forces which tied workers to capitalist war aims. He could not foresee that within two years the trickle would become a deluge foaming with the politics he now advocated; and, of course, that subsequent radicalization was itself a consequence of Easter Week. In any case, once set on insurrection, the requirements of military conspiracy took on an autonomous momentum, compelling Connolly to separate his ICA work from his union duties, which he never neglected.

In the months preceding the Rising Connolly's programmatic thinking edged further to the centre. His platform now demanded state direction of economic resources under a government of popular unity. The most advanced intellectual on the IRB side, Patrick Pearse, was approaching similar conclusions in *The Sovereign People*. At a deeper level, Connolly borrowed from Pearse's mystic concept of redemption through blood. Just as Pearse hoped to save the nation for another generation of struggle, so Connolly wished to redeem the anti-imperialist destiny of the working class. He was attracted too to Pearse's view of Irish history as a pattern of cyclical insurgency, which justified the role of exemplary action by a militant minority within a theory of recurrent revolution; and even employed the sacral imagery of faith, Calvary, and redemption in the advent to Easter. For Connolly therefore, Easter Week represented an eleventh-hour displacement of extraneous socialism for indigenous radical possibility. The signals failed to register with his followers. People saw in the Rising a native assertion of the militaristic nationalism rampant in Europe, and one more noble than the slaughter in the trenches. General Maxwell's executions and arrests dispelled indignation at the 'pro-Germans' and, in an entirely ironic sense, made Pearse's 'blood sacrifice'. Connolly's execution on 12 May gave labour a shrine in the national pantheon; it brought respect but no understanding.

The insurrection was planned in hope of victory, but after the capture of the *Aud* and MacNeill's countermanding order it is hard to see how participation could have been anything other than political suicide for Connolly.[43] When the ICA marched out of Liberty Hall on Easter Monday it left labour behind it. Even the ITGWU had come close to repudiating Connolly ten days previously for hoisting a green flag over Liberty Hall, and he, quite responsibly, did not implicate the union in the Rising.[44] Labour understood Larkinite myth because it was rooted in trade union practice. If Connolly's strategy merely recalled workers to their own history, it was too little, too late to reverse a generation of anglicization, and too premature to exploit the possibilities that unfolded with the conscription crisis. When rank and file pressure for political intervention finally bubbled inchoately forth after 1917, there was no Connolly to direct it. Substantially, 1916 ended the ICA's active service. Its most famous veteran, Countess Markievicz, hero-worshipped Connolly without grasping his ideas, whilst its most promising commandant, Michael Mallin, was shot by firing squad on 8 May. As Connolly anticipated, international socialist opinion was baffled by his involvement in a nationalist revolt, although Lenin and Trotsky appreciated the attempt to create revolutionary opportunity.[45]

The Rising threw Labour on the defensive. The British had shelled Liberty Hall, seized ITGWU and Congress files, and arrested trade union leaders. Into the vacuum stepped Belfast-based Tom Johnson and D.R. Campbell. When the first Congress since the outbreak of world war assembled in August, Johnson's presidential address trod delicately between pro- and anti-war opinion. After mourning the death of Connolly and other trade unionists killed in Easter Week, he invited delegates to stand in hushed tribute to those who had fallen in all fields 'for the Love of their Country'. The Congress report for 1916 refuted government and employer allegations of Labour involvement in the Rising and tried to dissociate the ITGWU from the ICA. Trade unions and trades councils kept their silence.[46]

5

Syndicalism, 1917–1923

Meeting the needs of Britain's war economy brought great prosperity to Irish employers.[1] Employees were less fortunate. Wage levels failed to match inflation from 1914 to 1916, causing hardship and accusations of profiteering against the propertied classes. But if the first half of the war stored up social grievances, production demands and the growing manpower shortage after 1916 provided the means of redress. The pre-conditions of wage improvement materialized in two ways; through government intervention to increase pay in war-related industries, and, later, through the all-round economic improvement. After the war, the release of 'pent-up' consumer demand generated a brief economic boom. Wages generally rose faster than prices from 1916, overtaking pre-war levels by 1919–20, until the economy hit a disastrous slump in 1920–21. Given the nature of capitalism, the money was only for those who could get it. Trade unionism exploded in all directions; from under 100,000 in 1916, membership affiliated to Congress reached 225,000 in 1920.[2] Moreover, it assimilated the aggressive class consciousness fermenting since 1914, and the unprecedented frequency of strikes during these years consolidated an exceptionally assertive spirit at the base of the movement. As workers spontaneously revived and developed pre-war Larkinite tactics, their leaders adopted Connolly's industrial unionism as an organizational strategy. To this was added the promise that through industrial unionism Labour would ultimately realize the Workers' Republic. The ascent of Sinn Féin also politicized wage militancy. In breaking the hegemony of conservative nationalism, separatists subverted the social consensus, creating the scope for native echoes of international radicalism to flourish. Reflecting this transition, and under the influence of syndicalism, Congress was itself transformed from a bunch of trade unions with no coherent politics beyond a few labourist assumptions borrowed from Britain into, potentially, an industrially and politically integrated movement, geared to tackling native reality. The confluence of tactics, strategy, and promise made the syndicalist moment.

THE WAGES MOVEMENT

State intervention remained a key determinant of wage movements for the first three years of the war. Though the initial effect of statutory control was to freeze wages, from 1915 onwards intervention became a means of securing war bonuses or minimum rates. Importance to the war effort and good organization were therefore essential for successful militancy. Ireland's piecemeal integration into the war economy created a time-lag in wage movements between employment sectors.[3] 'Old sectors', i.e., those with a history of trade unionism, were the first to recoup lost ground. Seamen and dockers won pay advances in 1915. The government took control of the shipyards and railways in 1916, making provision for the payment of war bonuses. Aerodrome and other military construction, together with the repair of Dublin's shell-torn city centre, revived the building line in 1917–18. Building became particularly strike-prone after mid 1918, with three general stoppages hitting Dublin and Belfast. Almost 19 per cent of all strikers between 1914 and 1921 were building workers.[4] The introduction of statutory minimum rates in agriculture in 1917 finally enabled 'new sectors' to join the wages movement over the next two years. Government regulation and the interventionist momentum persisted into the post-war era, partly in response to fears of class conflict. The recommendations of the Whitley committee, appointed to investigate wartime industrial unrest in Britain, led to the Trade Boards Act (1918). An Irish Department of the British Ministry of Labour was set up in July 1919, and fifteen new trade boards were established in little over a year. By August 1920, there were nineteen trade boards covering 148,000 employees, the bulk of them in Ulster's textile and clothing industries.[5]

The war mobilized industry without restructuring the workforce. Ulster was the main beneficiary. Textiles, clothing, engineering, and shipbuilding were soon harnessed to military needs, but no sizeable munitions sector developed in Ulster, while Unionist and British employer determination to freeze nationalist Ireland out of lucrative war contracts kept the south de-industrialized. The few munitions factories distributed to mollify nationalist outrage did not commence production until 1917, and employed a mere 2,169 persons by the armistice.[6] As a result of the bias in government policy, southern wage movements were compelled to be the cause as much as the consequence of state intervention. This, together with the more primitive condition of industrial relations in which they operated, gave them a more militant character, and strikes lit the path of trade unionism to new sectors and new regions. Strike activity increased steadily from 1915 to the armistice. The level of conflict declined in 1919 as rising unemployment yielded quickly to an economic boom, but militancy reached new heights in 1920, before receding sharply with the onset of the slump and the gradual fall in the cost of living towards the end of that year.

Railwaymen led the first big push for government intervention in the south. Inspired by British NUR men, who had emulated British munitions workers in developing a shop stewards' movement, Dublin and South Eastern Railwaymen spearheaded a threat of unofficial action in September 1916 for a 10s. per week wage rise. Most railwaymen still earned under 14s. weekly, a rate that ignored soaring prices since 1914. After inconclusive discussions, the NUR sanctioned a strike for 18 December. As private interests could not, or would not, meet the pay demand, the government stepped in to keep the war effort running smoothly and took control of Ireland's thirty-two railway companies shortly before Christmas. On 29 December, the men were awarded a 7s. per week war bonus. Over the next nine months the NUR's Irish affiliation rocketed from 5,000 to 17,000 members.[7] It was a victory not alone over the railway companies. Railwaymen developed the most sophisticated rank and file movement in Ireland during these years. Up to the rise of the ITGWU in 1918, they were the van of progress.

The major state intervention came in agriculture. Social conditions worsened alarmingly over the winter of 1916–17 as food and fuel supplies dwindled. With widespread talk of famine, the ITUCLP called a special congress in December to demand price control and a ban on selected exports. To provide more basic foodstuffs the government introduced tillage orders under the Corn Production Act, obliging farmers to bring at least 10 per cent of their arable land under the plough in 1917, and a further 5 per cent in

1918. As tillage was labour intensive, the act gave farm workers a scarcity value. Moreover, the Department of Agriculture accepted that if there was not an absolute manpower shortage on the land, the quality of labour suffered from the attraction of higher wages in Britain. Initially, the Department appealed to farmers' better nature. It was soon compelled to be serious. An Agricultural Wages Board was established in September 1917 to determine compulsory minimum pay and conditions. Tillage orders stirred the old rural labour unions and encouraged the formation of new local societies. Broadly, these bodies had three main objectives: wage improvement, land redistribution, and government aid for plot-holders. Land hunger remained strong, but agricultural trade unionism gradually turned aside to the more urgent goal of wage improvement. After January 1917, labourers aimed at parity with their urban counterparts, requesting pay rises of up to 100 per cent. Though the introduction of the Agricultural Wages Board reduced the likelihood of conflict, where organization was strong, labourers sought to ensure that 'legal minimums' did not become 'legal maximums'.

The developments in agriculture were of seismic importance, and 1917–18 witnessed a sea-change in the character of Labour. The food supply crisis gave Congress a social purpose and widened the ambit of industrial struggle. Workers responded to profiteering by setting up consumer co-operatives which, though limited in scale, and mostly of brief duration, were of demonstrative importance for the inchoate anti-capitalist sentiment welling up in popular consciousness. As unrest spread, the coincidence of pay claims from so many disparate occupations turned wage movements into the wages movement. Trends towards general action first cohered in Dublin in October 1917 when strike notices affecting 2,000–3,000 employees were pending. The *Irish Independent* feared another 1913. Dublin trades council offered to co-ordinate demands and promote the convening of unions in industrial groups. If the promise of inter-union co-ordination at the grand level was never realized, generalized action re-emerged to enable the ubiquitous 'miscellaneous' workers to become militant. It was the ITGWU that grasped the potential of this development.[8] Reorganized after Easter Week in February 1917, its executive had again come out in favour of sympathetic action by 1918. From the beginning of that year its organizers were in the countryside, mopping up the rural labour unions as farm workers threw in their lot with the urban working class. By 1920 the union mustered 60,000 members in agriculture, the bulk of these in the twelve south-easterly 'tillage counties'.

Surmounting the enormous difficulties of organizing farm workers copperfastened trade unionism in the provinces, and was of immense pyschological importance in taking Labour from the more anglicized urban fringe to the very heart of the Irish condition. It also facilitated an equally remarkable rise of general unionism in the towns; as did the conscription crisis. Whilst workers had been divided on the question of support for the war, there was, among nationalists, decisive opposition to conscription. Congress had no hesitation in joining the resistance committee *Comhdhail Chosanta Gaedheal* with Nationalists and Sinn Féin.[9] On 20 April 1918, 1,500 trade union delegates assembled in Dublin's Mansion House to call a general protest strike for 23 April. Though hardly a controversial initiative, the success of Ireland's first general strike made labour seem a power in the land. The next three months witnessed a tremendous upsurge of membership, chiefly within the ITGWU, which mushroomed from 5,000 members in 1916 to 120,000 four years later. Craft and clerical unions expanded too, with the latter displaying a strong and unusual affinity with the labour movement. Trades councils multiplied, to fifteen by 1918 and forty-six by 1921. Symbolic of the new awareness was their titular rejection of 'trades and labour' in favour of 'workers" council. Reflecting the myriad of minor struggles making up provincial wage movements, the proportion of strikes in Dublin and Belfast fell from 50 per cent between 1914 and 1918 to 20 per cent from 1919 to 1921; the corresponding proportion of strikers fell from 67 to 57 per cent.

Under the impact of nationalism and industrial unionism, growth reshaped the movement.[10] Nineteen of the thirty-seven affiliates to the 1916 congress were British. Five years later, the number of Congress unions had risen to forty-two, but the amalgamateds had dropped to thirteen, and now represented under 25 per cent of total membership. Between 1917 and 1923, eleven new unions were founded by breakaways away from the amalgamateds, and four of these adopted an industrial union structure. An articulate rank and file movement within the NUR blended nationalism with industrial unionist arguments to secure a semi-autonomous Irish executive. Partially successful ventures in industrial unionism resulted in the formation of the Local Government

Officials (Ireland) Trade Union and the Irish Union of Distributive
Workers and Clerks. In its drive to become the OBU the ITGWU
absorbed numerous small societies. The tiny scale of organization,
which had formerly caused native unions to atrophy, now acted as
an incentive to consolidation. Only the ITGWU endeavoured to outline formally an industrial unionist policy for general consumption.
Guided by Connolly's *Socialism Made Easy*, it set out to become the
OBU; the single, all-powerful voice of labour which would realize
the workers' republic through winning control 'at the point of
production'. On 1 July 1918, Liberty Hall issued *The Lines of Progress*,
a pamphlet intended to 'advance Connolly's OBU idea' in order to
develop 'a scientific solution to the Labour question'. The pamphlet
argued that all workers should be represented by one union, organized in industrial sections. It also held out the syndicalist promise
that complete economic and political freedom could be achieved
through the OBU. Syndicalist influences also pervaded the strong
rank and file movement in the NUR and had a broad impact
throughout the labour movement. But it was the ITGWU that
matched aspirations with a visionary professionalism, building up
an organizing staff of twenty-one by 1920. Liberty Hall also revived
pre-war ideas on alternative morality. Its annual report for 1919
directed members to conceive of the union 'as a social centre, round
which they can build every activity of their existence, and which,
wisely used, can be made to remedy all their grievances'.

The 1919 'land campaign' in particular, when the ITGWU responded to a big push for improvements in agricultural wages with
a series of fights in Munster and Leinster, including two county-
wide strikes in Meath and Kildare, established its credentials as
the one, true OBU, the ultimate, invincible weapon of industrial
unionism. At the base, its members were to the forefront in revolu-
tionizing tactics. That unique trait of contemporary agitation, the
general local strike, of which there were eighteen during the
advance of the wages movement, twelve of them taking place in
1919, reflected the grip of OBU solidarity in the small towns.
Workplace seizures or soviets, almost all involving the ITGWU,
emerged from November 1918 onwards, substantially as strike tactics but indicating too a political ambition.[11] The most extensive
seizure, that of thirteen Limerick creameries in 1920, known as the
'Knocklong soviet', was a well-planned affair directed by three
socialist ITGWU officials. It was significant, and not alone for

Knocklong, that few ITGWU officials were tested bureaucrats. Having risen from the ranks in the great advance, their instincts as yet lay with the membership rather than the organization. Despite William O'Brien's managerial abilities, and propaganda extolling the OBU as a finely marshalled machine, the union grew too quickly and too spontaneously for Liberty Hall to establish effective central control. In rural areas especially, success in strikes came to rely increasingly on co-ordinated violence and sabotage, which could only be used in revolutionary conditions. Liberty Hall indulged—indeed its journals the *Voice of Labour* and the *Watchword of Labour* encouraged—revolutionary action as long as it appeared to pay dividends. But when the economic boom gave way to slump in 1920, and the Anglo-Irish Treaty heralded a return to political stability, the ITGWU would encounter problems with its dangerously independent rank and file.

The post-war years confirmed the divergent evolution of northern and southern trade unionism.[12] Ulster wage movements never gelled into the wages movement. In the key engineering and shipbuilding sectors, war production brought few changes in working practices. Skill displacement or dilution, which pushed west Canada craftsmen into the Canadian OBU and created 'Red Clydeside', were resisted successfully by the craft unions. Government control of shipbuilding did lead to a narrowing of wage differentials between skilled and unskilled, and a big increase in membership of the NAUL and the Workers' Union. However, the craft unions went some way to restoring the differential in 1917, and the issue provoked the only major strike of the war years in Belfast. In the uncertain aftermath of the armistice, it looked briefly as if sectionalism might be rattled. On 25 January 1919, 30,000 Belfast engineering and shipbuilding workers struck unofficially for a 44 hour week. Soon the trouble spread to municipal employees. Control of power supplies gave the strike committee some administrative authority and the establishment of a permit system, enforced by pickets, led journalists to refer to the 'Belfast Soviet'. Alarmed at the contagion of 'Bolshevism' and the prospect of Sinn Féin winning Protestant support through it, Dublin Castle sent in troops on 15 February to restore municipal services. The strike collapsed within a few days, and marked a deceleration of northern wage movements. In truth there was little cause for alarm. Sensitive to its fragile base, the strike committee had strained to moderate radical impulses. Offers of help from Congress and the ITGWU met with no response. Though 1919–20 were paramount years for Belfast Labourism, the massive dispute carried a tentative import.

There were possibilities of bringing unskilled and textile operatives into communion with Dublin. Their bargaining problems approximated to those of southern workers. Like the mass of southern workers, they had historically proved too difficult for the British unions to organize, and the small craft societies in textiles had, of all unions in Ulster, been most supportive of Congress. Whilst Protestants held Dublin unions in suspicion, there was no enthusiasm for loyalist alternatives. The Ulster Workers' Trade Union, launched in December 1918 by James Turkington, a founder member of the Ulster Unionist Labour Association, encountered stiff opposition from *bona fide* unions on all sides. Faced with the option of Irish or loyalist unions, Protestant workers might have chosen the former. However, the earlier mobilization of the northern and British economies for the war effort allowed the amalgamateds to preclude this dilemma and then camouflage sectarianism with a veneer of British secular ideology. When Liberty Hall was ready to push north in late 1918, the NAUL and the Workers' Union had already established a firm presence among general workers outside Belfast. With textile operatives, the story was similar. The ITGWU recorded some successes in recruiting Protestant and Catholic workers in Monaghan and Caledon, but otherwise its resolute Ulster campaign found itself sided into the nationalist ghetto. Less enterprizing Dublin unions, such as the Brick and Stonelayers, the Irish National Teachers' Organization, and the Drapers' Assistants, lost northern branches after Labour's general strike against conscription.

CONGRESS POLICY

Against a backdrop of burgeoning membership, the food supply and conscription crises led Congress to assume a leading role in the movement for the first time, with Tom Johnson and William O'Brien exerting a guiding influence on political and industrial strategy respectively.[13] More than any other figure Johnson characterized the temper of the modern Labour Party. Born in 1872, of

'Liverpool English' stock, he became connected with Irish trade unionism in 1903 after obtaining work as a commercial traveller in Belfast. He first attended Congress in 1911 as a delegate of the National Union of Shop Assistants and Clerks, and therafter rose steadily to prominence, impressing his colleagues as the archetypal 'decent Englishman'. Alone of all the post-Connolly Labour leaders, Johnson was not a trade union power-broker, which left him free to focus on politics, and in deference to his literary talents in a fraternity desperately short of intellectuals, he emerged as Labour's ideologist. Although a member of *Cumannacht na hÉireann*, Johnson remained a labourist at heart, holding a Fabian view of progress at odds with the quicksilver politics of revolution. In any case, he lacked a bargaining instinct. Johnson was a conciliator, who liked to present himself as the honest servant of the movement, but invariably beavered away quietly to moderate radical impulses; a duplicity that infuriated his radical critics in the 1920s. O'Brien, by contrast, was a manager; he was a poor agitator and no idealist, despite a record of activism in Dublin socialist groups since 1899 and an almost filial devotion to Connolly. *Cumannacht na hÉireann*, of which he was now president, he allowed to lie moribund. Although a member of the Amalgamated Society of Tailors until 1918, O'Brien had always been close to the ITGWU and joined its No. 1 branch in 1917, rising quickly to become the union's first full-time general treasurer and its most powerful officer. Here he found his *métier*. Unlike Johnson, O'Brien had vision and grasped the need for de-anglicization. However, he was not big enough to prevent a narrow regard for Liberty Hall's short-term interests encumbering his goal of one union for all. Similarly, his work in Congress was for the union, not the movement.

The impact of transition at the base was unmistakeable at the 1918 congress. Two hundred and forty delegates attended, compared with 99 the previous year. O'Brien's presidential address strained to strike a historic note, enshrining Connolly and his influence on 'the great Russian Revolution'. Equally conscious of history, the delegates passed unanimously a motion entwining support for the Bolsheviks, peace in Europe, and self-determination for all peoples. With thirty-five delegates holding ITGWU cards, O'Brien exploited the occasion to consolidate both his leadership within the union and Liberty Hall's stamp on Congress policy. In a shuffle to prevent P.T. Daly from being elected secretary to Congress, O'Brien cornered the position himself, switching the pliant Johnson to candidacy for treasurer.[14] In reality, Johnson continued to act more as secretary; indeed he and O'Brien swapped posts three years later. A more comprehensive Labour policy now began to take shape. The congress took as its objective the promotion of working-class organization socially, industrially, and politically in co-ops, trade unions, and a party. Liberty Hall subsequently formulated a scheme to develop the co-operative angle to this trinity in syndicalist style. Taking its cue from the workers' co-ops formed to combat profiteering, it recommended branches to start by forming distributive outlets, connecting ultimately into a 'Workers' Food Committee laying down food policy for the country'. The annual congress also called a special conference to prepare for political action. Predominently native in organization and Fenian in mind for the first time since the 1890s, with the old dependency on the rhythm of British militancy finally broken, Labour seemed set to make its mark. However, in three crucial areas the post-1918 leadership was to prove unable to surmount the legacy of colonialism.

The most immediate failure occurred in relation to nationalism, where Labour semaphored an abiding concern to walk within the bounds of consensus and constitution. All of the major parties were nervous about the anticipated post-war radicalism. Highly suspicious of labour independence, the Unionists re-cast the Ulster Unionist Labour Association as a vehicle of Tory paternalism. For the Nationalists, Joe Devlin proposed a 'New Democratic Movement', committed to co-partnership in industry and profit-sharing.[15] Perceptibly closer to labour, Sinn Féin took the direct approach, offering Congress a clear run in four Dublin constituencies if it would not fight elsewhere, and providing its candidates pledged support for the Republic and abstention from Westminster. Abstention was the crux. It remained uncontroversial in wartime; since the enactment of conscription the Nationalist MPs had joined Sinn Féin in boycotting Westminster, and on 10 September the Congress executive committed Labour candidates to abstention. A peacetime election upset this cosy *entente*. Nationalists proposed to attend parliament, which would leave Labour stranded with Sinn Féin and unconstitutional agitation. Johnson especially saw trouble in all this. He was as anxious now as he had been in 1916 to keep Labour within the prevailing consensus but out of revolution, while most of his colleagues were apprehensive at tying their unions to the wheel of the Republic. Hesitancy reigned at the base; in consequence of its long depoliticization, membership signals were neither clear nor strong. If Labour contested independently and fared badly it might burst the bubble of confidence generated by the wages movement; if it did well, it was still stuck on the hook of abstentionism. At a special conference on 1 November, an executive recommendation to stand down from the next general election was approved by 96–23 votes.

The famous fudge was justified on grounds of giving electors a free hand in what was presented as a referendum on the constitutional status of Ireland. Opposition came from the more radical republicans, like Thomas Farren and Cathal O'Shannon, who saw no reason for not pursuing the Workers' Republic, and from northern labourites whose politics invariably aimed to prevent the primacy of constitutional issues. Typically, the north acted independently in any case. The Belfast Labour Party, which had been formed in 1917 from a conference of trades council, trade union, and ILP delegates, ran four candidates in the city. They polled a respectable average of 22 per cent of the vote in each constituency, but the only 'Labour' victors of the 1918 election were three token Ulster Unionist Labour MPs.[16] In the long term, the Congress decision to stand aside confirmed in left thinking the presumed dichotomy of the social and national questions. In the short term, it appeared to radicalize the leadership, who rifled syndicalist arguments to rationalize their funk. The November conference symbolically re-named the ITUCLP as the Irish Labour Party and Trade Union Congress (ILPTUC), and adopted Labour's first socialist programme, demanding collective ownership of wealth and democratic management of production.

A second great challenge came on the industrial front. As wage movements approached a crescendo, pressure mounted for co-ordinated action. In February, the Congress executive responded with a special conference on minimum pay and conditions. The conference set as its objectives a 44-hour week, a 50s. weekly minimum wage, and a general 150 per cent increase on pre-war wage levels.[17] To match the mood, the executive reminded employers that wage increases could be an interim palliative only, pending workers' control of production. Mayday was set as the deadline for employers' compliance, but no practical steps for action were taken and, not surprisingly, nothing happened. The Congress executive then served employers with a Mayday manifesto, explaining its case and warning of dire consequences if the manifesto were ignored. Affiliates were circulated with a document on a 'Proposed United National Wages and Hours Movement'. These papers merely represented an appeal to others to act and served to underline the executive's inefficacy. Embarrassed into further initiative, the executive appointed a sub-committee to examine ways of strengthening the movement. Their report came before the annual congress in August. It recommended affiliates to reorganize in ten industrial sectors with the intention of making Congress 'a single, all-inclusive Irish Workers' Union' which, through its political and industrial activities, would eventually realize 'the taking over control of industry by the organized working class'. Opposition came from the amalgamateds. Not for the last time, their British ties could not be reconciled with the trajectory of industrial unionism. Though the report was approved by a majority of eighty-one votes, nothing was done to implement it. Again, the Congress executive shirked responsibility, urging affiliates to introduce the scheme at local level first. But wasn't that the whole point of putting the scheme through Congress: that singly, trade unions were unwilling or unable to act effectively?

The failure to grasp opportunity in 1919, when labour all over Europe stood on the crest of a wave, was historic. The dynamic and talent of the movement continued to rest in individual unions, in contrast to whom the Congress leadership appeared unbelievably inept. Without direction, the wages movement became more reliant on militant tactics that could be sustained only in conditions of boom or revolution. Congress leaders played with fire in cloaking inertia with ever more radical rhetoric, endorsing direct action and soviets. The slump would show that they had painted themselves into a corner from which there was no escape with honour.

It was through the independence struggle that an interplay evolved between rank and file movements and Congress action. Once Sinn Féin's electoral landslide had created a new consensus, Labour gave freely what it had just refused to sell. Johnson cheerfully drafted the Democratic Programme adopted by Dáil Éireann as its social and economic policy on 21 January 1919. Though watered from down Johnson's original paper, which elaborated on principles in Pearse's *The Sovereign People*, its request and adoption testify to Republican anxiety about popular feeling and malleability on social issues. In return, Johnson and Cathal O'Shannon argued Ireland's claim to statehood at the first post-war international socialist conference at Berne. Labour also lobbied its French and British counterparts on Ireland, persuading the latter to substitute self-determination for home rule as its position on the Irish question. In lesser ways, Congress assisted Sinn Féin by nominating delegates to Dáil commissions and to the White Cross, which aided victims of the Anglo-Irish war, and helping to enforce the 'Belfast Boycott'. Yet Labour never recognized Dáil Éireann, lest it would prejudice industrial relations with British state agencies, and its stand on the national question spoke of 'Ireland's right to self-determination' as if it were an item of foreign policy. Nor did it seek to cultivate influence within Sinn Féin, despite the presence in Republican cabinets of people like Constance Markievicz and Sean Etchingham, who battled to re-organize the fishing industry along co-operative lines in the face of proprietary opposition.[18] This detached exchange was ideal for both Sinn Féin and Labour elites. The former wanted no more than moral and indirect political support from radicals. The latter acquired the benevolent neutrality of Dáil arbitration services towards the wages movement—in contrast with the Republic's suppression of land agitation by small farmers in the west—as well as unprecedented prestige and a breezy toleration of red flaggery which Congress leaders indulged to the full. In Berne, for example, Johnson and O'Shannon sided with the far left minority, voting for a resolution demanding a 'dictatorship of the proletariat' rather than one supporting parliamentary democracy, on the ground that the latter 'tended to condemn the Soviet system of government'. At home, Congress declared Mayday 1919 to be a 'general holiday' for international self-determination and proletarian solidarity. Inevitably, this use of nationalism as a safe outlet of radicalism raised membership expectations, the more so as Labour leaders excused their refusal to participate in the revolution with the plea that Sinn Féin was out for a republic, whereas Labour stood for a workers' republic.

Reality provided a less shambolic education. In building its republic Sinn Féin demonstrated the political nature of the state, whilst the Irish Republican Army subverted the legitimacy of institutional authority and paralysed state agencies, making direct action in wage movements more attractive. Labour analysis evolved from militant trade union, to social democratic, and, ultimately, revolutionary concepts. Pressure from the base challenged Congress to substantiate its rhetorical pretentions. In April 1919, Limerick trades council co-ordinated a nine-day general strike 'against British militarism'. The Irish Automobile Drivers' and Mechanics' Union struck in November in protest at the introduction of compulsory permits for vehicle drivers; a move by the authorities designed to asssist the monitoring of transport. Dockers, and then railwaymen, commenced a seven-month selective stoppage in May 1920, refusing to handle or convey British munitions. In all cases, the Congress executive intervened to snaffle these actions, indicating no greater enthusiasm than Sinn Féin for distinct class participation in the national struggle.[19] However, the push/pull of direct action and the consolidation of the Republican consensus brought Labour into unofficial, but open, alliance with Sinn Féin. The 1920 local elections, in which Labour did spectacularly well despite a Congress manifesto which ignored the independence struggle, saw widespread collusion with Republicans.[20] The authorities reacted with raids on union offices and arrests of Labour leaders, suppressing the *Voice of Labour* in September 1919 and its successor, the *Watchword of Labour*, in December 1920. In Cork, the ITGWU hall was burned and Tadg Barry, an outstanding organizer of rural workers, was arrested and later shot. This was just what trade union leaders had feared in 1918, but by now the political dividends and wage advances far outweighed the price of disruption.

The dialectic of direct action and nationalism climaxed in 1920–21. In March, dockers threatened to black food exports in response to the government's decontrol of food prices.[21] Congress intervened to secure a modification of the embargo pending talks. Meanwhile, trades councils were advised to form food control committees and be prepared to enforce price fixing. After conferences with farmers and bacon curers, an arrangement was reached whereby 30 per cent of certain produce would be retained for the home market. It was the first time that Congress had sanctioned direct action on a purely social issue. Coincidentally, a hundred political prisoners in Mountjoy jail began a hunger strike on 5 April, generating a huge emotional response. On 12 April, Congress called a general strike for their release, to start the following day. The call was immediately effective outside Ulster, inspiring the declaration of soviets in many towns as trades councils assumed administrative authority for the two-day duration of the stoppage. The soviets broadcast a ringing signal of membership confidence. Direct action on social issues was raised again the following year in *The Country in Danger!*, Labour's response to the looming economic crisis and a recent Dáil Éireann commission on labour policy. This most detailed and practical programme yet to come from Congress disturbed the Dáil cabinet with threats against any reduction in tillage acreage. A series of meetings took place in April 1921 involving representatives of the cabinet, the Irish Farmers' Union, and Congress. Nothing positive emerged, but *The Country in Danger!* indicated that Labour was belatedly awakening to the need to confront the national revolution with social demands.

The third area of policy failure related to Ulster. During the negotiations for the Anglo-Irish Treaty, Labour made three demands of any settlement: withdrawal of British forces, self-determination for Ireland as a whole, and the maintenance of Irish unity.[22] Given the record of Congress in dealing with the partition of its own movement, this was rich. Belfast had been included in Labour's anti-conscription campaign; Tom Johnson had his head split by a piece of cement for his troubles.[23] Such loyalist thuggery and the southern disposition of the trade union movement discouraged further forays north, and Dublin left northern labourites to themselves. The Congress response to the 1920 workplace expulsions was particularly feeble. Once again, it shrank from independent action, and then tucked in behind Sinn Féin. Throughout the national revolution, Congress policy scarcely noted that six-county colleagues were primarily concerned not with Ireland's constitutional status but with preventing themselves from being corralled into a sectarian *laager*, and it did nothing to maintain the left political unity achieved by Connolly in 1912.

THE SLUMP

Massive expansion of the world's productive capacity during World War I, followed by a further increase in output to meet the first demands of a peace-time market, led to a crisis of overproduction in the autumn of 1920.[24] Food prices were the first to tumble, causing a severe depression in agriculture. During 1921, Irish manufacturing trade was almost halved. By December, over 26 per cent of workers were idle. Rising unemployment depressed consumer demand, sending the economy tail spinning into long-term recession. Employers clamoured for the restoration of pre-war wage levels. In Britain, wages were getting 'back to normal' following the collapse of the Triple Alliance of railwaymen's, miners', and transport unions on 'Black Friday' and the subsequent isolation and defeat of the miners' strike against pay cuts. A similar pattern was anticipated in Ireland, with the railwaymen providing the initial sacrifice following government decontrol of the railways on 14 August 1921. Largely fulfilled in Northern Ireland, employer expectations were frustrated in the south by the effect with which militancy could be deployed in the near anarchic conditions obtaining during the Anglo-Irish truce and the Civil War.

To avoid a death of a thousand cuts, the 1921 congress signalled a desire to square up to the impending struggle with syndicalist pessimism. Clearly shaken by Britain's 'Black Friday', speaker after speaker affirmed conviction in industrial unionism as a strategic riposte to the employers' counter-attack, pledging that there would be no 'Black Fridays' in Ireland. Trapped between employer obduracy and membership militancy the leadership indulged the latter, resolving, with reckless naivety, to 'hold the harvest' of wage gains. Forecasting 'the greatest industrial upheaval in the history of the Irish Labour movement', Thomas Foran, President of the ITGWU, alluded to the general strikes of 1918 and 1920 as a way forward: 'they had shown imagination and determination in the Mountjoy hunger strike and conscription issues, and something like that would have to be done to meet the coming trouble. . . . We may as well all go down together now as drag the thing on'. Foran's prediction did indeed come true, but Labour failed dismally to meet the challenge of unity. Typically, the Congress executive threw the onus of action back onto the unions, urging the formation of inter-union committees on a local and industrial basis to co-ordinate resistance. It did propose direct intervention to assist the railwaymen, the first major sector into the breach, only to learn that the railway unions had agreed to arbitration under the Carrigan tribunal and meanwhile had no need of Congress. Thus ended the first and last effort to forge a united response to the slump. In reality the deadly rivalry between the ITGWU and the NUR made joint action unlikely. From this on, employers held the initiative; they would dictate the pace and pattern of events as best they could.

J.H. Thomas had persuaded a reluctant membership to accept the Carrigan tribunal as an alternative to a national strike and the 'railway crisis' produced six months of tense uncertainty as union leaders battled to restrain sporadic unofficial disputes. It was precisely to avoid such divisive and ultimately unsuccessful conflict that NUR men appealed for national action. Their fears were confirmed when the Carrigan tribunal found in favour of reductions and an extension of hours. Under strong rank and file pressure, the NUR's Irish council opted to fight for the eight-hour day, calling an unofficial national stoppage from 15 January 1922. In Cork, industrial unionists formed the Industrial Co-operative Workers' Committee to co-ordinate a take-over of local lines. Intervention by the Belfast and Dublin governments secured postponement of action pending further negotiation. On 10 February a settlement was announced which suspended the Carrigan award for six months and guaranteed the eight-hour day in principle. Lunging at the heels of a vanishing era, the Industrial Co-operative Workers' Committee seized all four railway systems in Cork on the following day, and ran its own timetable for twenty-four red hours: a belated gesture of what might have been. Strikes continued and in August the threat of serious unrest prompted further state intervention to delay proposed wage cuts, but the 'railway crisis' was over.

The 'railway crisis' had not tumbled the domino effect anticipated by employers, and a second false dawn of decisive conflict following the ratification of the Anglo-Irish Treaty on 7 January 1922 confirmed the dependency of the wage cutting offensive on state help. Disdaining to exploit this situation, the Congress executive sidled into constitutionalism as fast as decency permitted. The *Voice of Labour* promptly advised neutrality on the Treaty, and neutrality became official policy at a special conference in February. As the *Voice* acknowledged, Labour had more in common with the social and political opinions of the anti-Treatyites, and an early draft of the executive recommendation to the February conference envisaged supporting the Republicans should Labour deputies hold the balance of power in Dáil Éireann.[25] As in 1918, however, confusion at the top, hesitancy at the base, and the contention that neutrality meant unity, allowed Tom Johnson to realize his abiding concern to keep the movement out of unconstitutional politics. Quite exceptionally among his colleagues, Johnson positively favoured the Treaty, and was not embarrassed to canvass for it privately. A constitutional settlement promised a road forward into the simulacrum of British Labourism which framed Johnson's mind. On the day the Provisional Government replaced its revolutionary predecessor, Johnson led the first ever Labour deputation to Dáil Éireann, to protest about unemployment. Swinging Labour *de facto* behind the Treaty, the February conference agreed to contest the next elections, defeating an abstentionist resolution by 115–82 votes.

The absentionist case rested on two distinct grounds, and illustrates the disarray among critics of executive policy. First, there were those who dismissed electoral activity as a vain diversion from the industrial front. Secondly, there was the argument, tendered by straightforward separatists, Larkinites who despised the Johnson-O'Brien axis, and Communists, that entering Dáil Éireann and taking the controversial oath of allegiance would legitimize the Provisional regime. Communist opposition stemmed from a coup within the mothballed *Cumannacht na hÉireann* in September 1921. Led by James Connolly's son, Roddy, radicals had expelled the 'reformists', including Cathal O'Shannon and William O'Brien, reactivated *An Cumannacht* as the Communist Party of Ireland (CP), and affiliated to the Comintern. The move was less a reflex of organic forces than a mirror of faraway trends. As Connolly later lamented, the executive contained only one member who was 'nearly a proletarian'.[26] From the outset, the party and its spiky organ, the *Workers' Republic*, encountered endless difficulties. Initial membership did not exceed a hundred and dropped to fifty or so activists by 1923. Whilst Communists organized unemployed protests and had contacts with some of the Munster soviets, their 'anti-imperialist' perspective accorded priority to socializing republican militancy. If this policy proved remarkably fruitless, a comment on the sterility of Civil War republicanism rather than anything else, a switch to class politics in 1923 yielded no greater bounty. Even in contemporary Ireland, building a revolutionary opposition was beyond party resources. To protect its left flank, Congress camouflaged its funk on the Treaty with a token general strike, the last of that vintage, 'against militarism' on 24 April 1922. Coevally the ITGWU moved to incorporate the ICA within a bigger Workers' Army, ostensibly to defend Labour neutrality but probably to prevent Labour entanglement in a civil war. The initiative failed and some pro-Communist ICA men did take arms on the anti-Treaty side.

Labour amazed itself in the general election, returning seventeen of its eighteen candidates, including Paddy Gaffney, who disdained to take the oath of allegiance and joined the CP.[27] Undoubtedly, the circumstances of an election in which pro- and anti-Treaty Sinn Féin colluded to ensure that many constituencies went uncontested were exceptionally favourable to third parties. To some it seemed that Labour, with a handful of Farmers' Party and independent candidates, offered the only alternative to continued Sinn Féin dictatorship. None the less, the votes showed that despite the slump, the bulk of trade unionists were in fighting form, and revealed to the extent to which Labour leaders had underestimated their strength. Pleased with events, the 1922 congress in August devoted most of its time to political affairs, but Congress failed to connect its political influence, soon to be an important constitutional prop in providing the official opposition in Dáil Éireann, with industrial policy. As deputies railed across the Dáil chamber, it was clear that the Provisional Government was amenable to less diplomatic forms of pressure.

For most of 1922, illegal direct action had kept employer ambitions in check. Following the abolition of the Agricultural Wages Board in October 1921, violence and sabotage became more important in farm strikes, and played a crucial role in enabling the ITGWU to settle four major disputes in Dublin, Meath, Cork, and Waterford. In late January, the first of about eighty soviets that year took place at Mallow, where the Quartertown Mills were seized. With such minimal scope for compromise on wage grievances, soviets now acquired a serious revolutionary intent. All were disowned by the ITGWU and created friction within the union. Unable to guarantee property protection, the Provisional Government tried to restrain employers, hoping to minimize disorder by staggering wage deflation. Dáil Éireann's Labour Department intervened widely in disputes during the first quarter of 1922. The cabinet approved the formation of conciliation boards to deal with unrest in printing and dairying, and sponsored commissions of enquiry into the railways, canals, tailoring, and the postal service. Most remarkably, the right-wing Provisional Government over-ruled objections from the Cleeve company, owners of an extensive combine of mills, bakeries, and creameries in Munster, and appoint-ed two ministers to a sub-committee to formulate a scheme that would enable employees to buy out proprietary creameries. By mid May, neither ownership nor Cleeve's demand for wage cuts had been resolved. When Cleeve's locked out its 3,000 operatives on 12 May, a workers' Council of Action directed the seizure of thirty-nine creameries, together with mills and other company plant. As the red flags fluttered along the Suir valley it seemed initially as if the soviets might realize their motto 'the sovereign people'. Even Liberty Hall offered tacit assistance with the storage and export of butter. However, the economic and infrastructural disorder which facilitated occupation frustrated the financial success of the soviets. Moreover, farmers had now become violently hostile to 'Russian methods'; most withheld milk supplies, some resorted to arson or sabotage. The end came in August as the Free State army rolled up the 'Munster Republic' along the Waterford-Limerick line. By September, the Provisional Government had established its autho-rity over virtually all of the twenty-six counties. Its new-found confidence revealed itself in a willingness to face strike action in the civil service. Since February, the cabinet had played for time in negotiations with postal workers. In September, it rejected the find-ings of its own commission of enquiry into the cost of living for postal employees and fought a tough eighteen-day strike to enforce pay cuts. In the spring of 1923, state defences were reviewed to enable more effective intervention against popular unrest. The Criminal Investigation Department's intelligence system was redir-ected against 'agrarian irregularism', and, to avoid compromising the Civic Guard in such nastiness, or promoting a combative atmos-phere, a Special Infantry Corps was raised from the army to act as 'armed police'. Six hundred Specials were subsequently deployed in the Waterford farm strike.

As the noose tightened, the ITGWU completed the corruption of industrial unionism. The union still held 100,000 members in 1922, and most retained peak wage rates: a remarkable record. Seasonal farm labourers accounted for most of its losses since 1920, while gains came from poaching and the absorption of smaller societies unable to withstand the employers' offensive. If this process sustained the OBU idea, it differed in character from the pioneering advance before the slump. Now the ITGWU was sheltering the remnants of a retreating army, and its morale began to corrode. The number of organizing staff fell to nine by July 1922. Efforts were made to augment officialdom at local level and strengthen central control. Within head office, dissatisfaction mounted. Perplexed at the dilution of the OBU's revolutionary heritage, the idealists drifted out. A strategic shift was evident too. Notwithstanding some efforts to retrieve lost ground, the ITGWU aimed to compensate for reverses by intensifying its drive into traditional trade union sectors. In particular, it exploited the amalgamateds' disposition to accept wage cuts in line with the more rapidly falling cross-channel rates. Poaching was not new, nor was it novel for Irish unions to portray the amalgamateds as bureaucratic and conservative. But by 1922–23 a needling anglophobia vitiated the rivalry, aggravated by the inaction of British labour in the face of northern sectarianism and its stubborn intention to remain in post-colonial Ireland. Whilst arguments for an OBU held an iron logic, other unions, both British and Irish, had come to regard them as thin camouflage for empire-building: the OBU, they jibed, meant 'O'Brien's Union'. Hopelessly at odds with itself, Labour's woes were complete when Jim Larkin sailed home on 30 April 1923. Larkin had maintained an ambiguous attitude to events from his New York prison cell, but everyone expected trouble on his arrival. Moves were immediately afoot to establish a tenuous accord between ITGWU leaders pending some arrangement as to how so volcanic a personality could be accommodated within O'Brien's administration. In June, the fragile truce was shattered when Larkin publicly denounced O'Brien and was suspended as General Secretary by his executive. Despite his involvement with the Communist Labor Party in America, and contacts with Moscow, Larkin made little effort to rationalize his action ideologically, prosecuting a vituperative, personalized power struggle through the revived *Irish Worker*. Neither did he seek to rally support nationwide, sticking instead to Dublin, as if nothing had changed since 1913. In these bizarre circumstances, the final act of the drama unfolded.

There were omens in the spring of 1923 that Labour hopes of weathering the storm without general conflict might be realized. Agricultural workers in Wicklow and Cork were settled with little difficulty. Nine thousand labourers struck in Dublin, Meath, and Louth to hold weekly rates of 30s. or more. But as the smoke of civil war began to clear, the most desperate protagonists entered the arena with impatient aggression. A convergence of strikes brought matters to a head in the autumn. The wages crux in the portal trades had hung fire for two years as stubborn resistance prevented a conclusive adjustment of rates. On Friday 13 July, employers announced a reduction of 2s. in the dockers' average daily rate of 16s. About 3,000 dockers and others struck on Monday. The strike dealt a body blow to the economy. Cattle exports fell by 60 per cent. The meat industry virtually shut down, reducing staff and lowering wages in the process. With trade depressed, employers had little to lose in industrial action. By late September, Dublin was experiencing a series of selective strikes. A violent farm strike in south Kildare approached its first anniversary. Since May, Waterford had been convulsed in a major farm strike that had extended to urban employees, and on 21 August 6,000 workers in building, manufacture, distribution, and transport turned out against demands of the Cork Employers' Federation for staff cuts. About 20,000 trade unionists were affected by the autumn unrest. Here was the general challenge dreaded by Congress since 'Black Friday', and rampant sectionalism left it ill-placed for a response. In the key dock dispute, Larkin assumed direction of ITGWU men in Dublin, compelling a grudging executive to subvent a strike it came to regard as a vehicle for his ambitions. Taking on the O'Brien dominated Congress, he also sought to prevent the ILPTUC annual conference that August.

To make embarrassment doubly sure, Larkin endorsed five candidates for the August general elections. Larkinite bluster and sporadic collusion between trade unionists and Sinn Féin at constituency level isolated Congress leaders. Targetting them, Johnson especially, as the underbelly of Saorstát Éireann, Republicans attacked mercilessly; the more critical they became of Cumann na nGaedheal, the more abusive Sinn Féiners became of them. Being in the eye of the storm at least dealt Labour an ace; it could turn the tables on all its detractors and trump the cabinet's dismissal of republicanism as a cloak for anarchy by raising the spectre of industrial agitation merging with 'irregularism'. Financial opinion in Britain, which the government was anxious to reassure, believed that Republicans might commence a campaign of economic sabotage, aided and abetted by Larkin and his communist friends. The cabinet took seriously a threat by Larkin to prevent the general election failing a settlement of strikes. Concluding that 'an atmosphere of industrial unrest, necessitating, perhaps, the presence of bodies of military to prevent breaches of the peace during the elections should be avoided at all costs', the cabinet agreed on 1 August to request that employers postpone wage cuts for three months, during which conferences would be convened under government auspices. Again, Labour ignored reality and sailed into the hustings with pamphlets entitled *How to Get Houses* and *If You Want Your Child to Get a Fair Start in Life*.[28] The results demonstrated parliamentary Labour's irrelevance to wage conflict, clipping it to fourteen deputies. Only 60 per cent of electors bothered to vote. It was a measure of its detachment from such popular disillusion that the leadership had expected a big increase in representation. Yet the game was not up. Though vilified for the Civil War, Sinn Féin had polled surprisingly well in the election, and the government's position worsened over the next two months. Despite vigorous pruning of public spending, war expenditure had created a deficit of £2.5 million. With the first Saorstat loan to be floated, public confidence needed to be bolstered urgently to meet this fiscal test of statehood. Congress pleaded for an across the board settlement of strikes, based on mutual economic co-operation, but refused to imperil democracy by pulling its deputies out of Dáil Éireann. Indeed, both Larkin and the Congress leadership stooped to bidding against each other for government favour. With no compulsion to do otherwise, President Cosgrave rejected general discussions, arguing that a resolution of the dock dispute would pave the way for industrial peace. An ignominious end to the dock strike in early November did just that. Within two weeks the spirit of post-war trade unionism had been crushed.

Labour had known defeat and disillusion before. But the depth and scale of the 1923 catastrophe was unique. It poisoned the memory of the syndicalist era, and laid the seeds of enduring internal enmity.

6

Unfinished Business, 1924–1938

As peace settled nervously on a partitioned island, Labour could reflect on the unfinished business of its formative years. With a more effective Congress, an active political party and a larger number of trades councils, the movement retained the framework of its post-1917 structural advance. Indeed, the modern labour movement was formed between 1917 and 1923. However, whilst the principle of organization, for the labourer and the clerk as well as the craftsman, was now established, the 1923 defeats had led to the collapse of general unionism in small towns and on the land, and contraction elsewhere. Craft and clerical unions suffered too, if less severely, and Congress membership dropped from 175,000 in 1924 to a low of 92,000 in 1929.[1] Therefore, the great question first posed by new unionism, how to build a bargaining power for the mass of workers, remained unanswered.

Prospects for recovery were poor in the 1920s. Once the social shocks of world war and revolution had passed, the pre-1917 consensus reasserted itself, creating a climate of hostility to radical thinking. Though the worst of the slump was over, trade remained sluggish. Saorstát Éireann inherited a small, undeveloped, open economy, tied to Britain. Agriculture employed over half the labour force, and food and drink accounted for 85 per cent of merchandise exports. Crucially, the UK market was all-important, taking 98 per cent of exports in 1924. Faced with such crushing dependency, and beholden to the ranchers and the handful of major capitalists, the cautious Cumann na nGaedheal government chose to leave well alone, jettisoning industrialization through a self-sufficiency aim indelibly associated with Sinn Féin. Reliance on exports, especially beef exports, as the engine of economic progress produced an impressive rise in farm incomes for the Saorstát's 25,000 or so graziers, but little growth in employment.[2] Neither could Labour place much hope in government intervention. Cumann na nGaedheal opposed public enterprise on principle, and state sponsorship of ventures like the Shannon hydro-electric scheme reflected the weakness of the private sector. Subjectively, Labour added unstintingly to its own misfortune with a suicidal sectionalism. Superficially, the blame lay with self-serving, egotistical elites; but the fault was rooted in models of organization and politics that ill-suited native conditions.

These deficiencies in structure and outlook became clearer after 1932 when re-industrialization under Fianna Fáil's policy of economic protectionism unfolded a two-pronged challenge to Congress. In the short term, membership recovery revived inter-union disputes. In the long term, the state queried the voluntary basis of industrial relations. Fostering native industry behind tariff walls intensified the cycle of high production costs leading to high wage rates, low profit margins, high prices, and low real incomes. Though *per capita* income grew by 15 per cent in the inter-war years, compared with 25 per cent in Britain, and was less than half of that in Britain in 1939, money wages for craftsmen exceeded British rates from the early 1920s.[3] With the exhaustion of the import substitution phase of industrialization, the implications of wage levels for manufacturing competitiveness came under scrutiny. Now, the unfinished business was back on the Congress agenda.

THE LARKIN SPLIT

Strike activity in Saorstát Éireann fell steadily after 1923, and the most important dispute of the decade was internal to the movement.[4] In February 1924 the Master of the Rolls dismissed several legal actions taken by Jim Larkin to show that ITGWU rules were invalid. On 14 March the ITGWU executive voted unanimously to expel Larkin from the union. Larkin still clung to his hopes, and an opportunity arose in May when members at Dublin Gas struck over a personnel issue. Refused official backing from the executive, they invited Larkin to represent them. Within a week he had won the strike and his supporters occupied Liberty Hall until ejected by the army. Leaving for Moscow on 27 May, to address the Comintern and the Red International of Labour Unions, he told his brother, Peter, to stick with the ITGWU. Instead, Peter moved quickly to tidy up the chaotic tangle of union affairs. A Port, Gas, and General Workers' Provisional Committee was established to receive all union monies and Larkinites were directed to ignore the executive. On 15 June, the split was formalized with the creation of the Workers' Union of Ireland (WUI). Sixteen thousand members, two-thirds of the ITGWU muster in Dublin, defected to the WUI, along with 23 of 300 provincial branches. The great bulk of branch officials, Dublin and country, stayed with Liberty Hall. Exasperating jurisdictional disputes ensued, with animosity reaching new depths in the 1925 coal strike when WUI men pelted ITGWU dockers at the Alexandra Basin with a hail of stones and lumps of coal.

The split accentuated the defensive, bureaucratic mentality already evolving within the ITGWU. The loss of Dublin branches diluted the influence of the union's more conciliatory, and more intuitively radical, General President, Tom Foran, whereas William O'Brien consolidated his grip on the movement, succeeding Larkin as General Secretary and accepting the Presidency of Congress for the third time in 1924.[5] Feeling vindicated in his rule-bound response to 'disruption', O'Brien pursued ITGWU interests with minimum militancy and maximum internecine politicking, opposing all moves at *rapprochement* with Larkin and keeping the WUI barred from Congress. This was dangerous, self-defeating self-righteousness. In blaming Larkin for labour's woes, O'Brien disdained to identify with his members in their agony, and Larkin was patently not the primary cause of decline. The ITGWU claimed 40,000 members in 1926, when Larkin had done his worst. Three years later, enrolment had dwindled to 15,500.[6] For its part, the WUI remained very much a Dublin and Larkin-centred union, so short of funds that it did not affiliate to the 'Larkinite' Dublin trades council; one positive result of which was a *detente* in relations with the rival Dublin workers' council, culminating in unity and affiliation to Congress in 1929. It was the only contemporary rank and file initiative of any consequence.

The 1920s saw Dublin divided not alone between two trades councils, or Larkin and Liberty Hall, but also between craft and general, and Irish and amalgamated unions. Provincial centres tended to be dominated by one or other of the protagonists, but here the movement was now very thin on the ground. The number of trades councils, a good indicator of the geographical spread of trade unionism, fell from forty-six in 1921 to ten by 1930. Congress stirred itself in 1927 with a special conference on re-organization and recruitment. Delegates agreed to consider the merger of cognate unions and urged the amalgamateds to grant greater autonomy to their Irish sections, yet refused to appoint a committee on re-organization.[7] Once again, nothing happened. A few 'Back to the Unions' campaigns were mooted at local level in the mid decade, particularly after the British general strike of 1926, which quickened the pulse of Irish workers. The ITGWU enjoyed a minor recovery in 1925–26, notably in Dublin. But efforts to organize labourers on the Shannon hydro-electric scheme were undermined by the use of unemployed workers, despite widespread protest and a Labour Party call for a boycott of the scheme.[8] When the economy again dipped into recession in 1927, it proved impossible to halt the continuing slide in trade union membership.

LEFT POLITICS

The typical Labour TD (*Teachta Dála*) of the early intake was a union official, preoccupied with dwindling membership and wage rates. Most had been elected on their record as agitators in the heyday of direct action. When trade unionism disintegrated about them, they shrugged philosophically and rebuilt their electoral bases on clientelist lines, leaving Tom Johnson to shoulder the brunt of parliamentary duties.[9] Johnson was a polished performer. An assiduous contributor to Dáil debates, he never missed a division until overwork forced him to take a short respite in 1927. His interest in policy formulation and personal example helped to make Labour a disciplined, united party, superior to the other minnows in Dáil Éireann, and worthy of its status as official opposition to the government. But if Johnson discovered his *métier* as a parliamentarian, he was no chief or tactician. After 1923, Labour needed not alone to restore credibility in its role as the 'political wing' of Congress, but to expand beyond it. On both counts, Johnson made no progress. The ILPTUC format did little other than entangle the party with the quarrels of union leaders, and as the fountainhead of sectionalism, Dublin remained embarrassingly barren electoral territory. Passive reliance on a contracting, faction-ridden trade union movement for ideological stimulus produced a pedestrian Labourism which mistook 90,000 or so trade unionists for the people. Johnson's aversion to nationalism locked Labour within this narrow, increasingly peripheral politics. The catatonic post Civil War Irish Republican Army (IRA), which claimed over 20,000 members in 1926 and held a rich source of radical energy, was left to remain a formidable alternative locus of dissent until tapped by Fianna Fáil.[10] Convinced that democracy depended upon it, Johnson kept Labour basically pro-Treaty. 'We have had one revolution and one revolution in a generation is enough' was his rebuttal of Fianna Fáil's stand on the Oath of Allegiance.[11] Yet, he was happy to modify the Saorstát constitution where it conflicted with any proven consensus. As the shaping of consensus was left to others, Labour became the reluctant but undemanding servant of Cumann na nGaedheal or Fianna Fáil. That Johnson could repeat the tactical blunders of 1917 to 1923 with such facility reflected on Labourism generally. Although party systems structured around the question of relations with the former imperial power were typical of economically dependent post-colonial countries, Labour never understood this politics as anything other than irrational. Articulating assumptions infused into the movement by its assimilation into British labourist sub-culture during the late nineteenth century, Johnson argued that Labour should stick to purely social and economic issues. Sooner or later, political stability and modernization would 'clear the decks' for a class oriented party system.

Once again, colonialism turned everything upside down. The quest for an integral nationality fueled the industrialization drive of the 1930s, Fianna Fáil captured urban trade unionist votes, and the strongholds of the modernist Labour Party receded to the largely unorganized rural proletariat of the tillage and dairying constituencies of Munster and Leinster. Class divisions were vivid in rural society, where land was everything. And though a generation of urban workers had been depoliticized by the ITUC's disengagement from nationalism after 1894, farm labourers had retained a political consciousness through the Land and Labour Associations. The Labour deputies who nurtured their bailiwicks on rural workers effectively revived and intensified the incrementalist politics of the old associations. With a highly personalized constituency machine, a deft hand in brokerage, diligent attention to local issues, and transferred votes from other candidates, such 'dacent men' could scrape together an electoral quota. Ideology, if they considered it, meant siding with the underdog. Anything else was a threat to their re-election prospects. Ideologically committed members or branches operated on the fringe. As party organization was built from the top down, rank and file revolts were little less unusual than a puppet chastising the ventriloquist.

During the fourth Dáil, the first to meet in peacetime, Labour evolved as a mild social democratic party, doing the usual social democratic things, like opposing cuts in public spending and demanding state intervention in the economy. A special conference of Congress in 1924 narrowly endorsed tariff protectionism, those against stressed the implications for higher living costs, and Labour gave qualified support to the selective tariffs introduced incrementally by Cumann na nGaedheal.[12] Such tentativeness in economic strategy, coupled with ambivalence on the national question, prevented the party from projecting a clear political stance. In public perception, it slipped into a marginal role as defender of social welfare recipients. This in itself was an onerous task in the teeth of a regime which clipped a shilling off old-age pensions and denied any responsibility to provide unemployment benefit at a time when one in four insured workers were idle and insurance benefit was being exhausted at an alarming rate.[13] Overworked and guilty at the inability of parliamentary methods to make any impression on Cumann na nGaedheal's stonehearted conservatism, Johnson offered to resign as party leader and secretary of Congress in 1925. It was a measure of Johnson's personal stature and the lack of alternative talent that he was prevailed upon to withdraw his resignation.

Hopes of mounting a challenge from the far left were stymied by Larkin. In 1924 the Comintern had dissolved the Communist Party to confer its *imprimatur* on the Irish Worker League, which Larkin had launched some months previously as a social auxiliary to the *Irish Worker*.[14] It seemed an obvious move, given 'Big Jim's' leadership and a promising attendance of 500 at the League's inauguration. As Dublin would show repeatedly in the 1920s, a communist constituency existed in the city, small but solid against the odds. The League's London branch displayed some political consistency. However, apart from a few social events, and despite the WUI's affiliation to the Red International of Labour Unions, Larkin confined Dublin operations to prosecuting his vendetta against Congress. Disgusted with this 'dog in the manger' attitude, serious minded elements set up the propagandist Connolly Workers' Educational Club, from which emerged, in 1926, the breakaway Workers' Party of Ireland. Efforts by the party to secure Comintern recognition, and its criticism of Larkin's line that Fianna Fáil, not Labour, deserved Communist support, led to bitter clashes between the two groups. When Larkin secured a decisive Comintern adjudication against the Workers' Party in 1927, it sank into decline. Whatever his record, Larkin was still an important man in Dublin or Moscow.

There were indications in the mid 1920s that Cumann na nGaedheal and the Republicans, in their self-destructive straitjackets of severe statism and abstention, would allow Labour to prosper by default. Indeed, the threat of an effective pro-Treaty opposition was a factor in timing de Valera's decision to launch Fianna Fáil.[15] Good results for Labour in the 1925 local elections and subsequent by-elections were followed by the record achievement of returning twenty-two deputies in the general election of June 1927. De Valera had escaped from the sterility of Sinn Féin metaphysics into politics, but he still baulked at swallowing the oath of allegiance. Then the assassination of Kevin O'Higgins upset all calculations, throwing Cumann na nGaedheal, already rattled by a disastrous electoral performance, into paroxysms of reaction.[16] Johnson promptly offered to join a government of national stability. President Cosgrave dismissed this soother and introduced bills to toughen public safety legislation and require Dáil candidates to abjure abstention. When de Valera moved to elude his impending pickle, both Larkin and Johnson scrambled to help him, seeing here the carrot to tempt Fianna Fáil into Dáil Éireann. De Valera and Larkin proposed a conference of opposition groups to discuss an alternative government. Labour ignored the conference of course, but Johnson loved intrigue. Within a week he had cobbled together support for a Labour-led coalition government, sustained from the back benches by Fianna Fáil. It was an unlikely scenario that would harness such adversaries as Fianna Fáil and the Redmondites. Yet had it not been for the inexplicable absence of the Redmondite deputy for Sligo, the famous Mr. Jinks, the opposition would have defeated the government in a confidence vote. President Cosgrave quickly dissolved the 'short Dáil', went to the country, and won his majority. The September general election squeezed the smaller parties. Labour lost nine seats. Remarkably, the three candidates fielded by the Irish Worker League polled well, with covert and overt assistance from such unlikely auxiliaries as Fianna Fáil and two British Communist stalwarts, Willie Gallacher and Shapurja Saklatvala. James Larkin Jr helped to unseat Johnson in County Dublin. Larkin Sr was returned for Dublin North; the only Communist TD ever elected to Dáil Éireann, though as an undischarged bankrupt he could not take his seat. Loyalties were now polarizing around Cumann na nGaedheal and Fianna Fáil. Between them, Larkin and Johnson had manoeuvred Labour back to the margins.

After 1927, politics assumed a classic post-colonial form. Deepening its ties with ex-Unionists and the 'stake in the country' people, Cumann na nGaedheal became the party of those who favoured the maintenance of existing political and economic links with Britain. By adopting radical socio-economic policies, Fianna Fáil nationalism matured into a critique of dependency with a pronounced urban working-class appeal. Labour wilted. Thomas J. O'Connell outdid his predecessor in shunning constitutional issues. As secretary of the Irish National Teachers' Organization, a very political union, O'Connell expected the party to be reciprocally fine-tuned to internal trade union sensitivities. Weeks before succeeding Johnson, he had asked that teachers' opinions be respected through 'strict neutrality' on 'purely political' questions.[17] Once Fianna Fáil accepted the role of official opposition, neutrality became impossible and discipline crumbled. Five TDs bucked the whip to vote with Fianna Fáil on a land annuities motion; two more suffered expulsion for supporting Cumann na nGaedheal's public safety legislation during the red scare of 1931.[18] Identity faded as circumstances pushed both Labour and Fianna Fáil into the same division lobbies. Party-union relations within Congress also deteriorated under the luckless O'Connell. Amicable divorce proceedings, designed to improve organization, were concluded in 1930; Congress carried on, the party established its own branches and an administrative council. Successive steps in this direction had been taken since 1923, in pragmatic acknowledgment that few trade unionists voted Labour. Labour still represented itself as the 'political wing' of Congress. Its policies, calling for an industrial development commission, nationalization of banking and transport, and progressive taxation, were broadly those of the ITUC. Yet, just thirteen unions bothered to affiliate to the new-look party.

SOCIAL REPUBLICANISM

Between 1927 and 1934, the dynamo of far left politics was driven by a synergy of republicans and Marxists. From the United Irishmen to the Provisionals, reliance on the 'men of no property' was the standard separatist fallback position, but contemporary zealots were slow to lower their gaze from the mystical *de jure* republic established in Easter Week. In May 1922, the IRA approved, but never applied, a policy of seizing land on behalf of the people.[19] Subsequently, it ignored appeals from the CP, Liam Mellows, and Constance Markievicz to activate a social policy.[20] Peadar O'Donnell, the outstanding agitator of his day and a central figure in the maturation of social republicanism, began the push to the left in 1925, when he persuaded the IRA to break with Sinn Féin's 'Second Dáil'.[21] One year later O'Donnell started a campaign against the payment of land annuities in his native Donegal. The IRA remained sceptical until defections to de Valera's heresy, combined with a slow revival of the far left, induced a rethink. Leftist republicans developed contacts with international communism in 1927 and at home a plethora of organizations emerged to link the IRA with trade unionists, the unemployed, and small farmers. As the Comintern explored new links with Ireland, communism itself was embracing a more exclusive position. Known as 'class against class', the revised line depicted reformist labour as a tool of capitalism, 'social fascist', and an obstacle to the coming revolution. At one level, 'class against class' contributed to the revival of communist politics in Ireland. Marxists re-opened the Connolly Workers' Club in Dublin in 1928 as a cadre school.[22] Twelve graduates, including young Jim Larkin, were enrolled at the Lenin College in Moscow, where his father's credit was finally running out. Following the creation of a preparatory committee for the formation of a Workers' Revolutionary Party in March 1930, the Comintern instructed Irish comrades to proceed with or without Larkin Sr and, for once, the big man stood aside, retiring gradually from communist politics. The Revolutionary Workers' Groups (RWG) formed in Belfast and Dublin in November set out to build a rank and file movement among the unemployed and in the strikes against wage cuts that followed the 'Wall St crash'. From a remarkable record of struggle, with outdoor relief workers in Belfast, miners in Castlecomer, building workers in Dublin, and small farmers in Leitrim, the RWG could claim to be Ireland's most vigorous communist movement ever. Larkin Jr won a seat on Dublin Corporation in 1930. In general however, relentless clerical hostility contained the RWG to flashpoints of militancy. At this level, 'class against class' did little to ease its marginality, or enable it to cultivate social republicanism.

The IRA Army Council kept its distance from left tendencies until the depression hit the agricultural economy in 1931. Having melted to a core of 5,000 or so, membership now began to pick up, and support for the land annuities campaign encouraged IRA approval of its quasi-communist progeny Saor Éire, launched in September by O'Donnell, George Gilmore, and Frank Ryan to unite socialists and republicans.[23] Against a background of social unrest, IRA drilling, intimidation of juries, and shootings, the government reacted on 17 October, proscribing twelve radical groups. The intent of this essentially anti-republican move was camouflaged in a hysteria about 'godless communism', prepared in consultation with the Catholic hierarchy, which weighed in on 18 October with a pastoral letter condemning Saor Éire and, implicitly, the IRA. Thus, the proscription affected not only the IRA and Saor Éire, but obscure or defunct organizations like the Workers' Revolutionary Party. Similarly, widespread Garda raids included 'communist fronts' like Russian Oil Products Ltd. Curiously, the one genuine centre of communist politics, the RWG, was scarcely touched.[24] As Cumann na nGaedheal hoped, a fear that the IRA would play Lenin to de Valera's Kerensky animated the 1932 general election. But despite its best efforts to play the religious card, at a time when the Papacy was attempting to posit Catholic social action as a political creed, the government had sealed its fate with untimely austerity measures, clipping the wages of public employees, and introducing a marriage bar for women national school teachers.[25]

Fianna Fáil's historic victory created a moment of truth for social republicanism. Power allowed de Valera to cut his politics to a more conservative cloth. There would be no more Fianna Fáil flirtation with red republicanism, as the unique decision to deport Jim Gralton demonstrated. Gralton was deported in August 1933 for communist/republican activities in south Leitrim.[26] Sloughing off the revolutionary roots was a delicate but clinical operation. Republicanism was not necessarily a social ideology, and de Valera could always exploit the confusion about its social aims. Typically for the time, republicans were prominent both in defending and opposing Gralton. With the red scare intensifying, the IRA leadership recoiled from the Marxist embrace. It accepted the suppression of Saor Éire and had it wound up at the 1932 army convention. When a Catholic mob attacked RWG and WUI head offices a year later, the Dublin battalions stood aside. For some on the left, the answer was to counter Fianna Fáil's bourgeois republicanism with socialist republicanism. For others, notably Peadar O'Donnell, social republicanism was not a new left politics, but real republicanism. A republic for the people, he argued, could be not achieved under capitalism. Thus, the task was to expose the limits of de Valera's politics by crystallizing 'real' republican politics in a broad congress of progressive forces. Either way, social republicans found IRA Army Council prevarication intolerable at a time when, they believed, action was needed to confront Fianna Fáil and the Blueshirts, who emerged in fascist garb in April 1933.[27] Moreover, a fear of fascism was producing a momentum for unity on the left. Particularly influential was the shift from 'class against class' to a 'united front' line in the CP, which the RWG had re-established in June.[28]

In March 1934, resolutions from Michael Price for a socialist republic, and from O'Donnell for a republican congress, were narrowly defeated at the IRA army convention. The old Saor Éire leadership then withdrew to set up the Republican Congress. A sprouting network of rank and file support pitched into a hectic campaign of class agitation in preparation for a conference on strategy, fated to take place in Rathmines Town Hall. On 28–29 September, the old Town Hall hosted a remarkable 'who's who' of Irish militancy; arguably, Europe's first Popular Front.[29] The Labour Party leadership was pointedly excluded, but delegates attended from fourteen trade unions and trades councils, together with comrades from almost every shade of radical opinion, under the chairmanship of William McMullen, a senior ITGWU official and vice-president of the ITUC. A particular achievement was the attraction of Northern Protestant support. The Congress adopted a programme including demands for land redistribution, minimum wages for farm workers, equal pay for women, and an Irish based trade union movement structured along industrial unionist lines. However, the bifurcous nature of social republicanism booby-trapped the debate on strategy. The majority of the Congress organizing bureau, led by Price and Roddy Connolly, proposed to declare clear cut for a Workers' Republic and build a political party. O'Donnellites, on the other hand, pursuing their 'real' republican path, wanted to continue the 'United Front' approach towards 'the Republic', and were backed by the strong communist contingent who favoured unity on immediate issues, such as anti-fascism, but opposed the creation of a new party. By 99–84 votes the 'United Front' prevailed. But the Congress never recovered. Stricken internally, and isolated by the IRA, it limped to dissolution in 1937. The social republic, as a serious concept, was dead for thirty years.

IN LEAGUE WITH FIANNA FÁIL

The Labour Party's political 'neutrality' attained farcical dimensions in the watershed election of 1932. O'Connell requested 'five or ten years truce' on questions relating to the Treaty. On tariffs, Labour speakers approved a 'low wall', going half way with Fianna Fáil. On land annuities, the party programme pleaded: 'political parties [are] not qualified to pronounce judgment'. Extreme moderation in a moderately extremist climate paid no dividends. Seven Labour deputies were returned, and the party's immediate requirement in the seventh Dáil was a replacement for its unseated leader. The succession fell to William Norton.[30] Freshly elected and thirty-two years young, he was an inspired choice. A postal messenger boy at sixteen, Norton was general secretary of the Post Office Workers' Union seven years later. In 1926 he became the first Labour candidate to win a by-election. Losing the seat a year later, he switched constituencies to Kildare. Politically, Norton was professional and pragmatic. He had argued strongly for the separation of the party from Congress in 1930. Unencumbered with the constitutional hang-ups of Johnson or O'Connell, he soon ditched Labour's ambiguity on nationalism for a straightforward acceptance of consensus republicanism, dismissing the oath of allegiance as a 'relic of feudalism'. Labour and Fianna Fáil met to discuss co-operation on 8 March. Next day, Norton pledged backbench support for a minority Fianna Fáil government. In return, Labour expected work or maintenance for the unemployed, the construction of 40,000 houses, pensions for widows and orphans, the re-organization of transport on a national basis, protection for the flour milling industry, control of food prices, and economic development.

Trade unions were no less sympathetic to Fianna Fáil. The international depression had strengthened their belief in protectionism, and a convergence of labour and Fianna Fáil views was evident at the 1931 congress. To rally the movement against unemployment, the congress adopted an 'Industrial Charter' demanding a living wage; a forty-hour week; work or maintenance for the unemployed; national programmes of house and road building, and afforestation; public ownership of banking, power supplies, and transport; and import controls and the establishment of an exports boards. Congress instructed the executive to pursue implementation of the Charter through parliamentary channels.[31] According to protocol, this meant the Labour Party. But of course, Fianna Fáil were the only ones who could deliver. Not only did Congress not have effective leverage in politics, but its impact was invariably softened by disunity or sheer fuzzy thinking. Thus, Louie Bennett's presidential address to the 1932 congress warned that the 'tariffs, and taxes, powers assumed to promote certain industries' introduced by Fianna Fáil 'may be excellent but they bring us perilously near to a dictatorship'. At the same time she called for a national economic council to give unions an advisory role in state policy making![32] That kind of corporatism lay thirty years in the future, but by 1934 Congress could list nine items of legislation on housing, welfare, or industry featuring some labour input.[33]

Fianna Fáil more than met Labour expectations. A comprehensive tariff policy created opportunities for enterprise that expanded industrial employment from 110,000 in 1931 to 166,000 in 1938; proportionately a performance comparable with Stalin's massive industrialization programme, the Second Five Year Plan. New semi-state industries and public spending programmes were launched, agricultural policy laid greater emphasis on labour-intensive tillage, and working conditions were improved through the introduction of Joint Industrial Councils, new trade boards, and the Conditions of Employment Act (1936). A notable prize for rural Labour TDs was the re-appointment of an Agricultural Wages Board in 1936 to set minimum rates for 150,000 farm workers.[34] While real national income virtually stagnated as the Economic War depressed farm prices, incomes of those in industry and services increased. Fortuitously, the slump in livestock exports during the Economic War improved diet for the urban poor. Between 1926 and 1936, consumption of cattle rose by 79 per cent, of lamb by 37 per cent, and of eggs by 14 per cent.[35] Greater efforts were made to tackle the housing problem. Twenty-seven per cent of the population lived in bad housing, i.e., a density of more than two persons per room, in 1926. State credit schemes allowed 17,680 local authority houses to be built between 1932 and 1936, over twice the number completed during the previous seven years. By 1936, the proportion of people badly housed had fallen to under 23 per cent. And it may be added that members of the Irish National Teachers' Organization made a unique long-term contribution to the housing problem in 1935 when they subscribed over £5,000 to float the Educational Building Society.[36] The Unemployment Assistance Act (1933) provided for all unemployed men, insured or not, introducing the 'dole' in April 1934. A Land Allotments Act subsidized local authority in letting plots to the unemployed for food cultivation. It became easier to qualify for blind and old age pensions, and widows' and orphans' pensions were introduced in 1935.[37]

There were limits to Fianna Fáil achievement, and basic differences with Labour would surface before the decade closed. The growth in total employment, from 1,220,284 in 1926 to 1,235,424 in 1936, was unimpresssive. The extra jobs created were insufficient to absorb rural depopulation, whilst the world-wide depression discouraged emigration, severely so in the case of America. Rising unemployment figures reached 145,000 in January 1936.[38] And once the great industrial leap forward was over, new growth areas were not obvious. Efforts to diversify the export market met meagre results. High input costs for industries in a small home market meant high consumer prices. None the less, from a labour viewpoint, short-term trends at least were encouraging. If unemployment remained high, the workforce was being restructured in a way favourable to organization, while the Control of Manufactures Acts, designed to promote native ownership of industry, enhanced trade union bargaining power. Congress membership rose from 95,000 in 1933 to 161,000 in 1938.[39] Norton gave unwavering support for the Economic War, making representations to British Labour leaders during negotiations over the land annuities issue, and arranging a meeting between de Valera and the British Prime Minister, Ramsay MacDonald. The first Fianna Fáil administration also paid Labour the compliment of regular consultation on legislation. Flattered and elated, Labour men wondered if both parties were headed for unity.

The political pitfalls to the alliance became clear when de Valera called a snap election in 1933 to win a slim Dáil majority. Labour's vote slipped to an all time low of 5.7 per cent, although the parliamentary party increased from seven to eight deputies. Still, no had one expected Labour to do well. After a decade of Cosgravian reaction, at a time when European labour movements were being crushed by mass unemployment and fascism, it was not difficult for Norton to convince his colleagues that ideological and tactical imperatives offered no option but backing for Fianna Fáil. Labour lacked the numbers, the vision, and the guts to tackle the social and economic objectives set by Fianna Fáil, and de Valera seemed the best bulwark against fascism and red republicanism. Though General O'Duffy's National Guard was proscribed in August 1933, fascism acquired a deadlier import in September when Cumann na nGaedheal, the National Centre Party, and the Blueshirts, now called the Young Ireland Association, merged as Fine Gael under O'Duffy's leadership. Labour then agreed to support the government in return for concessions on pensions, unemployment benefit, housing, and working conditions. A joint Labour-ITUC manifesto on the 'Fascist Danger' appeared in October and Congress, after some prodding from Dublin trades council, sponsored a series of anti-fascist rallies in May.[40] O'Duffy finally over-reached himself in the local elections of June 1934. When his promised big advances failed to materialize, Fine Gael pressured him into resigning.

The fascist menace had never tempted Labour into any truck with red republicans. Weeks after the schism in the Republican Congress, Labour's annual conference slapped down a motion of Roddy Connolly's to unite republicans, Communists, and Labour in a common anti-fascist, anti-imperialist alliance, resolving instead to resist the introduction of 'anti-Christian communist doctrines into the movement'. Subsequent popular front overtures from the CP met a similar response.[41] None the less, a relaxation of the red scare encouraged Labour to attract the remnants of the Republican Congress and distance itself from Fianna Fáil by edging left. In 1936 the party adopted a constitution committing it to a 'workers' republic'. The Spanish Civil War soon put a stop to that. Many trade unionists joined the Christian Front rallies for Franco, leaving republicans and communists to dominate the pro-Spanish government lobby and the 'Connolly Column' that fought with the XV International Brigade. Facing an unequal contest, the CP folded its own paper to ally with republicans behind Peadar O'Donnell's short-lived *Irish Democrat*; it marked the swansong of the popular front idea.[42] Under pressure from Catholic actionists to dissociate itself from international socialism, the Labour Party published William Norton's pamphlet *Cemeteries of Liberty, Communistic and Fascist Dictatorships* in 1937. Norton revealed his touchiness on the subject at the 1938 party conference, interrupting Conor Cruise O'Brien to dismiss criticism of the Spanish Nationalists as irrelevant. Norton also endorsed a request from the Irish National Teachers' Organization to have Labour's new constitution vetted by the Catholic hierarchy. Two sections found 'contrary to Catholic social teaching' by the hierarchy were amended and the workers' republic objective deleted.[43] Thus trapped between a government that was more radical, in practice if not in theory, and its own fears of being 'misunderstood', Labour reverted to the defensive. Norton could justly claim to have guided the party from the verge of oblivion and buried the pre-1932 inanity about its political nature. The general elections of 1937 and 1938 saw Labour recover votes lost to Fianna Fáil earlier in the decade. However he failed to break with the practice of tailing the prevailing hegemony. In opposing the enactment of *Bunreacht na hÉireann* for not declaring the second republic, Labour affirmed a nominal independence on constitutional questions with the sterile formalism that characterized Tom Johnson's stewardship during the heady days of the first republic.[44]

INDUSTRIAL UNIONISM THIS TIME?

Recovery in depressed conditions triggered a significant escalation of trade union militancy. Yet despite Communist, and even IRA, involvement in some disputes, industrial struggle carried little radical import.[45] In contrast with the syndicalist era, labour was fatally divided; primarily, expansion meant new opportunities for inter-union rivalry. Sometimes unions fought over their respective merits, sometimes over the advantages of craft or industrial unionism, sometimes over the principles behind Irish or British based unionism; always they fought over members. The most strike prone sectors, transport and construction, were also the most faction ridden areas of trade unionism. Sixteen unions operated in transport, twelve of them British based, making it a cockpit of the general friction in the movement between the ITGWU, the WUI, and the amalgamateds. A protracted tram strike in 1929 prompted Congress to adopt a system of adjudication for inter-union disputes, and show greater concern to discourage the affiliation of small or splinter unions.[46] Such tentative action became hopelessly inadequate in 1934 when moves by the Amalgamated Transport and General Workers' Union (ATGWU) to block the defection of Dublin tramwaymen to the ITGWU provoked a renewal of opposition to British-based unionism *per se*. Preoccupied with Larkin, William O'Brien had been fairly conciliatory towards the amalgamateds over the preceding decade. *Three Men and Three Days; A Fight For Irish Trade Unionism*, the ITGWU's version of the tramway dispute, indicated that the gloves were off, again. Moreover, the ITUC executive sided with the ITGWU and the annual congress that August uncovered a broad opinion among Irish unions that the accelerating economic and legislative divergence between both countries should cause the British unions to review their position in Ireland.

In 1936, Sean Lemass advised Congress that the government would intervene unless something was done about the continuing internecine friction.[47] Congress responded in April with the appointment of a highpowered Commission of Inquiry to examine five main areas, of which the most important was the merger or grouping of unions, a delicacy that kept repeating; previous committees had toyed with it in 1927 and 1930. Forty-nine societies represented the 134,000 workers in Congress; two had more than 10,000 members; seventeen had under 500. None were strong enough to play a leading role; the ITGWU's share of Congress membership had fallen from over 40 per cent in 1919 to under 25 per cent. Taking his colleagues by storm, William O'Brien dusted off a relic of old glory and recommended that Congress membership be regrouped in ten industrial unions catering for building and furnishing; engineering, shipbuilding and vehicle building; the marine; transport; printing and paper works; bakeries; distributive, clerical, and supervisory staffs; teaching; the civil service; and general employment. To accommodate the sensibilities of loyalists in what were to be all-Ireland structures, Northern Ireland would receive 'the fullest measure of autonomy', an idea later vindicated by the creation of the Northern Ireland Committee. O'Brien's goal was less ambitious than the semi-syndicalist resolution for a 'single

Irish Workers' Union' adopted in 1919, but more specific. It envisaged that Congress should take the initiative in implementation, and whereas the 1919 resolution stemmed largely from the 'pull' of ideology, 'push' factors were now much stronger. In addition to the demarcation disputes which caused internal annoyance and external calls for statutory reform of trade unionism, a broader question materialized with increasing menace in the late 1930s. With the import substitution phase of industrialization evidently nearing its limit, would further advance be at the expense of living standards? Employers said yes, arguing that wage costs should compare with rates in agriculture rather than in British manufacture. Initially, the more important partner in economic direction seemed to say no; the Conditions of Employment Act (1936) allowed for the registration of wage rates throughout a given industry. Then, to trade union dismay, the government resisted application of the act in this respect, raising apprehensions that Fianna Fáil's policy of 'ruralizing' industry would serve as a cover for the pursuit of industrialization on a cheap wages basis. It was a serious grievance for the more geographically dispersed bodies, the ITGWU and Distributive Workers in particular, and threatened to generate a fundamental tension between unionization and job creation.[48] O'Brien believed that industrial unionism would enable labour to outflank the government 'through a large accretion of strength from the general re-organization of all workers', that re-organization to include a bluff, vintage 1919 demand that 'all within the industry must be either in their respective union or out of the job' by a certain date. Others were less sanguine, but the emergence of the first major difference in perceptions between unions and government at a critical time in national economic history, when labour-state relations were still in their infancy and fascist or corporatist ideas were advancing in Europe, made O'Brien's plan look all the more attractive. The Commission encoded it as Memorandum 1.

The ubiquitous canard that O'Brien's secret goal was to eliminate the British presence and make himself king of the movement is patent nonsense. True, the British would have to go: that was unavoidable. But O'Brien specifically declined to press for a giant 83,000 member marine, transport, and general union to allay fears of empire-building, opting instead for three industrial unions to cater for these workers. Under his own proposals, the ITGWU would hive off members to some industrial groupings, and merge the remainder with the remnant of nine other unions. O'Brien would swap control of a 35,000 member union for, presumably, a less dictatorial seat within a 38,000 member industrial union. Far from making himself king, O'Brien stood to lose more from the shakeout than probably any other senior officer. If there were accusations of anglophobia and empire-building, there were also testimonies to O'Brien's *bona fides* from amalgamated officials, and Memorandum 1 secured remarkably wide support. No alternatives appeared until eleventh-hour backpedalling from the amalgamateds. In what became Memorandum 2, Sam Kyle, the senior ATGWU man in Ireland since 1932, rejected O'Brien's scheme as impractical, suggesting instead that Congress formulate plans to merge small unions, and that unions agree to recognize each other's cards. The blunt closed shop ultimatum, he feared, would merely provoke a hostile reaction! Kyle's intervention split the twelve-person Commission between five Irish union delegates for Memorandum 1, five amalgamated delegates for Memorandum 2, one undecided, and William Norton, who agreed with Kyle but diplomatically tendered cognate recommendations as Memorandum 3.

It no longer looked as if Memorandum 1, the only genuine reform proposal, would carry the movement. Since 1934, the amalgamateds had taken a livelier interest in Congress, boosting their delegate numbers from about forty to eighty. Affiliates with headquarters outside Éire now mustered 77,000 members, compared with 83,000 for unions based in the state.[49] Just a few defections from the more sectionally conscious Irish societies would scupper O'Brien's plan. So, to debate the Commission's reports might deepen internal dissention; to shelve them would certainly fortify employer calls for statutory reform. A special conference finally convened on 9 February 1939. Irish unions had met earlier to discuss a joint approach but they were outmanouevred on the day by John Marchbank, the NUR general secretary, and O'Brien's old antagonist, P.T. Daly, who chaired the session. Daly let Marchbank present Kyle's memorandum as the key motion, refusing to allow a ballot on Memorandum 1. In a card vote, twenty-one unions representing 85,211 members voted for Memorandum 2; eighteen unions representing 70,836 members voted against. That was it, Daly decided: no more voting. After a debate which took the motion at face value to begin with, but touched increasingly on the glaring breach between Irish and British unions, Daly's ruling was dangerously insensitive. O'Brien walked out, furious that the amalgamateds should batten on Irish sectionalism to hamstring the movement for their own vested interests; furious that he, the one visionary in a mess of mediocrities, should be belittled by Daly. On 23 May, a Council of Irish Unions was formed to pursue national policy interests. Fissures criss-crossed trade unionism at various angles, but the fault line was now the divide between Irish and British conceptions of strategy.

7

The Chronic made Acute, 1939–1945[1]

The Emergency is often recalled in a cosy, nostalgic light; a time when a brave little country cheerfully shouldered its crosses to chart its own path through danger, oblivious to the great turmoil swirling about it. The quaint character of wartime social hardship is conveyed in tales of the ubiquitous glimmerman; while the plain people of Ireland's good humoured response is summed up in the jingle 'Bless de Valera and Sean MacEntee, for giving us brown bread and a half-ounce of tea'. Reality was not so funny. Over these years, the cost of living rose by two-thirds whereas wages increased by one-third. Unemployment, poverty, and, above all, the social inequality of the Emergency regime, swung public opinion to the left. Neither was Éire so isolated. Though not a belligerent, it experienced a common social consequence of war; the percentage of illegitimate births increased each year from 3.18 in 1939 to 4.03 in 1944, a peak figure not exceeded until 1977.[2] British newspapers and newsreels circulated freely. People saw what war meant, and if they blessed de Valera for anything, it was for keeping them out of it. At the same time, they knew of the Beveridge report, Britain's blueprint for a post-war welfare state, and of Europe's hopes for a fairer society after the war.

The Emergency was a period of experiment in labour-state relations, a pivotal era which harvested the historic conflict of philosophies between native and British unions, and seeded the post-war industrial relations system. The replacement of the consensus-oriented Sean Lemass with the trenchantly right-wing Sean MacEntee as Minister for Industry and Commerce from 1939 to 1941 set a bruising opening agenda. As workers battled against falling living standards, MacEntee extended state regulation to wages and trade unionism itself. On returning to his old portfolio, Lemass took a softer line, but welcomed the Emergency controls as the groundwork of options for post-war economic policy. Because this challenge to the traditional voluntary mode of organization and industrial relations impacted directly on the fault line within Congress, labour's response was disastrously self-damaging. Irish unions in the fragile private sector economy took a positive view of state intervention, and began to look more towards government, and less towards Congress, as a mechanism of progress. In yielding some advantage to the lower paid, statutory wages orders deepened this process. So too did expectations of the government's post-war labour policy. Contrariwise, the amalgamateds clung to the traditional *laissez faire* outlook. This was not purely for ideological reasons. Having filleted the workforce in the nineteenth century the amalgamateds tended to represent better paid employees, wage militants who sniffed an incomes policy behind state intervention. Public sector unions shared this apprehension. But whilst the widening gulf in the movement was really about attitudes towards the role of the state in labour affairs, the Irish-British divide crystallized the division; the more so as Irish unions lacked an ideology to clarify and legitimate their search for a modification of voluntarism. The debacle over the Trade Union Act (1941) convinced Irish union leaders that British based unionism, the fount of labour's anglified mindset, embodied a mental bloc to the evolution of a national labour policy. It was a view reinforced by the prevailing political climate and given a bizarre turn when the last twist of William O'Brien's vendetta against Larkin split the Labour Party in 1944. By 1945 it seemed, at a glance, as if nationalism had become an end in itself.

EMERGENCY

Once Hitler overran Czechoslovakia on 15 March 1939, few doubted that a general conflagration could be avoided. P.T. Daly's presidential address to the 1939 congress deplored the growing Nazi danger and regretted that 'acts of aggression have not been met by the strong and persistent opposition that should have taken place'.[3] The fraternal delegate from the Scottish TUC also dwelt on the approaching war. International affairs peppered the congress agenda. The National Executive's report condemned Japanese militarism in China and urged affiliates to make effective Congress's boycott of Japanese goods! A donation of £10 was made to the Irish Committee for the Relief of Austrian Refugees. Larkin vainly tried to raise Frank Ryan's imprisonment under the Franco regime. War clouds over Europe recalled memories of shortages and profiteering during World War I. While Daly's speech noted the difficulties which war would create for labour's social programme, already the International Labour Organization had shelved a demand for a forty-hour week, there was little to reassure delegates that Congress was any better prepared for World War II than it had been for World War I. Congress subsequently joined with the Labour Party in publishing the pamphlet *Planning for the Crisis*, and proposed the creation of a consultative Economic Council of representatives of government, industry, labour, and agriculture. Naturally, though it was not without irony in retrospect, this invitation to corporatism got short shrift from the cabinet.[4]

If war itself never came, its social and economic consequences were inescapable.[5] Prices increased immediately, and people were soon complaining bitterly about inadequate price control, profiteering, and the black-market. Selective rationing of imports like petrol was introduced incrementally from 1939, and general ration books came into operation in June 1942. However, as Ireland produced most of the foodstuffs it consumed, the basic problem was not scarcity but price. Inflation produced a high level of strike activity over the first eight months of the Emergency, but increasing use of the Emergency Powers Act to restrain wage demands, slackening trade, and industrial dislocation had gradually depressed wage movements and union membership by late 1940. The proportion of strikes in which workers were wholly or partly successful dropped sharply. Nevertheless, the government moved steadily towards statutory control of wages. Civil service salaries were frozen in May 1940, and from August MacEntee argued in cabinet for a general pay freeze. With the proviso that protected industries and essential services only should be affected, he got his way. On 7 May 1941, Emergency Powers Order no. 83, more usually known as the Wages Standstill Order, introduced an absolute wage freeze for employees in these sectors and removed legal immunity from trade unions in respect of action in breach of the order.[6] Conditions really began to bite from this point on. Adding to the distress, an outbreak of foot and mouth disease suspended cattle exports from January to October that year, and Britain retaliated for its failure to obtain trans-shipment facilities at Irish ports by restricting vital imports. By 1943, petrol supplies had dwindled to 20 per cent of pre-war levels, gas to 16 per cent, and textiles to 22 per cent. Domestic coal was unobtainable. Unemployment and emigration rose steeply. Already the building industry had virtually shut down. Railwaymen were laid off as train services were curtailed. Deep-sea docks lay idle, and cross-channel shipping fell. Factories closed for want of fuel or raw materials. Output slumped by 27 per cent between 1938 and 1943, reducing industrial employment from 166,000 to 143,000. The gap between wages and prices continued to widen. In February 1942, prices were 37 per cent above the pre-war level; wages had increased by about 10 per cent. By 1945, the average weekly industrial wage stood at 70s. 8d, an increase of just under 30 per cent on the 1937 figure. The cost of living rose by 74 per cent over the same period. The hard reality of these figures did not stop at frugal sustenance; they meant disturbing levels of malnutrition, infant mortality, and tubercolosis.

The one group of workers to benefit from the adversity were rural labourers. Price controls in Britain denied a repeat of the World War I profit boom, but farmers at least held their own; prices for agricultural products rose by 90 per cent from 1937 to 1945. Furthermore, to meet the food shortage, orders were introduced from 1940 to 1948 requiring three-eighths of arable land in each holding to be under tillage. Tillage acreage rose from 1.5 million acres in 1938 to 2.6 million in 1945. The coal shortage also created an urgent demand for turf cutters. The need to keep labour on the land compelled the government to make a relative improvement in agricultural wages. The Agricultural Wages Board weekly rate rose from 27s. in 1939 to 30s. in 1940 and 40s. 3d. by 1945, an 82 per cent advance on the 1937 level. However, the improvement was from an abysmally low base rate and did not keep pace, in absolute terms, with industrial earnings.[7] So serious did the want of skilled agricultural and turf workers become that the government pro-hibited men ordinarily resident outside towns of over 5,000 in population to emigrate.[8] The shortage of rural labour, together with the evident scope for improvement in wage levels, raised the question of reviving trade unionism on the land. A motion that 'all roadworkers and bog workers should be members of the union' was put to the ITGWU annual conference in 1942. Recalling the painful experiences of 1923, however, the executive quashed the idea.[9] Larkin took up the gauntlet in 1943 and in 1946 the WUI reconstituted its agricultural section as the Federation of Rural Workers, with Sean Dunne as organizing secretary.[10]

FIGHTING WITH SHADOWS

From early 1940, the focus of the government's labour policy expanded from wages to industrial relations, and there were sympathetic nods at employer calls for statutory intervention. Pay restraint remained the primary concern of course; in the short term to check inflationary pressures, and in the long term to improve the competitiveness of exports to Britain. When Dublin Corporation workers struck for an extra 8s. per week in March, threatening municipal services and cattle exports, the government effectively broke the strike, and MacEntee seized the opportunity to prepare legislation to deal with similar disputes.[11] A draft bill, based on Britain's Emergency Powers Act (1920) and Trades Disputes and Trades Union Act (1927), proposed that if strikes disrupted public utilities or essential services, the government be empowered to introduce a state of emergency. Employees might then be instructed to perform normal work by Ministerial order; failure to comply could lead to fines, dismissal, imprisonment, or loss of welfare benefits, including pension rights. This emphasis on economic penalties reflected MacEntee's conclusion that physical force would be counter-productive. One breathtaking stroke of vindictiveness recommended that traders might be debarred from supplying goods to recalcitrants. Any strike could be declared illegal, and deprived of the protection of the Trades Disputes Act (1906), if its objects were other than a trade dispute or if it inflicted hardship on society, and one month's notice was to be given of all strikes or lockouts. MacEntee's draft alarmed his colleagues, who considered some of its provisions to be provocative or unworkable. Surprisingly, a second draft, confined to 'lightning strikes' in essential services as the cabinet had directed, was also rejected by the government, this time without any alternative guidelines. Possibly the reason was that trade unions were now aware that something was afoot and the ITGWU annual conference in June had threatened to fight restrictions on the right to strike. On the other hand, the cabinet endorsed the principle behind the second draft, quibbling mainly with its provisions for the loss of pension and social security rights.

Either way, MacEntee was in a quandary. He still hankered after tough measures, and in August suggested that the legislation be extended to imposing demarcation lines on unions. This was a departure in theme, and it prompted civil service advice for a consultation with William O'Brien. O'Brien had initiated secret contacts with a principal officer of the Department of Industry and Commerce in May, sending him a copy of the Memorandum 1 submitted to the special ITUC conference in 1939. If this wasn't hint enough, O'Brien later forwarded, again 'in strict confidence', extracts from a speech he delivered to the ITGWU conference in June, in which he warned that the ITUC's inability to reform itself 'was a direct invitation to the government to interfere in their movement'. MacEntee authorized meetings with O'Brien and Tom Kennedy, the ITGWU President, in August. When the Department finally discussed its proposals with the ITUC executive in October, O'Brien had already shifted the content of the bill from industrial disputes to trade union regulation. Though MacEntee drafted a separate anti-strike bill, it was never presented to the Oireachtas. O'Brien also supplied his civil service confederates with a rationale for their action, locating the origins of the bill not in the Dublin Corporation strike, but in the failure of the ITUC commission of inquiry to heed Lemass's stricture of 1936. It was a neat mutual accommodation; O'Brien nudged the state away from coercion of industrial relations, while allowing the government to say it was implementing a trade union agenda. However, he could not claim credit for derailing the initial anti-strike thrust of MacEntee's proposals. Though later to be the source of speculation, his contacts with the Department remained secret; for William O'Brien had committed the unpardonable sin of inviting the state to meddle in labour's affairs.

The published bill had three aims: to clarify the legal position of trade unions, to whittle away the smaller unions, and to eliminate trade union multiplicity. Part II of the bill stipulated that to enjoy legal immunity and the right to negotiate for wages and conditions, unions must obtain a licence. This in turn required them to register under the Trade Union Acts of 1871–1935; or be a union under the laws of another jurisdiction; to maintain a registered office in Ireland; to submit details on rules, officers, and members to the

Minister for Industry and Commerce, and to lodge a deposit of between £2,000 and £10,000 with the High Court. Part III proposed to establish a tribunal with powers to grant one or more unions sole rights to negotiate for a category of workers where that union, or unions, represented a majority of those workers. Radical as these measures were, the government believed them to be broadly palatable to labour. The tribunal was O'Brien's own idea, though he demurred at the requirements for lodging a deposit. Both the Council of Irish Unions (CoIU) and the ITUC executive were briefed by the Department of Industry and Commerce on the basic points of the draft bill in late October 1940. Far from tendering reservations, both bodies indicated an acceptance of the legislation in principle. Congress affiliates were warned to expect a curtailment of organizational rights in 1941, but were given no details. Twenty years on, the state was about to make its first attempt at revising the form of trade unionism inherited from the colonial era. Internally at odds, cross wired with an alien mentality, Congress had no idea of how to handle this novelty.

Observers detected no unease in labour circles when the terms of the bill were published on 30 April 1941. The feared encroachment on union rights had not materialized. Congress deferred comment to a special conference, scheduled for 16 May. Then, on 6 May, Dublin trades council condemned the bill outright and started a snowball of rank and file dissent that led the special conference to express its 'emphatic opposition' to an 'unwarrantable invasion of the constitutional and historic rights of the Trade Unions'.[12] Whatever obligation O'Brien felt to defend the bill evaporated with the untimely promulgation on 7 May of the Wages Standstill Order; given the government's record on price control and its slack attitude to profiteering, this was downright inflammatory. The left promptly spancelled the two as a concerted attack on labour. Yet, if the ITGWU baulked at an endorsement of state intervention, O'Brien's covert sympathy for the bill was sufficient to dissuade the Congress executive from taking a strong line. The special conference, which widened the agenda from the bill to the Wages Order, implied that the burden should fall to the Labour Party. Labour obliged quite happily but, to the Congress executive's embarrassment, the dynamo of resistance sprang from a Council of Action formed by Dublin trades council. The council was uniquely placed for united effort as the ITGWU had disaffiliated following its decision to admit the WUI. With no internal diplomacy to worry about, the Larkins led the council's fight against what many suspected to be 'O'Brien's bill'.

Critics of the bill were therefore divided into many camps and two layers of thinking. At one level, there were the pragmatic, focused objections of the CoIU. Contrary to common recollection, the original bill was not anti-British and the effective riposte came from Irish unions; London's outposts were usually slower on the uptake. On 17 June, the CoIU requested MacEntee to withdraw the bill, pleading that its requirement for a financial deposit discriminated against the small unions and treated Irish societies unfairly as the British could borrow funds from London. Liquidating the small fry, of course, was the whole point of the exercise. Moreover, MacEntee's mandarins had hoped that the absence of a corrective pro-Irish bias would be seen positively as a signal that the bill was not designed to 'nationalize' the movement. In what amounted to a fateful revision of policy, MacEntee not alone agreed that the deposit might be reduced by up to 75 per cent for Irish unions in straitened circumstances, thereby blunting the impact of the legislation considerably, but explicitly and gratuitously re-directed the venom of the bill from the small unions to the amalgamateds. Speaking in Dáil Éireann on 4 June he had recited the familiar case for rationalization in order to end internecine conflict without apportioning blame to any quarter, in line with government advice to attract the widest possible trade union assent. However, in late June and July he vilified the amalgamateds as the root of industrial disruption, the obstacle to efforts of patriotic Irishmen to secure voluntary reform in 1939, and the source of the campaign against the bill. When William Norton pointed out that amalgamateds might obtain sole nego-tiation licences under Part III of the bill, MacEntee introduced a second crucial amendment reserving such licences to Irish unions only. This change of tack was patently intended to spike the unex-pected, and mounting, resistance to the bill. On 22 June, the day the *Wehrmacht* crashed into Russia, members of 53 trade unions marched from Dublin's Parnell Square to College Green, where Larkin dramatically burned a copy of the bill before an estimated 20,000 people. Impressed by the biggest demonstration of working-class resolve since 1923, Norton pledged that Labour would escalate its selective criticism of the bill into blanket opposition.

Ironically, this was the climax of the dissident campaign. But it seemed at the time as if Congress would be trundled into action against the government. Given the notorious tensions between Irish and British unions—Tom Kennedy's presidential address to the ITGWU conference in June complained that the bill would not 'confine the organization of Irish workers to Irish unions'—and the more constructive attitude of the CoIU, the gritty, confrontational MacEntee could not forego a tempting opportunity to divide and conquer. The government would learn eventually that a bifurcated movement was not in its interest.

The events of 22 June bolstered the ideologues. At this level, a trident of hostility sprang first from a sectionalism which confused a circumscription of individual trade union liberty with an assault on trade unionism *per se*; secondly, from a conflation of the bill with the Wages Standstill Order; and finally from a conviction that free trade unionism depended on a minimal engagement with the law and the state. This last mentality, anchored philosophically in English liberalism, underpinned all ideological criticism and was pervasive enough to transcend the structural Irish-British or craft-general divide. Dublin Council of Action projected the bill, with the Wages Standstill Order, as the first step towards 'corporative organizations made up of both workers and employers under the control of the government'.[13] Superficially, this seemed plausible. De Valera had appointed a Commission on Vocational Organisation in 1939 to examine 'the practicability of developing functional or vocational organization in the circumstances of this country'. Comprising twenty-five leading persons from the fields of industry, trade unionism, agriculture, social studies, and the churches, the commission collected extensive evidence from voluntary bodies and presented a weighty report in 1943, recommending the creation of six vocational chambers representing agriculture, industry, commerce, transport, finance, and the professions. These in turn would elect a National Vocational Assembly to operate parallel with existing political structures.[14] The Federation of Irish Manufacturers offered a gothic view of labour, productivity, and economic development in its submission to the commission. The problem, it contended, lay in the character of the Irish worker; the answer in his subordination to the needs of a fragile developing economy, a mental re-adjustment which the British unions militated against.[15] One feature of the Emergency labour regime had already introduced an uncomfortable element of moral re-education. Plans drawn up by the Department of Industry and Commerce for labour camps for the unemployed were partially implemented in 1940, in response to the shortage of turf workers. Out of this initiative emerged *An Cór Déantais*. *An Cór* recruited boys, mainly from deprived urban backgrounds, and set them, in army fashion, to work 'of national importance'. It was an experiment in social rehabilitation as well as an attempt to mobilize labour for necessary but unattractive employment. At its peak in 1943, *An Cór* was 2,000 strong. The concept was badly mismanaged by the authorities and met with dogged unco-operation from unemployed men themselves, despite loss of welfare benefits.[16] Leftists were not reassured by the qualified approval given *An Cór Déantais* by the Congress executive, granted after a meeting between de Valera and William O'Brien, or by the ITGWU's loan of £50,000 to the state to help it through the Emergency.[17] It all implied a corporatist collusion between O'Brien and Fianna Fáil that made the Trade Union Bill's bias against the smaller unions and the amalgamateds appear sinister.

In truth, there was no connection between the wage freeze and the bill, no fascist corporatism in government policy, no Machiavellian ploy to 'nationalize' labour, even after MacEntee's amendments; and, whatever the justification for shopfloor suspicions, the Congress executive should have known this or made it its business to find out. Neither was the Commission on Vocational Organisation the fascist bogey of socialist paranoia. Certainly Larkin, who sat on the commission with three other labour representatives, never took it seriously.[18] The corporatist red herring caused labour to confuse a genuine threat of legislative intervention in industrial relations and a policy of wage depression with the question of rationalizing the movement. Instead of exploiting its consent to the bill as a bargaining chip in a power play against the wage freeze, union leaders confronted the rationalization issue with such ineptitude as to make the government's case for it. O'Brien regarded allegations of corporatism as hypocrisy. The ITGWU remained scathingly critical of Fianna Fáil's 'criminal' record on wages and prices. It had led the charge against statutory control of industrial relations in Éire at the 1940 congress, whereas the amalgamateds worked hand in glove with Stormont to maintain war production, though wartime regulations in Northern

Ireland effectively debarred strikes. Yet this never came before Congress.[19] As for campaigns against the bill, that was just Larkin stirring things up again. Outside Dublin there was little street protest. Speaking to the 1941 congress in July, O'Brien condemned the Wages Standstill Order, but implied that if one could not commend the Trade Union Bill, it should be accepted as an inevitable consequence of the movement's incapacity to reform itself. O'Brien's cynical, 'take it or leave it' attitude as chairman of the congress suggested that the old dog was tired of playing games. He had tried repeatedly to persuade from within. It remained only to let the law, or 'the surgeon's knife' as he put it, take its course. From here on, Congress became of lesser consequence to O'Brien, and the process of alienation was exacerbated by a hardening of opinion against the ITGWU. In a break with convention the 1941 congress saw a contested election for vice-president, with Michael Keyes, NUR, defeating Tom Kennedy, ITGWU, by 101–84 votes.[20]

When the Trade Union Bill was enacted, a joint meeting of the Congress executive and the Labour Party administrative council asked the Congress executive to recommend unions not to take out negotiation licences. The party was understandably bullish; the trickle of recruits since the beginning of the Emergency had swelled in response to the bill and the Wages Standstill Order. Kicking to touch, the executive summoned a special conference in October. The move merely pushed the CoIU closer to the government. To steal some of the conference thunder, the Council made a prior approach to the government to amend the act. At the conference, where London's foreboding was evident in the presence of twenty-three British delegates, nothing conclusive emerged on the thorny question of taking out negotiation licences. Resigned to his failure to carry Congress opinion into some accommodation with the government, fatigued with the endless fudge, O'Brien said nothing in the debate, and the ITGWU did not obstruct a motion from William Norton for a joint campaign with the Labour Party against the act. Implicitly, it sidestepped the licence issue. As O'Brien anticipated, the campaign drummed up little enthusiasm in the provinces.[21] Unions were eventually compelled to treat with the act. Sean Lemass, who had added the Department of Industry and Commerce to his brief as Minister for Supplies in August 1941, relaxed the pay freeze on 9 April 1942. Emergency Powers Order no. 166 allowed wages tribunals to award cost of living bonuses in certain circumstances. Turning pay restraint from a source of hostility to a lever for compromise, Order 166 recognized licensed unions only in applications for bonus awards. Outmanouevred, the 1942 annual congress agreed *nem con* to tail the CoIU in parleying with the government. Lemass responded quickly with the Trade Union Act (1942), which made a few minor amendments to the parent act but was of symbolic importance in restoring a consensual style to labour-state relations.[22]

Lemass had no intention of allowing Congress to undo the substance of MacEntee's work. Appointed to a cabinet sub-committee on post-war planning with de Valera and Sean T. O'Kelly in November 1942, he envisaged the long-term retention of Emergency controls on labour to advance the 1930s industrialization drive, and had drafted proposals for a Ministry of Labour to co-ordinate all aspects of policy, including wages, industrial relations, unemployment, emigration, and welfare services. In addition to the anticipated problems of demobilization and the return of emigrants from Britain's war economy, Fianna Fáil were anxious about the likely impact of Britain's Beveridge report on mass expectations; a concern borne out by the public enthusiasm for Bishop Dignan's paper on radical reform of social security. In the teeth of resistance from the Department of Finance, Lemass and de Valera pushed through a scheme for children's allowance payments in 1944. Though MacEntee gave short shrift to Dignan, separate Departments of Health and Social Welfare were created in 1947.[23] Lemass believed that if Ireland could not match British living standards and levels of welfare benefit, it could achieve full employment through a policy of economic self-sufficiency embracing extensive state direction of capital and labour. In placing priority on wages, the unions, he held, militated against full employment. It was no longer tolerable that they should pocket a dividend from Ireland's relatively high degree of state economic regulation without conceding changes in the voluntary basis of labour relations. By 1943 Lemass was thinking of a totally new conception of trade union-employer-state interaction, geared to creating, not redistributing, wealth. Now was the time to entice unions into that framework. Whilst Lemass proposed draconian controls on labour, such as legal restrictions on wages, industrial relations, trade unions, labour mobility, and access to unemployment benefit, his was not the corporatism of the Commission on

Vocational Organization. If Dublin Council of Action's talk of assault on trade union liberties stumbled blindly over a truth, the knee-jerk reflex to defend voluntarism obscured rather than clarified the issues. There was a conflict of interests in a post-colonial, unevenly developed economy between wage militants with a stake in the *status quo* and those without; the lower paid, the unemployed, and emigrants. Lemass intended to offer something to the have-nots and to proceed through consensus. The wages tribunals set up under Order 166 were granted approval to link pay to the cost of living index; an important gain in principle for the lower paid. For the very first time, the bulk of workers did not need to establish a bargaining power through militancy. And as licensed bodies alone could apply for bonus orders, the tribunals acted as an incentive to join trade unions, contributing to an expansion of membership to new sectors after 1942. Circumstances remained difficult. Unions criticized the procedures under Order 166 as deliberately cumbersome. Above all, there was seething resentment at the absence of a comparable system of price control. 'No government in Europe', declared the ITGWU's annual report for 1942, 'has done more to depress the standard of living of the members of the working class than the government of Éire . . . Grave dissatisfaction pervades all ranks of the workers at the unbridged gap between wages and prices.' Labour's most successful campaign of the Emergency mobilized a series of protests in the autumn, and trade union nominees on the tribunals helped to secure over 800 pay awards in 1942/43. Lemass responded on 2 March 1943 with Emergency Powers Order no. 260, which made a significant concession to Congress in providing for a further relaxation of pay restraint, and encouraged a convergence of views between Lemass and trade union leaders on mechanisms of wage adjustment in peace time.[24]

Hopes that none would dare invoke the controversial Part III of the Trade Union Act, scheduled to take effect in April, were raised by a short *rapprochement* between the two big general unions following the appointment of a Congress committee on inter-union friction. In a gesture sympathetic with the ITGWU's well-known position on Larkin, the executive departed from custom to list its reasons for rejecting the WUI's regular application for affiliation at the 1942 congress, citing the WUI's 'record as a cause of disruptive action . . . and a promoter of libels against officers'—Larkin had recently been back in court for libelling Denis Cullen, a Bakers' Union official and member of the executive. Emphasising his solidarity with O'Brien on the point, Sam Kyle, ATGWU, proposed that Congress exclude members of unaffiliated unions, a move intended solely to remove Larkin who normally slipped in the back door with a nomination from Dublin trades council. Again, Congress grappled with the old chestnuts of eliminating multiplicity and encouraging mergers— with the same old results. By 1944, time was running out. Applications had been made under Part III. All were refused. More would follow.[25]

DIVISION

Reaction to the inequity of wartime social hardship, and what looked like a bout of union bashing from Fianna Fáil, reaped rewards for Labour. The party made a breakthrough in the 1942 local elections, becoming the largest group on Dublin Corporation. Labour consolidated its progress in the 1943 general election, winning 15.7 per cent of the vote, its best showing since 1922, and raising its Dáil representation from nine to seventeen deputies.[26] In one respect, however, success was to be its undoing. Larkin's role in the campaign against the Trade Union Act had done much to reconcile him with the Dublin left. In December 1941, he was readmitted to the Labour Party and later selected as a Dáil candidate. The administrative council refused to ratify the nomination, but only because the absence of two persons gave ITGWU members a majority. Larkin stood successfully none the less, nominated by a Dublin caucus and openly supported by William Norton. That was the year the ITGWU published the pamphlet *Nineteen Thirteen; Its Significance* without once mentioning Larkin's name, and admitting the unperson to the Dáil party was more than O'Brien could stomach. Immediately, the ITGWU demanded his expulsion. When Norton's efforts to cool the passions failed, the union disaffiliated from the party in January 1944 and told its members in the Oireachtas to do likewise. Five of the eight TDs sponsored by the ITGWU seceded to form the National Labour Party. To counter accusations that union members had not been consulted on the split, and camouflage its vindictively personal root with a veneer of ideology, the ITGWU alleged communist infiltration of the Labour Party, and National Labour challenged the party to accept an investigation by 'the bishops or any impartial body'. There was a thin pretext for the scaremongering. Larkin, of course, had led the communist movement in the 1920s, and when the Nazi invasion of Russia jolted the CP line from a pro-neutrality to a pro-war stance, the party dissolved its shrivelled organization in Éire—in effect, its Dublin branch—and advised the rump to join the Labour Party to work covertly for an alliance with Fianna Fáil to bring Éire into the war. Though thoroughly sceptical of the sudden concern with entryism, Norton thought it prudent to appoint an internal enquiry. Yielding to the pressure merely inflated the red scare. With coverage worthy of the later McCarthyite inquisitions from the influential Catholic weekly, the *Standard,* the inquiry resulted in expulsions, resignations, and recriminations. Despite continuing use of the anti-communist theme at the hustings, National Labour showed little evidence of its supposed fears of communism, opposing only one outgoing Labour TD, Larkin, in the 1944 general election. National Labour deputies largely stuck to their bailiwicks, leaving other constituencies virtually untouched by the split, and relations between both parliamentary parties remained amicable.[27] Credibility was the chief casualty. The Labour vote sank to 8.8 per cent in the 1944 general election and the Dáil party dwindled to eight deputies. National Labour held four seats, with 2.7 per cent of the vote. At a time of quickening interest in social questions like housing, full employment, health, and welfare as potential goals of national policy, when Labour had seemed poised to displace Fine Gael as the main opposition, it was a disastrously inopportune reverse.

The split confirmed the ITGWU's imperious isolationism and prepared the drift of allied unions from the prevailing, anglified, labour thinking towards a pointedly indigenous labourism, distinguished by emphases on corporatism, nationalism, Catholicism, and anti-communism. This retreat into authenticism was driven too by Northern Ireland's embarrassingly good war. The stark contrast with Éire's proud but painful neutrality was hammered home to Irish unions in the more rapid expansion of the amalgamateds. The former affiliated 80,000 members to Congress in 1944; the latter 108,000, an increase of 40,000 on the 1937 figure.[28] Congress elected Bob Getgood as president in 1943, the first Belfast-based delegate to hold that office since Tom Johnson in 1917, and for the first time since 1918 British unions secured a majority on the executive in 1944.[29] As the bulk of amalgamated membership lay north of the border, there was no real threat to Irish domination of the movement in Éire. Nor did the amalgamateds indicate any desire to control Congress. Indeed the true outcome of these trends was the creation of a special Northern Ireland Committee in 1945 to activate the ITUC presence in the six counties. But in terms of prestige, of competition for members, and of the fading prospects for collaboration between Congress and the government to restructure trade union organization, developments were deeply frustrating for the CoIU. Adding insult to injury, the reactionary, sectarian Tory statelet of inter-war imagery metamorphosed as *Hibernia antifascista* to tilt with neutral Éire for the moral high ground. This was too much for the jealousies endemic in cross-border exchange. With little ado, Congress condemned fascism in 1939, but similar resolutions in 1942 and 1943 trod unwittingly on sensitivities about neutrality. Speakers from Irish unions made plain their dislike of taking sides publicly on the war.[30]

Here was the nerve-end of a visceral clash of world views: between the inchoate *Weltanschauung* of Irish unions, an unprepossessing offspring of their mismanaged quest for a labour strategy geared to native conditions, and all the more techy for its immaturity; and the hegemonic anglo-centrism of the amalgamateds. In January 1944, the Congress executive declined an invitation to attend a world trade union conference on the war economy and reconstruction to be hosted in London by the British TUC. Although the TUC proposed to restrict congresses from neutral countries to the debates on reconstruction, and the ITUC was invited as a neutral, Irish unions objected to representation at an assembly identified with the allied powers. When Sam Kyle tabled a motion regretting the decision, William O'Brien warned that were it passed, it would be 'the first step in the break-up of this Congress'. Passed it was, by 96–51 votes, and the incoming, amalgamated controlled executive reversed the decision and appointed two delegates to the London conference, which met in February 1945. Fifteen unions, ten of them affiliated to the ITUC, then resolved that a British dominated congress could not represent 'the opinions and aspirations' of Irish labour. On 25 April they agreed to constitute a separate body, and withdrew formally from the ITUC. The CoIU, together with its new accretions, became *Comhar Ceard Éireann*—the Congress of Irish Unions (CIU).[31]

The schism hardly ruffled Northern Ireland, where the CIU presence rested entirely in the ITGWU's 2,500 or so members; a trifle compared with the ITUC muster of over 70,000. But the southern cleavage went deep, with the CIU claiming 75,000 members to the ITUC's 72,000.[32] The ITUC retained support from three groups: the amalgamateds; public sector unions; and a few unions at odds with CIU values for special reasons.[33] The alignment of most public sector unions strengthens the conclusion the split was not fundamentally about nationalism or socialism. Noted for their patriotic corporate culture, these bodies boasted an exceptional level of *fíor Gaeil*. Nor could they be accused of fellow-travelling with the left.[34] Their relations with the state however, were of a very different order to the CIU affiliates, who favoured legislative intervention to protect memberships and stabilize industrial relations in the choppy waters of the private sector. Here was the nub. The ITUC represented those with vital interests in the *status quo*; the amalgamateds, who had creamed off the better-paid workers in the late nineteenth century and were well situated for wage militancy in free collective bargaining, and who feared that a shift from the voluntary principle of industrial relations would carry an attack on their British roots; and the public sector unions who had maximized their membership and had little to reap from trade union rationalization. The CIU comprised elements with something to gain from change; those, like the ITGWU, with a membership potential closely dependent on national industrial policy, or, like the Distributive Workers, with a high proportion of members for whom wage militancy was not a viable option. Reflecting its presence in frontier sectors, the CIU expanded more quickly than its rival in the post-war recovery. Around the core division there were also unions who sided with the CIU for its nationalism, or with the ITUC for its broad-left 'internationalism', or who were guided simply by pro- or anti- ITGWU sentiment. In all cases, the proclivities of union executives dictated the decision.[35]

The split implied a major challenge to neo-colonial labourism. Formerly, Irish unions had sought to revise the British model of union organization. Now, they questioned the principles of industrial and political strategy. British labour was based on a strong trade union movement in a strong economy, capable of pursuing

workers' interests through a voluntary system of industrial relations, and a political agenda through a powerful Labour Party in a
party system divided along class lines. None of these conditions
applied in Ireland, yet ITUC values took no cognizance of this.
However, the CIU failed to sustain the challenge with a radical critique, lapsing instead into reliance on the prevailing political forces,
chiefly Fianna Fáil and popular nationalism, to enforce its increasingly narrow case against the amalgamateds. In consequence, the
rhetorical divergence between the Congresses has shrouded the
split in complexity; for the reformist CIU seemed positively right
wing, whereas the conservative ITUC held to a watery socialism.
Without a radical appeal to workers' interests, the schism evoked
little shopfloor enthusiasm. The rank and file scarcely demurred at
being marshalled behind the competing claims of de-colonization
and progressive internationalism, regarding it as a matter for their
leaders. Most trades councils remained united until CIU affiliates
received instructions to form separate Councils of Irish Unions.
Inured to the contradictions of a British paradigm and native reality,
of a leftish elite directing Fianna Fáil voting masses, of a secular
movement in a Catholic society, and of an all-Ireland Congress
embracing the loyalist North, workers accepted that there were
things in trade unionism one simply didn't question. Whilst a
treacherous signpost to ideology, and derivative ideologies are
usually deceptive in post-colonial societies, the split says much
about the inability of labour to cultivate an organic politics, and it
speaks volumes about the lack of internal union democracy.

8
Labour in Twain, 1946–1959

Nineteen-forty-six is a watershed in labour history. Before the Emergency wages orders, trade unionism was characterized by struggle for survival; not always and everywhere, but, basically success depended on militancy. The Industrial Relations Act (1946) made unions a part of the social furniture. The act set up the Labour Court to offer services of conciliation and adjudication in the rush of wage claims that would follow the revocation of Emergency Powers Order no. 260. The court consisted of employers' and workers' representatives under a neutral chairman appointed by the government. In providing for wages orders, the Labour Court made it possible for low-paid employees to pursue pay claims without first establishing a combative bargaining power. As the court recognised licensed trade unions only, it not alone accorded a more secure status to unions, it was a direct incentive to join them. Voluntary reform of industrial relations was taken a step further when statutory wage control yielded to joint agreements on wage levels under the national pay rounds. Like the Labour Court, the pay rounds encouraged a broader acceptance of unions and the standardization of rates for comparable employment. A third factor behind the rapid expansion of membership after 1945 was, of course, economic. The economy recovered at an impressive rate after the war. Industrial output was double the 1943 level before the end of the decade, and by 1953 there were 228,403 people engaged in industry.[1] However, ambitions to keep pace with European economic reconstruction came unstuck in the 1950s. Agricultural output and exports did not match the growth in consumption. Record levels of imports led to successive balance of payments crises. Large budget deficits in 1951 and 1955 were followed by deflationary policies and a credit squeeze, causing economic stagnation and a fall in gross national product between 1955 and 1958. By 1958, industrial output barely exceeded the 1953 level; industrial employment had fallen to 210,324. Unemployment again became a major problem. Emigration reached figures not seen since the 1890s. With the rest of Europe enjoying the novelty of sustained full employment, Ireland's undevelopment created a crisis of national self-confidence, culminating in the abandonment of protectionism by Fianna Fáil.

POST-WAR TRADE UNIONISM: EXPANSION AND STAGNATION

The origins of the Industrial Relations Act lay in a proposal from Lemass in 1944 for a public Commission of Inquiry on wage policy and its relation to economic development, comprising representatives of Congress and the Federated Union of Employers (FUE).[2] Congress responded positively in 1945, indicating an enthusiasm for wage negotiation machinery, but a desire to deal separately with matters of economic development. Following the split, Lemass confined his initiative to the more urgent problem of securing agreement, especially trade union agreement, on negotiation machinery. He now believed that wage control could not be imposed forcibly, rejected FUE and Civil Service suggestions for a strong compulsory element in the Industrial Relations Bill, and accepted requests from both Congresses not to grant transitional wage control functions to the Labour Court. Reflecting the greater leverage of organized labour over the weak private manufacturing sector on state policy on industrial relations, Lemass developed a closer liaison with the Congresses than with the FUE, though ties with the CIU were strongest, and while both Congresses endorsed the bill, the ITUC's gut reaction against trucking with the government was evident in negative speeches from the floor at its 1946 annual conference.

Simultaneously with the Industrial Relations Act coming into effect, Emergency Powers Order no. 260 lapsed on 23 September. The 'general adjustment of wages' over 1946–47 came to be known as the first national pay round. On average, wage increases of about 25 per cent were secured as unions sought to make up the ground lost since 1941.[3] Discussions on a second round commenced on 1 December 1947. Representatives of both Congresses met the FUE under the auspices of the Labour Court. On 11 March

1948, the parties issued a 'Joint Statement on Principles to be Observed in Negotiations for the Adjustment of Wages'. Wage claims for men were not to exceed 11s. per week. Claims for women were to be 'in accordance with existing practices'. The second national pay round lasted from 1948 to 1950. On average, weekly rates for men rose by 8–10s, and for women by about half these amounts. Up to the establishment of the Employer-Labour Conference in 1970, subsequent pay rounds followed the practice of one or other of the first two. Demands for pay increases mounted in 1950, and talks on a general agreement were opened under the auspices of the Labour Court. As economic trends worsened, the FUE refused to negotiate a new arrangement. Both Congresses then ended their commitment to the 1948 'Joint Statement on Principles' and the third national pay round took the form of a general wage movement. The fourth was partially negotiated, being preceded in May 1952 by an agreement between the CIU and the FUE. Again reverting to a general adjustment, the controversial fifth round brought an upsurge of strike activity and widely diverging wage advances. The sixth round involved a 'Joint Agreement on Guiding Principles relating to Wage Claims', while the seventh emerged from another general movement.

The national pay rounds were a long way from the centralized bargaining of the 1970s, but they marked an important decline in the autonomy of local industrial relations. Plant level bargaining continued, but within a national matrix strung together with a new jargon of parity, differentials, inequities, and anomalies. Guidelines of the fourth pay round for example, though endorsed by one Congress only, were generally implemented. This process of standardization, in wage claims and wage bargaining, together with the work of the Labour Court and the easier acceptance of trade unions by employers after 1945, initiated a change in the character of unions and branch officials. Their operations became more businesslike, more bureaucratic, more taxing intellectually, and less demanding of physical stamina and courage. In acknowledgment of the times, the ITUC appointed a research officer in February 1949, the post going to Donal Nevin, and issued the first bulletin of *Trade Union Information* in May.[4]

Although the national pay rounds reduced the likelihood of conflict over wage levels, difficulties persisted, compounded by inflationary trends in 1947 and again in 1950–51 when a wave of price hikes caused by the outbreak of the Korean war led to an upsurge of wage militancy, including a six-week bank strike.[5] Workers also began to use the strike weapon more readily in protest against conditions, dismissals, or personnel grievances. Before the Emergency, about half of all strikes involved wage questions. After 1945 this proportion fell, significantly so in the 1950s. Unofficial strikes also became more common. The frequency of disputes, especially of lightning or unofficial action, and the greater use of strikes over personnel issues, led to calls for statutory control of industrial relations. Voluntary reform enjoyed undoubted success, although the Labour Court's role under R.J.P. Mortished, its first chairman, attracted criticism, notably in 1950. Both Congresses were dismayed when the court endorsed the FUE's rejection of a joint agreement for the third pay round. More generally, the CIU complained that the court was concerned more that judgments conform with national pay trends and the requirements of government economic policy, than with assessing each case on its merits or resolving disputes. According to the Congress 'a large proportion' of its findings were meeting rejection from trade unionists. Mortished resigned as chairman in May 1952.[6] Economic conditions gave his successor an easier tenure as, with the exception of the opening months of the fifth pay round in 1955, strike activity remained low for the remainder of the decade.

From 1945 to 1950 trade union membership in Éire rose from 172,000 to 285,000, with general unionism the great beneficiary. General unions represented 80,000 members, or 46.7 per cent of all trade unionists, in 1945, and 163,000 members, 57.2 per cent of the total, in 1950. The ITGWU accounted for the bulk of this growth, swelling to an estimated 120,000 members. By contrast, British based unions expanded marginally, despite significant advance in the six counties, and their proportion of Éire membership fell from 22.9 per cent to 16.6 per cent. These trends, in their different ways, embarrassed both Congresses, leaving the CIU looking like a shoal of minnows tailing a whale and the, still southern oriented, ITUC with 60 per cent of its membership north of the border. After 1951, trade union growth slowed considerably and in some cases was reversed. Having rocketed from 146,000 in 1945 to 211,00 in 1951, ITUC national affiliation stood at 226,333 in 1958. The respective figures for the overwhelmingly southern based CIU are even more arresting: 77,500 to 170,601 to 187,969.[7]

A NEW MACHINE IN NEW TIMES

Up to 1953 the CIU adopted a stiff line towards unity overtures from the ITUC. Its more rapid expansion raised hopes that time would see it displace the other Congress, and the ITGWU rammed home the point with a militant recruitment drive among road and rail staffs, rattling the British based Railway Clerks' Association and the NUR.[8] In general, however, CIU unions did not use wage militancy as a strategic weapon, but looked to changes in labour law and closer relations between government and unions to wrongfoot the amalgamateds and thereby weaken the ITUC. The founding manifesto of the CIU had stressed this point.[9] Trade unions, it argued, must be part of a 'new machine for new times', alive to 'a newer and greater power and status' which they would enjoy through a more productive engagement with government. A foreign controlled congress could not be expected to secure influence over state policy, the more so as legislative reform was likely to undermine further the already 'shaky' legal status of British based unions. That, of course, was a prophecy which the CIU intended to fulfil. From the outset it refuted all claims of the ITUC to represent Irish workers, and sought to ensure that labour law would favour Irish unions.

Ideological differences with the ITUC acquired a fresh intensity from the Cold War. Though the tiny CP, revived in 1948 as the Irish Workers' League, presented no conceivable danger to anything but itself, the international climate exerted an immense impact through two world-shrinking developments; the collapse of great power rivalries into a bi-polar balance of atomic terror, and the more public pontificate of Pius XII.[10] As the first 'media Pope', and a symbol of the global conflict, Pius brought Irish Catholics into the front line. The arrests of Archbishop Stepinac of Zagreb and Hungary's Cardinal Mindszenty generated huge popular protest. During the Italian general election of 1948, church gate collections raised nearly £20,000 for the Christian Democrats. Over the next decade, indignation was kept on the boil over the Korean War and the Soviet invasion of Hungary, when union branches and factories collected for the 'Help Hungary' fund and dockers offered to boycott Soviet ships.[11] Exceeding opposition to communism or anger at Eastern bloc persecution of Catholics, a neurotic fear of communists *per se* gripped the public, with infiltration theories giving substance and immediacy to an otherwise remote prospect. As the bulwark against this evil, the Catholic Church enjoyed an unprecedented degree of hegemony. Whereas in the 1930s the Church had courted workers with debate on social action, trade unions now sought clerical protection from the red octopus. Facing no social challenge, contemporary Catholic action focused mainly on direction of thought, devotion, and spirituality. The most important initiatives came in the area of ideas and education. In 1946, Professor Alfred O'Rahilly introduced lectures in Catholic social teaching for trade unionists at University College Cork and, with CIU backing, a similar programme later developed at University College Dublin. The ITUC adopted a more independent line, launching the People's College, a title which confirmed suspicions of Eastern European influence, to offer courses based on those run in Britain by the Workers' Educational Association. To forestall the extension of education modelled on British secular lines, O'Rahilly expanded his programme at Cork into a Diploma in Social and Economic Science, offered extramurally to trade unionists throughout Munster, while the Jesuits founded the Catholic Workers' College, later the National College of Industrial Relations, in Dublin in 1948.[12] The ITUC's proclivity for a nominally secular approach contrasted with the CIU's loyal devotion to Catholic social teaching. And having started its own Cold War in 1944, the ITGWU and allied unions needed no prompting to exploit this situation. In reality, both Congresses lived in a simulacrum of their respective positions. Clerical influence and anti-communism were sufficiently pervasive to make negligible the differences between the masses of either body. Among activists however, the divergent orientations could generate some passion, and the rivalling value systems of anglified labourism and nativist Catholicism were there to be tapped.

Legislative reform, the CIU believed, was the key to success, and early pointers were encouraging.[13] In 1945 the High Court rejected a constitutional challenge by the NUR against the crucial Part III of the Trade Union Act (1941). Lemass filled both Irish seats at the 1945 conference of the International Labour Organization with CIU delegates. And despite vehement protest from the ITUC, the precedent was continued under the Inter-Party government. Also, the Industrial Relations Act (1946) precluded worker representatives to the Labour Court being nominated by foreign unions. Lemass told the ITUC plainly that while the cabinet had no plans to force the matter, they should seek unity with the CIU through facilitating the voluntary withdrawal of amalgamated societies. For rather different reasons, his advice was taken seriously by two influential men within the ITUC; the veteran Tom Johnson, recalled to front line service after the split, and ever the voice of *via media*, and young Jim Larkin, now maturing as the greatest mind of the post-war movement. Larkin Jr appreciated the merits of the CIU analysis. He welcomed the opportunity to influence government policy and was ready for the responsibilities it conferred. Not alone was the largely British based ITUC badly placed in that respect, but a divided trade union movement could never take full advantage of the promised dispensation. If sacrificing the amalgamateds was the price of a new era in labour-state relations, so be it. At the request of its Irish counterpart, the British TUC convened a conference to discuss the options on 15 May 1946, where Johnson proposed that in questions of public affairs, British unions devolve autonomy on Éire while retaining a connection through federation. However, the British TUC made it clear that it would not direct its affiliates on Irish policy, and for their part the amalgamateds saw no reason to budge. On 4 July 1946, the Supreme Court dropped its bombshell; overturning the High Court decision, it declared Part III of the 1941 act to be in contravention of a citizen's right of free association. When the ITUC opened its annual congress five days later the amalgamateds had their tails up, and Johnson came under fire for his 'defeatism'. In their eyes, the judicial judgment exposed the brouhaha for what it was: an inter-union conflict, prosecuted by the ITGWU par excellence to dominate the movement.

Still the CIU remained sanguine. Ironically, the demise of the O'Brien-Larkin quarrel deepened its resolve. On William O'Brien's retirement as ITGWU General Secretary in February 1946, the succession had passed to Thomas Kennedy, who tended to invert O'Brien's rationale for the split, placing nationalist differences with the ITUC above trade union reasons. Jim Larkin's death the following year promised to strengthen his son's voice; and young Jim marked the occasion with a moving appeal for unity. Above all, the CIU believed that developments in law would sustain a tempo for a national trade union centre. The appointment of worker representatives to the Labour Court showed this assumption to be dangerously complacent. The ITUC asked Lemass to nominate one from each Congress; the CIU demanded both seats. Lemass eventually circumvented the problem by appointing Cathal O'Shannon, secretary of the CIU, and Tom Johnson as nominees of individual unions; Johnson being proposed by the Bakers' Union, an Irish affiliate of the ITUC. Initially, CIU unions refused to make joint submissions to the Labour Court with ITUC colleagues, until membership common sense caused the practice to be abandoned. Such procedural problems and the CIU's insistence on dealing with government separately were a nuisance to Lemass. If still pro-CIU in principle, he became less sympathetic to its arched stance on unity.

The incongruity of CIU and government interests sharpened in 1947 when Lemass unveiled his plans for a new industrial order. It was an exceptionally difficult year, ushered in with freezing temperatures that caused fuel shortages and factory closures. Popular unease at the erosion of real wage gains by inflation crystallized in January. Dublin Trade Union Council sponsored a conference to set up a Lower Prices Council, evoking a tremendous response from political, social, and women's groups. Some provincial trades councils followed suit, and the campaign later scored a minor success when the government appointed a Prices Advisory Board in January 1951.[14] One day after the Dublin conference the government imposed bread rationing, and on 22 January de Valera announced that a state of emergency still applied, with the possibility of greater hardship ahead. As strikes and price hikes continued, there were conflicting calls for statutory intervention. In May, Lemass prepared to use the Special Powers Act to prevent a strike of flour millers.[15] Against this backdrop, he moved also to replace the tattered Trade Union Act.[16] Because the law could not constitutionally circumscribe a worker's right to join a union, Lemass aimed to regulate those unions which he might join, through an independent registration authority, empowered to deregister any unions acting in a disruptive manner towards other unions. Workers would be given rights of appeal against unions in cases of inequity, expulsion, or refusal of membership. Only unions conforming to statutory restrictions would receive the protection of the Trades Disputes Act (1906). All new unions required approval from the authority, and would have to be Irish based. The CIU pleaded that the proposals did not go far enough in ensuring native control of the labour movement, but neither Congress warmed to measures that exceeded the 1941 act in departing from the voluntary principle, and CIU craft unions were particularly uneasy about workers securing rights of appeal against admission to the trade. The CIU did broach one reform of industrial organization with Lemass. Owen Hynes, Building Workers' Trade Union, outlined a scheme for the creation of industrial groups and joint industrial councils within each industry.[17] The group would convene delegates from craft or occupational sections to act as a negotiating body. The joint council would comprise the workers' industrial group and the employers' industrial group. That Hynes's was the only attempt to apply recommendations of the Commission on Vocational Organization to industrial relations demonstrates the reactive nature of CIU thinking. Now that the Labour Court had improved the position of private sector unions, the CIU was little less suspicious of structural reform than the hidebound ITUC.

Lemass, however, still saw the Labour Court as a step towards a national wages policy, and intended to nudge unions along that road with anything short of compulsion. Alarming price rises in August opened an opportunity. As the ITUC threatened a general strike, Lemass first requested restraint. Then he seized the moment to offer unions a prices and incomes policy, with price control to be introduced through the Industrial Efficiency and Prices Bill, Lemass's blueprint for post-war growth. Primarily the bill aimed at deepening state intervention to promote efficiency in a protected economy. Joint development councils, involving employers, workers, and others, would be set up in each industry to monitor all aspects of production, management, and marketing; a rich prize for trade unions, and bitterly resented by employers. There would also be a commission to regulate prices and deal with restrictive practices, and trade unionists would receive strong representation on a related price advisory committee. Discussions with the Congresses on an incomes policy commenced in October, Lemass's intent being to index-link future wage increases to the cost of living. These initiatives lapsed when de Valera decided to forestall the gathering momentum of Clann na Poblachta with a general election. Wages talks continued under the Labour Court, and led to the general agreement of March 1948 that governed the second national pay round. Employer opposition deterred a revival of the Industrial Efficiency and Prices Bill by later administrations.

MUDDLING ON

Founded in July 1946 under Sean MacBride, Clann na Poblachta evolved from republican prisoners aid committees and combined nationalism with a programme demanding state-led economic development, repatriation of capital invested abroad, and a break with sterling. To many, the Clann appeared as a revitalized Fianna Fáil of 1932 vintage, brimming with the vigour the elder party had lost. Ninety-three Clann candidates contested the 1948 election. Though other opposition groups looked decidely feeble, the mood for change was strong after years of austerity. Despite Fianna Fáil's red scare tactics, Clann na Poblachta won 13.2 per cent of the vote, with Labour taking a further 8.7 per cent, and National Labour holding 2.6 per cent. The Clann's ten deputies were not the break-through it had expected, but enough to stop Fianna Fáil six seats short of a majority.[18] Eyes turned to National Labour, now the political wing of the CIU. A special CIU conference had pledged full support for the National Labour campaign, and the Congress circulated other parties on their attitude towards British-based unionism. As Fianna Fáil alone had replied in favour of 'an Irish self-contained trade union movement', the CIU-National Labour Party Joint Committee instructed its five TDs to re-elect de Valera as Taoiseach. To the committee's disbelief, the deputies joined the combined opposition to form the first Inter-Party government, pleading that their constituents put welfare reform before the intricacies of inter-union politics.[19] The incoming cabinet allotted the social portfolios to the left, placing the Labour leader and Tanaiste, William Norton, in Social Welfare; party colleague T.J. Murphy in Local Government, and Dr Noel Browne of Clann na Poblachta in Health.

Loans and grants of £46 million from the US Marshall Aid programme, most of it earmarked for land reclamation, enabled the government to make strides in tackling infrastructural and social development.[20] None the less, it could justly claim kudos for redressing neglect of public services, notably housing. Housing was currently the chief concern of Labour Party members, who directed heavy criticism at Fianna Fáil's tardiness in reviving the building industry after the Emergency. Though the Department of Local Government estimated the requirement of new dwellings at

110,000 in 1948, a mere 1,602 houses were completed with state aid that year, compared with 14,297 in the year ending 31 March 1938. T.J. Murphy's quiet dedication surmounted the problems of skilled labour supply, the lack of speculative construction, and the banks' reluctance to loan capital. After his death in April 1949, the work was continued by M.J. Keyes, who boosted the number of dwellings built with state aid to 3,418 in 1949 and 12,305 in 1951. Housing acts were introduced also to increase grants for private construction, loans for buyers, and the powers of local authorities to deal with housing problems. Less impressive was the cabinet's handling of the economy and in May 1951 the government fell. Its position had been crumbling since late 1950. Devaluation of sterling in 1949 and the Korean War had raised the cost of imports severely, aggravating the balance of payments problem. But the controversy over the 'Mother and Child' scheme delivered the fatal blow.

Dr Noel Browne had accrued immense admiration for his crusade against the dreaded tuberculosis. Initially it appeared that his proposals to provide pre-natal and child care were being delayed by objections from the Irish Medical Association. On 30 March 1951, the ITUC executive, dismayed at the widening gap between social services in Northern Ireland and the Republic, called for the scheme to be implemented urgently. In reality, the crucial hurdle confronting Browne was the Catholic hierarchy, and on 5 April the bishops informed the cabinet of their judgment, ruling the scheme to be 'opposed to Catholic social teaching'. The cabinet then refused to back Browne, and he agreed to consider resigning. But when an ITUC lobby urged him to modify his policies instead, Browne let it be known to the press that he was open to suggestions. This merely worsened his relations with the Taoiseach and Sean MacBride. With no alternative, he resigned on 11 April. If Browne's prickliness had contributed to his isolation, MacBride's handling of events brought little credit to Clann na Poblachta, and the next election crippled the Clann politically. Labour slipped from 19 to 16 Dáil deputies—not a bad result in the circumstances, but the loss of power soured party relations with union leaders. Norton resented the ITUC's pressure on the government during the Browne affair, and subsequently complained that electoral defeat had aborted his own plans for welfare reform. Working-class betrayal at the ballot box would become a theme in Labour rhetoric over the next two years. Browne returned to Dáil Éireann as an Independent and supported a minority Fianna Fáil government, which enacted a modified version of the 'Mother and Child' scheme.[21]

The Inter-Party government had pursued a more even-handed approach to the Congresses. After all, the Tanaiste's own union was an ITUC affiliate. He himself had not supported O'Brien's memorandum to the Congress special conference in 1939; O'Brien had split the Labour Party in 1944; and the CIU's rhetorical conservatism alienated left-wing activists. In any case, Lemass's ineffectual ministerial successor in Industry and Commerce ensured that nothing disturbed the routine of labour-state relations. However, external developments intervened to give the ITUC a buffetting. In September 1948, the Taoiseach confirmed that Éire would become a Republic and sever the Commonwealth connection. The British Labour government responded with reassuring signals to Northern Ireland. These moves served to intensify support for the campaign being waged by the Anti-Partition League set up by six-county nationalists in 1945. In January 1949, government and opposition combined to launch an All-Party Anti-Partition Committee to seek re-unification by peaceful means. The Republic was duly proclaimed on Easter Monday, and the south bid farewell to the Commonwealth. London reacted with its Ireland Act, guaranteeing the constitutional status of Northern Ireland as long as Stormont so wished. Coming from a Labour government, this was indeed a bombshell; for on the Northern question, as on amalgamated unions, opinion tended to be naively normative. Neither the government or the labour movement had done anything to anticipate the likely repercussions of leaving the Commonwealth, and they now blundered on with crass ineptitude. It was all acutely embarrassing for the ITUC. Amalgamateds in the North welcomed the Ireland Act and played a big part in pushing the Northern Ireland Labour Party to adopt a partitionist policy. Humiliatingly, the British TUC disdained to pass on to the British Labour Party an ITUC resolution condemning the Ireland Act.[22]

Because trade union division in the south was not really about nationalism, these events failed to rumble the inertia of amalgamated membership. But they did seem threatening. In his capacity as ITUC President, Larkin Jr appealed to the fragmented movement for a co-ordinated response. Though some delegates to the CIU annual congress that year warmed to Larkin's overture, others suspected it as a damage limitation excercise and pointed to attitude of amalgamateds north of the border. With time unfolding CIU logic, the ITGWU reverted briefly to a vintage OBU stance, favouring fraternal appeal before coercion to induce workers out of the amalgamateds, and re-stating the case for industrial unionism. In November, the National Labour Party proposed that Congress unity talks commence on the understanding that the movement ought to be Irish based. Despite the misgivings of amalgamated unions at this concession, discussions opened in February 1950, only to founder on a poaching wrangle between the ITGWU and the NUR. After parallel moves had succeeded in fusing both Labour parties in June, the search for a Congress *rapprochement* began again; with the same result. This time however, twelve Irish unions within the ITUC signalled their frustration by querying the CIU about shifting Congress allegience. The coming months brought flickers of hope that the British might go voluntarily. Since the Trade Union Act (1941), the National Union of Boot and Shoe Operatives' executive had favoured the establishment of a separate union for its Irish sections. Most members were reluctant to terminate their association with the bigger British body, but the executive saw little future for the union in Ireland. In 1951, members in the Republic balloted to form the Irish Shoe and Leather Workers' Union. Against executive advice, Northern members insisted on sticking with the National Union. Soon afterwards, the NUR voted to withdraw from Ireland, also against the wishes of Irish members. In this instance, cross-border unity was maintained. Most NUR men joined the successor National Association of Transport Employees. At the 1952 annual Irish Trade Union Congress the WUI persisted with a contentious motion that other amalgamateds follow suit. Leading the opposition, Norman Kennedy, ATGWU, made it very plain that the remnant had every intention of staying put and that further withdrawals could only reinforce partition as Northern trade unionists were not likely to weaken their ties with UK wage bargaining.[23]

It was now patently clear that the CIU offensive had shot its bolt. The Congress had done little to effect the recasting of mentalities it purported to champion—ironically it reinforced anglicization in replicating the ITUC—and the paucity of CIU thinking was painfully evident in the poor calibre of debate at its annual congresses and the difficulties it encountered in energising its trades councils.[24]

The CIU's tactical hamhandedness played into the amalgamated canard that here was nothing more than inter-union rivalry masquerading as narrow nationalism. Moreover, the deceleration of economic growth after 1951 dented CIU hopes of dislodging its rival. Fianna Fáil suffered a particularly dismal term of office from 1951 to 1954. De Valera's orthodox conservative response to recessionary trends depressed industrial output. Unemployment climbed from 50,000 in 1951 to over 70,000 by 1953. In Dublin, an Unemployed Men's Association caught the public imagination with regular sit-downs on O'Connell Bridge, until the Catholic *Standard*'s McCarthyism exposed involvement by the Irish Workers' League.[25] Less exotic but more troublesome tensions developed over the fourth pay round in 1952. When the CIU's central council recommended a 12*s*.6*d*. per week ceiling on wage increases, affiliated craft unions expressed strong opposition and opened liaison with their ITUC counterparts.[26] There could be little point in having two British-type congresses at a time of mounting strain. Attitudes were already softening when, in April 1953, Lemass urged labour to settle its differences or face the consequences of legislative intervention. And the thaw deepened when another of the old guard, William McMullen, retired as general president of the ITGWU in the summer. A colleague of Connolly's in Belfast and a steadfast Protestant nationalist, McMullen still hankered after the industrial unionist ideal. His successsor, John Conroy, was more compromising. Conroy and young Jim Larkin would be the architects of unity.[27]

UNITY IN ADVERSITY

An inter-Congress correspondence opened on Mayday, with the CIU reiterating its demand for a wholly Irish-based, Irish-controlled movement. The ITUC accepted that discussions should be 'very largely concerned with questions relating to the interpretation and application of this principle'. This concession was nothing new, for the crux was how one defined 'Irish control'. But now the CIU chose not to press the point. Both annual congresses that year encouraged the *rapprochement*, and in September a joint committee commenced talks on unity. The committee presented a memorandum to conferences of the Congresses in April 1954. Technically, the CIU secured its demands for an all-Ireland, Irish-controlled movement. In practice, however, the memo endorsed ITUC *caveats* that any restructuring of organization must be implemented gradually, and with the consent of members directly concerned. Accepting this compromise in its Irish context, the CIU then turned to what it considered the source of its difficulties, and requested the British TUC to facilitate the withdrawal of amalgamateds from Ireland. Once again, the British put their own interests first, and refused to co-operate. To extricate itself from a highly embarrassing situation, the ITUC sought to deepen the unity process, persuading its Irish counterpart that overtures to the British would be more effective from a united trade union authority. In June 1955, a sub-committee met to prepare the way for the formation of the Provisional United Trade Union Organization (PUO) in January 1956; the umbrella beneath which both Congresses would later be reconciled.[28]

The PUO emerged amidst the pressures of the difficult fifth national pay round and a profound economic crisis. The 1954 general election had reduced Fianna Fáil to its lowest ebb since 1932. Fine Gael and Labour almost monopolized the second Inter-Party government, with Clann na Talmhan holding a solitary cabinet post, and the shrunken Clann na Poblachta supporting from the backbenches. Labour received four portfolios: Norton took Industry and Commerce, James Everett held Justice, Brendan Corish moved into Social Welfare, and Michael Keyes became Minister for Posts and Telegraphs. It was not a happy time for Labour. Irrespective of political change, the old economic policies continued. Rising imports and a fall in cattle exports in 1955 led to another balance of payments crisis. Again the cabinet reacted by deflating the economy, introducing austerity measures in February and July 1956. Then the Suez aggression reversed what had been an encouraging growth in manufacturing exports, plunging the economy deeper into trouble. Between 1955 and 1958, industrial output declined by 11 per cent. By now, state policies were attracting widespread opposition, and trade union criticism of the Labour Party's role included the authoritative voice of backbench Labour deputy Jim Larkin, secretary of the PUO. Up to July 1956, the PUO found itself preoccupied with economic affairs, entering discussions with government and employers on the economy in May, when the preliminary report of the Census of Population shocked the nation. Two hundred thousand people had emigrated since 1951, causing a net population drop of 66,000. Ireland, it seemed, was dying. The PUO responded with two special consultative conferences, one in Belfast to discuss the disturbing rise in Northern Ireland's unemployment, and one in Dublin, for which it issued *Planning Full Employment*, a programme demanding the maintenance of existing levels of current public spending, a National Investment Board to plan state investment in capital projects, repatriation of external assets, foreign investment, and a relaxation of the credit squeeze.[29] However, within weeks, the initiative passed to the rank and file.

On 12 January 1957, as the live register of unemployed swelled to 95,000, Dublin building workers formed an Unemployed Protest Committee, with *Planning Full Employment* as their platform. Whilst five of the Committee's twelve leaders were members of the Irish Workers' League, a palpable sense of historic national failure sufficed to make the movement acutely political. As if to amplify the swansong of old Ireland, the IRA had launched its border campaign 'Operation Harvest' in December 1956. The ensuing crackdown on republicans finally pushed Clann na Poblachta into opposition and the Taoiseach went to the country in February. Labour fought the election with little conviction. Unsure of its policy direction or its attitude to another coalition, the party vote slipped to 9.1 per cent, and the Dáil party to twelve deputies. By contrast, the Unemployed Protest Committee scored a famous victory in getting Jack Murphy returned for Dublin South Central. The incoming Fianna Fáil government promised to tackle unemployment and emigration. De Valera declared that one of its first objectives would be to revive the building industry. Having welcomed de Valera's priorities, it was with some astonishment that the trade union movement learned of his budget in May. Huge cuts were introduced in the housing programme. Public capital spending was to be reduced by one-third. The removal of food subsidies led workers to dub it the 'Famine budget'. Deputy Murphy and two colleagues responded with a hunger strike. The strike attracted huge publicity but created consternation in the Unemployed Committee. It was called off after four days, following PUO intervention. Agitation continued, and Unemployed Protest Committees were formed in provincial cities, but again the red scare struck. Under pressure from Archbishop McQuaid, Deputy Murphy dissociated himself from the Dublin Unemployed

Committee. Then he announced his intention to retire from agitation and concentrate on Dáil duties. The unemployed movement sank into terminal decline. If Murphy would not work with the movement, he was too conscientious a man to pretend he could do anything without it. He resigned from Dáil Éireann in March 1958 and emigrated to Canada. Trade unions meanwhile took up the running, shying away from protest, but keeping the unemployment question in the public eye. The PUO sponsored a conference on the issue in April, which generated much media coverage, but little else. At this stage, unemployment was falling and the economy stood on the brink of a fifteen-year period of expansion. Government measures to revive the building industry had already removed a core of activists from the protest movement. Trade union agitation abated as it appeared that the worst was over.

The economic crisis had initially disrupted the PUO's constitutional agenda but also reinforced the desire for unity, encouraging considerable progress to be made after July 1956. Twelve months later a draft constitution was ready, and in September the PUO consolidated its authority in negotiating with employers on a joint agreement for the sixth national pay round. In theory, the proposed constitution affirmed that the new congress would be an all-Ireland, Irish-controlled body. In practice, there were qualifications. The document made clear the subordination of the Northern Ireland Committee to national policy making structures, but to overcome Northern misgivings the PUO dropped a provision that the national executive appoint members to the Committee in favour of demands that it be elected by the Northern Ireland Conference. A similar compromise resolved the question of British involvement. Participation in the new congress was to be confined to Irish based delegates. Amalgamateds could affiliate only in respect of their Irish memberships. They were to leave purely Irish-affairs to their Irish sections and create structures to that end. Ten of the nineteen seats on the executive were to be reserved for Irish unions. Thus, with minimum guarantees, some of them cosmetic, the CIU secured the principle of native control, whilst the ITUC defined the terms. The amalgamateds would stay. Equally, the form and character of trade unionism would remain unaltered. If the CIU carried into the constitution a concern to relate trade unionism to national development and a proclivity for a more interventionist role in industrial relations, it was a slim intellectual dowry. Industrial unionism was indeed dead. On 10 February 1959, separate delegate conferences of both Congresses assembled to vote on the final draft. The jaded CIU scarcely demurred. British spokesmen for the amalgamateds put up strong opposition at the ITUC conference. Irish delegates however, from whatever quarter, North, south, native or foreign, were almost unanimously in favour, and the ITUC approved the constitution by 148–81 votes. On the following day the PUO was replaced with the Irish Congress of Trade Unions (ICTU). The CIU and the ITUC were dissolved at their annual conferences in July.[30]

Philosophically, the ICTU's constitution reflected a social democratic outlook. Clause 6(d) pledged Congress 'to work for such fundamental changes in the social and economic system as will secure for the workers of Ireland adequate and effective participation in the control of the industries and services in which they are employed'; a slightly more moderate phrasing than either of its predecessors had chosen.[31] At all levels of the newly spliced movement, a pervasive wariness discouraged a resumption of the old ITUC ties with the Labour Party. The ITGWU did not re-affiliate to the party until 1968, and the ATGWU until 1969.[32] None the less, the proportional representation referendum of 1959 prompted the ICTU belatedly to intervene in Labour's campaign against the 'straight vote', and in December the Congress appointed a committee to 'study the problem of political organization'.[33] However tentative, such gestures were eagerly grasped at by Labourites attempting to rebuild a party still shellshocked from the second Inter-Party government. In the backwash of the 1957 general election, the left appeared to be at a crossroads. The formation of the 1913 Club and the National Progressive Democrats in 1958 suggested a drift of intellectuals from Labour towards 'progressive unity'.[34] Left-wing frustration within the party boiled over at the following year's annual conference when William Norton received a barracking for an attack on young Jim Larkin. A youthful dynamo on assuming the party leadership in 1932, Norton had come to personify the achingly conservative, clientelist style of Labour deputies. Now tired and uninterested in political work outside constituency affairs, he might yet have held on, but resigned the leadership in February 1960. With the election of Brendan Corish to the succession, the long night of the 'Norton years' gave way to a pink hued dawn.[35] The making of the modern Labour Party had begun.

9

Avoiding the Issue: Northern Labour, 1920–1960

Trade unions in Northern Ireland had the advantage of operating in a relatively industrialized society. The 1926 census showed the six counties to have a population of 1.26 million, with about 25 per cent of the workforce engaged in agriculture. Manufacturing employment was highly aggregated. As late as 1952, after decades of efforts to diversify, shipbuilding and engineering and textiles and clothing still employed 44 per cent of insured male employees in manufacture, and 82 per cent of insured females; with men predominating in the first pair, and women in the second.[1] This made for easier co-ordination at industry level, and trade union federations covered shipbuilding and engineering, construction, printing, and, later, teaching and the civil service.[2] At the same time, women and unskilled grades generally were very badly organized during the inter-war years and it was not until the 1940s that unions gave any thought to addressing a public agenda. Few up to then identified with Congress, which itself had little inclination to pursue a Northern policy. The root of stasis lay not so much in divisions between Catholics and Protestants as in the conflict between labour and loyalist ideologies. With a mainly Protestant, anti-Unionist leadership and a mainly Protestant, loyalist membership, mutually dependent for their bread and butter, but otherwise at odds, the British unions who nearly monopolized trade union membership in Northern Ireland found themselves walking a tight line between their organizational interests and the politics of their members. The provincial status of Northern Ireland, its partial integration into the British economy and British wage determination, and the desire of its government to proceed 'step by step' with Westminster legislation, did much to offset pressures for a united labour voice. Though the inter-war depression and the establishment of a separate administration after 1920 disrupted the trend towards Northern inclusion in UK level wage agreements, partition reinforced the underlying orientation towards Britain.³ Both government and unions tended to submerge regional realities in a bland anglo-centrism. The desire to develop a labour-state relationship, so catalytic in the evolution of Congress, never became acute until the 1950s. Change in this provincial paralysis could only come from without; and it came from a combination of economic growth in the 1940s and after, and the threat to the amalgamateds in the south.

If the six county labour movement was made in the 1940s, and tempered over the next decade in a battle for government recognition, the making occurred at the level of officialdom only. Unions recognized, from bitter experience, the political limitations imposed by loyalism. Of its nature, the Northern Ireland Labour Party (NILP) had to be political. From 1937 onwards, the party's stance on partition, technically non-committal but in practice ambivalent, came under increasing strain. When a drift towards linkage with the British Labour Party became entangled with the post-war anti-partition campaign, Northern Labour divided into pro- and anti-partition camps. The result was decline and deference to sectarianism. A revival of NILP fortunes a decade later again foundered on the rock of Protestant privilege. Anti-partitionist Labour too succumbed to sectarian solidarity. Yet, the 1949 schism had its positive side. The NILP could never have been an agent of reform in Northern Ireland. By freeing the anti-partitionist left to join a nationally organized Labour Party, the split confirmed the displacement of the ineffective and conservative Nationalist Party in Belfast, and mapped out a new direction for minority politics.

THE HUNGRY DECADES

The post-war slump had a devastating impact on Northern Ireland. In June 1921, out of 260,000 insured workers, 65,500 were idle, and 43,500 were on short-time.⁴ Conditions improved a little after 1922, but the North shared the depressed state of the British economy in the inter-war years, with an average unemployment rate among insured workers of 19 per cent from 1923 to 1930, rising to 27 per cent over the next decade. To some extent, this common UK experience camouflaged problems peculiar to the region. Almost 60 per cent of its workforce were in declining economic sectors;

construction excepted, a mere 6 per cent worked in growth sectors. The over-capacity and over-supply created during the war continued to affect shipbuilding and agriculture, while changes in clothing and lifestyle were consigning linen to the status of a luxury good. The linen trade dipped into terminal decline after the peak production years of the immediate post-war boom.[5] The underlying crisis was concealed by the generality of recession in 1921, a strong demand from the American market up to 1927, and the Great Depression that followed the Wall Street Crash in 1929. Nearly 20,000 linen workers were idle in Belfast in 1930, when appalling levels of unemployment also afflicted the shipyards and engineering. Shipbuilding employed 2,000 workers in 1933, one-tenth of the 1929-30 figure. Workman Clark, Belfast's 'wee yard', closed in 1935. Shipbuilding and engineering began to pull out of recesssion in the mid 1930s, but linen would never regain its former pre-eminence.[6] Government efforts to diversify the economic base made little headway against the propensity of Britain's growth industries to locate in London and the English midlands. Of twenty-seven firms operating under new industries acts in 1939, only the Short and Harland aircraft factory, established in 1937, made a significant contribution to job creation. None the less, the workforce grew by about 12 per cent between the wars, despite high emigration, with additional jobs coming mainly in distribution, services, public employment, and construction. Incomes rose by 10–15 per cent, compared with a British average of about 25 per cent, leaving *per capita* income at 58 per cent of the UK average in 1939 compared with 61 per cent in 1924.[7]

For political reasons, the onset of the slump was made exceptionally traumatic for northern labour. The pockets of mainly Protestant labour representation that flourished in mid and east Ulster after 1917 generally sought to evade the national question through 'bread and butter' politics. However, almost all labour councillors opposed partition, and Unionist leaders detected here a trojan horse of 'Sinn Féin Bolshevism'. In particular, labour successes in the 1920 local elections were seen to weaken the case for six county exclusion.[8] Against a backdrop of violent rightist reaction throughout Europe, the extension of the IRA war to the north, and lethal disturbances in Derry, Edward Carson's 12 July speech urged no toleration of the labour enemy within. Whether a direct incitement or not, both Carson and James Craig applauded what followed on the shopfloor. On 21 July, the Belfast Protestant Association instigated workplace expulsions in the shipyards. Next day, the terror spread. To protect Protestant employment, smash the labour movement, and create a more homogeneous Ulster, over 7,400 men and women, one-quarter of them Protestants, were forced out of their jobs by the end of the year. Others deemed it wise to leave of their own volition. The degree of intimidation in Belfast became evident early on when Labour councillors D.R. Campbell and James Baird, himself expelled from the shipyards, called a meeting of the Corporation to discuss the situations. With loyalist workers packing the gallery, Campbell and Baird were the only members of the twelve-strong Labour group to protest against the expulsions. By 35–5 votes, the Corporation agreed to take no action.

Baird meanwhile helped to form an Expelled Workers' Relief Committee, which turned for aid to Congress and the British TUC. Neither were particularly forthcoming. Arguing that the key lay with the unions concerned, Congress did nothing to pressure the British movement, and while the Expelled Workers appreciated the limits of Dublin's leverage, Tom Johnson's plea that the executive had 'no right' to ask anything of the TUC carried his usual prevarication to the verge of crass humbug. Most of those who participated actively in the expulsions, in the shipyards at least, were low paid, non-union labourers and craftsmen's assistants. However, neither management nor unions were unhappy with the results. British officials did press their Belfast committees to work with expelled members, but buckled to a negative response. Only the Amalgamated Society of Carpenters and Joiners took resolute action, going so far as to strike companies which refused to re-instate expelled members. Of its 4,000 members in Belfast, up to 3,000 ignored the strike call and had their union cards withdrawn. In early September, the TUC annual conference had accepted a motion from an expelled workers' delegation calling on the Parliamentary Committee to summon a meeting of the executives of the unions concerned to pursue a 'common line of action'. The Parliamentary Committee then appointed a three-man commission of enquiry which finally crossed to Belfast in December. Adding insult to injury, their report deplored the expulsions as one more expression of the Irish tragedy; reason, it was hoped, would prevail. With Belfast sliding into communal violence that would claim 500 lives and 2,000 injuries between July 1920 and July 1922, the eyes of the TUC glazed over. It now became more anxious about the dispute within the Carpenters and Joiners, which was eventually resolved in favour of the renegades.

Most of the assistance given the expelled workers came from Catholic, nationalist, and Sinn Féin sources. Southern Ireland expressed solidarity through the 'Belfast boycott', officially a selective blacking of northern goods, but applied indiscriminately in some cases.[9] Already, there had been talk of an economic embargo to scuttle 'Carsonia', and a spontaneous boycott evolved quickly in August 1920, before coming under Dáil direction. It did little damage to those most at fault in the expulsions. Congress assisted in its enforcement, and the Expelled Workers' Committee vainly urged the British Labour Party to effect a similar action in Britain, where it might have had a real impact. In January 1922, the boycott was suspended as part of the Craig-Collins pact, in return for Craig's promise to endeavour to get the expelled workers reinstated. When the deal went unfulfilled—Collins repudiated but could not unmake the boycott, while Craig cited the boundary commission as the latest source of loyalist insecurity—a second pact in March included included a British grant of £500,000 for relief works in the Belfast area, one-third of which was to be earmarked for Catholics, with preference in employment being given to expelled workers.

Unionism threatened a permanent anti-labour mobilization. Vigilance committees were set up to confirm the new sectarian realities on the shopfloor, their leading figures drawn from the Ulster Unionist Labour Association. In politics, the British Empire Union and the Ex-Servicemen's Association performed a similar directive role in hounding Labour during the 1921 Northern Ireland elections. The Belfast Labour Party had largely gone to ground after July 1920, but Baird, John Hanna, and Harry Midgley stood on an anti-partition Labour platform, with covert funding from Sinn Féin. When loyalists prevented them from holding a rally in the Ulster Hall they folded their campaign. At the hustings, all three lost their deposits, as did a fourth independent socialist, Rev. Bruce Wallace.[10] None the less, so reactionary an ideology could build no enduring alternatives to labourism. Membership of both the Ulster Unionist Labour Association and the Ulster Workers' Trade Union remained small. Even the Unionist Party found its obsequious Labour Association to be quite useless. As the crisis receded, most of the five Unionist Labour MPs elected in 1921 faded from politics. Northern ties with the ILPTUC frayed in the 1920s, but no serious demand arose for a separate six-county congress. British unions with a substantial cross-border membership continued to locate their Irish offices in Dublin, and loyalist aggression made officialdom more inclined to maintain lifelines to London and Dublin.[11]

Whatever about values, the sectarian expulsions had a selective and short-term impact on trade union efficiency. The general assault on wage levels was in full swing in 1921, with twenty-three of the twenty-seven wage strikes that year being directed against reductions. Though shipbuilding workers opted out of UK stoppages against pay cuts in 1920 and 1922, engineers and printers joined UK strikes in 1922, and local disputes occurred in construction and many smaller occupations. High unemployment in the staple industries forestalled a resurgence in 1923, but when the decline in living costs bottomed out the following year, militants managed to restore 1922 conditions.[12] Wages fell steadily over the next ten years, before recovering their 1924 levels by 1937. However, the rate of decline was almost exactly the same as in Britain. Moreover, wages for craftsmen in Northern Ireland generally stayed above the UK average during the inter-war years. Reflecting the relative scarcity of skilled and abundance of unskilled labour in the region, it was the latter who fared worst, with rates well below the UK average. Equally, the drop in union membership from some 100,000 in 1920 to a nadir of 60,000 in 1933, conceals a major disparity in performance between skilled and general unions. Excluding agriculture, where trade unionism collapsed in 1920, the proportion of male insured workers in trade unions in 1931 was 40 per cent, little less than the UK figure; on the other hand a mere 7 per cent of insured female workers were unionized, compared with 21 per cent in the UK as a whole, though women made up 40 per cent of the employed industrial workforce.[13]

The odds facing low-paid workers in arresting the erosion of pay levels was demonstrated in the major dispute of these years, the 1933 rail strike. The NUR had conceded a 4 per cent pay cut in 1931, and was dismayed to find the railway companies seeking a further 10 per cent reduction twelve months later. When the companies refused to meet the union half way, the executive reluctantly decided to make a stand. An all-out strike on Northern based systems began on 30 January 1933. Of 3,478 members called out, 2,765 responded, along with 1,037 'nons'; crucially, the recalcitrants were mainly busworkers. Strike breaking by busmen and railway clerks provoked a violent reaction. A train was derailed, killing two blacklegs. Then the IRA started to bomb transport installations. On 6 April, the NUR executive caved in, unilaterally accepting most of the companies' terms, including the retention of strike-breakers, over the heads of its members. Six months later, there were still 599 NUR men awaiting re-employment.[14] As industry climbed out of the worst of the depression, union membership recovered. By 1937, shortly before another sharp rise in unemployment, there were about seventy trade unions in Northern Ireland, representing approximately 80,000 out of 300,000 insured workers.[15]

The misleading perception of inter-war trade unionism in Northern Ireland as timid and crippled by sectarianism is due largely to its policy failures—for which Congress cannot be exculpated—to confront sectarianism, to transcend sectionalism, to address the problem of building a bargaining power for the lower paid, and to unite as a movement in challenging public policy. Labour-state relations functioned in a haphazard, low-key fashion in Northern Ireland up to the 1960s. Craig liked a personal approach to government, and once described his role as 'distributing bones' to his supporters.[16] Unionists would listen to workers through patronage channels: the Minister of Labour from 1921 to 1937, J.M. Andrews, chaired the Ulster Unionist Labour Association, but an open relationship with an independent labour movement was not on. As a linen manufacturer, landowner, and railway director, Andrews was a typical Unionist MP; 85 per cent of them usually came from the business, professional or large farming classes.[17] For tactical reasons however, their conservative instincts were circumscribed by a desire to keep social services as close to British levels as possible, despite the additional financial burden of coping with greater housing, health, and unemployment problems. The result was a xeroxing of Westminster policy, with pennies pinched where possible. Civil service unions fought a long campaign before the Whitley process was finally extended to the North in 1945.[18] Whitleyism was also pruned out of trade board legislation in 1923, and the government acceded to employer demands for the abolition of the big flax and hemp trade board. Due largely to this move, the number of workers covered by trade boards was slashed from 115,000 to 51,000, over 80 per cent of whom were in the textile and clothing industries. Stormont showed no desire to keep pace with Britain in extending the system, rejecting a plea for a trade board for linen weavers, in response to a proposed 20 per cent wage cut in 1931, and a similar request from catering staffs, following the defeat of the Belfast hotel strike in 1936. Only one new board was approved in Northern Ireland between 1923 and 1945, on foot of a joint appeal from the baking industry in 1938. Trade board minimum rates, which offered no more than a subsistence income approximate to the local average wage for unskilled labour, fell steadily from 1924 to 1936, and did not recover their old levels until 1940. By then, employees covered by trade boards had fallen well astern of the average wage earner, and their counterparts cross-channel, with women faring worse than men. Stormont also declined to follow England or the Free State in re-introducing an Agricultural Wages Board, with the result that when the North's 19,000 farm labourers were brought under the Insurance Acts in 1936 they were almost as well off on the dole.[19] One area where the government was happy to emulate Westminster was in copying the Trade Disputes and Trade Union Act (1927), although Northern Ireland had not been mobilized in the British general strike which prompted the act. The act changed the procedure in paying trade union political levies from 'contracting out' to 'contracting in'; thus placing the onus on the individual member to choose to pay. Political strikes were outlawed, and public employees debarred from membership of Congress, compelling the Union of Post Office Workers to disaffiliate.[20] Though repealed at Westminster in 1945, and amended in Northern Ireland in 1958, the 'contracting in' stipulation remains on the six-county statute book.

THE LEFT

After its hammering in 1920–21, the Belfast Labour Party regrouped in 1923, with Harry Midgley as secretary. Elated with Midgley's excellent showing in the West Belfast Westminster constituency in December, the party met with delegates of the Confederation of Engineering and Shipbuilding Unions and country groups on 8 March 1924 to found the NILP.[21] From its inception, the NILP allowed members to hold their own opinions on partition while trying to soft pedal 'non-essential', i.e., constitutional, issues in order to unite workers around social democratic policies borrowed from British Labourism. In part, this reflected the fact that the problems of cultural identity so dismissed by the party were not exclusively external; the NILP embraced a medley of Connollyites, leftish nationalists, neo-Walkerites, and variations in between. Party unity demanded that the central questions in Northern politics were rarely confronted, and party activists became adept at tailoring their message to the religious geography of the occasion. The introduction of the 'straight vote/single seat' electoral system in 1929, and the creation of 'Catholic' and 'Protestant' constituencies, deepened Labour ambivalence.

The decision to scrap proportional representation was partly directed at the NILP. Against a background of widespread unemployed protest, Labour took three of the fifty-two seats in the Northern Ireland parliament in 1925.[22] Independent Unionists too were returned on social issue platforms, and Joe Devlin led the Nationalists out of their parliamentary boycott. It looked briefly as if parliament might become something more than a rubber stamp for Westminster legislation. Alarmed at the corrosion of 'border politics', Craigavon changed the rules. With two brief exceptions, the NILP was reduced to one or two MPs for the next twenty years, and none at all from 1949 to 1958. It would remain also a Belfast-centred party. Though active branches evolved in Antrim, Armagh, and Derry, only once did it capture a Stormont seat outside Belfast: South Armagh in 1938, won by default when the Nationalists abstained. Within Belfast, it variously represented five constituencies from 1929 to 1958: Pottinger, Dock, Willowfield, Oldpark, and Central, none of which could be called 'safe'. Pottinger alone was held in consecutive elections, and then by the maverick Jack Beattie, who flitted in and out of the party. Vital to NILP success in Belfast was the ghetto mentality of the Nationalists. Joe Devlin's National League adopted a fairly radical social programme and Devlin welcomed an alliance with Labour in the 1925–29 parliament. But as he saw it, Nationalists should dominate majority Catholic areas and Labour could have a go at the Unionists elsewhere. This formula gave the NILP the space to win mixed constituencies like Dock, Oldpark, and Pottinger, with a combination of blanket Catholic and radical Protestant support. After

Devlin's death in 1934, the Nationalist machine atrophied in Belfast, making life easier for Labour. Important too was Belfast's location as a centre of trade union officialdom, from which the NILP drew its MPs; just three of the thirteen MPs in its history were Catholics.[23] Crucial as the union input was, it did not guarantee a sound financial or electoral footing. With nearly 90 per cent of organized workers in amalgamated unions, political dues normally went to London, returning in the form of grants to members contesting elections. Proposals to the British Labour Party for a clawback arrangement were never resolved satisfactorily. The NILP received subventions from Congress in 1927 and 1928, but otherwise had to rely on unions making special provision for local dues.[24] In the circumstances, it was an achievement to secure the affiliation of about twenty unions to the party initially, and this figure declined in the years ahead.[25]

During the inter-war years, the NILP leadership was identified with a series of individualist trade union officials. Midgley worked for the National Union of Distributive and Allied Workers. Sam Kyle, of the Workers' Union and later the ATGWU, William McMullen, ITGWU, and Jack Beattie, of the Blacksmiths' Society and later the Irish National Teachers' Organization, made up its parliamentary party from 1925 to 1929. Kyle and McMullen took up union jobs in Dublin in 1932, leaving Beattie and Midgley to jostle for control.[26] Midgley had become party chairman months earlier. He entered Stormont as MP for Dock in 1933 and saw the expulsion of Beattie, for collusion with the Nationalists, in 1934. Just as Beattie was adopting a vigorous anti-partitionism, Midgley was moving in the other direction. During the decade he nudged the NILP closer to the British Labour Party, which was represented at an NILP conference for the first time in 1932. Efforts of anti-partitionists to ensure that external links gravitated instead towards Irish Labour could not offset the mesmeric lure of mighty Britannia; the more so as southerners responded kindly but with little understanding or interest. There had been no Free State input in the early NILP. Delegates to the 1924 congress demurred at the idea of a separate party for the six counties, and left it at that.[27] The NILP affiliated to Congress in 1927, and set up a joint council with the Labour Party following the latter's restructuring in 1930. But though the council was to convene bi-annually and publish annual reports, meetings were few and discussions confined to general exchanges of views.[28] The incremental divergence of the two Irish states, a trend given psychological impact by the Economic War and intensified customs control on the border, shaped a mentality in the south which was at once partitionist and irridentist.

Up to 1930, the NILP monopolized radical politics in Northern Ireland. The republican movement shared little of the socialism that permeated its southern wing after 1927.[29] An ILP branch existed in Belfast until 1932, when the ILP disaffiliated from the British Labour Party. The branch then reformed as the Socialist Party (Northern Ireland), but continued its role as a ginger group within the NILP. Ironically, in view of their own history, Socialist Party members were mainly Connollyite, and hostile to NILP links with the British Labour Party.[30] A challenge from the far left materialized in 1930 with the formation of a Belfast section of the Workers' Revolutionary Party, soon to become the RWG. As capitalism faltered throughout the western world, communist agitation on unemployment attracted hundreds of people, especially after the collapse of the MacDonald government in Britain. Revolutionary groups were formed in Ballymena and Ballymoney, while weekly sales of the RWG paper, *Workers' Voice*, topped 1,200 copies in Belfast. Much of this support was ephemeral, narrowly based on unemployed protest, and conditional on constant street politics, which the Ulster Protestant League and heavy policing made an onerous strategy for an organization with a core of about fifty cadres. Moreover, this was Northern Ireland, a state on permanent alert for subversion. In September 1930, the first of many communists was jailed for sedition under the Special Powers Act.[31]

The militant Ulster Protestant League was founded in 1931 to combat class politics with a 'jobs for Protestants' appeal. This standard loyalist response to recession was largely successful. Membership of the Orange Order expanded during the slump.[32] Even so, rising levels of long-term unemployment, adverse changes in the payment of benefit in 1931, and the example of violent protest in Britain against the changes, induced an attitudinal shift which caught Unionists napping. Roughly 100,000 people were idle in Northern Ireland at this time, half of them in Belfast. Of the total, about 43,000 were on benefit, 19,000 received transitional benefit, and 14,000 were eligible for the lowest form of assistance, outdoor relief.[33] Outdoor relief existed for married men only, and was administered by miserly Boards of Guardians under the Poor Law.

Cash payments were given to men on public works; others received food parcels. The Poor Law reeked of pauperism, and the introduction of a means test in 1931 for those on transitional benefit suddenly increased the number of people under its wretched care. A system geared to squeezing the pips from improvident Catholics now faced humiliating many of its own as well. As the NILP and Belfast trades council thrashed about with resolutions, deputations, and parliamentary questions, the RWG demanded direct action. Following the 'class against class' line, communists had little time for reformists. In July 1932, they helped set up an Outdoor Relief Workers' Committee to seek better pay and conditions, abolition of payment in kind, and relief for single people. After months of campaigning, the 2,000 men on Belfast relief works struck on 3 October. That evening, 20,000 people marched through the city in support. Mass meetings culminated in serious disturbances on 11 October when the Royal Ulster Constabulary tried to prevent a banned march. Catholic and Protestant workers united in battles with the Constabulary, who replied with gunfire, leaving two dead, fifteen wounded, and at least nineteen suffering other injuries. Belatedly, the government had begun to heed the tocsin sounded by Protestant clergy and businessmen. The Belfast Guardians were pressured to improve rates immediately. On 14 October, the Outdoor Relief Workers' Committee hailed a 'glorious victory'.

The outdoor relief strike marked the zenith of RWG influence. Its techy relations with the mainstream labour movement were further strained by recriminations over the October events. From the right, Midgley charged the RWG with making workers suffer for its irresponsible politics; from the left, the settlement was criticized for not including an extension of relief to single persons. Belfast trades council launched a moderate unemployed workers' movement, while the Ulster Protestant League redoubled its efforts. At the next elections for the Belfast Board of Guardians, in June 1933, the NILP won a solitary seat, compared with twenty-nine for the Unionists.[34] It was among dissidents that the remarkable class unity achieved in the outdoor relief agitation had some positive effect, as is evident in IRA intervention in the 1933 rail strike, and in the formation of Republican Congress clubs in the Protestant Shankill and Newtownards Road districts of Belfast; there was even a Shankill contingent at the annual Wolfe Tone commemoration at Bodenstown in 1934. Thirty Northern delegates attended the Republican Congress that year, including members of the CP, the ITGWU, and the Socialist Party.[35] Communist trade unionists won representation on Belfast trades council, and the Communist Party of Ireland, as the RWG had now become, continued to unite Catholics and Protestants through agitation on unemployment and housing rents.[36]

Leading Unionists hit back by endorsing the message of the Ulster Protestant League, and the League itself embarked on an escalating anti-left campaign, made more paranoid by the CP's adoption of a 'united front' line. Both the NILP and the CP headquarters in Belfast were attacked by Protestants in June 1935. Midgley's election agent complained of the impossibility of holding public meetings since the start of the Royal Silver Jubilee celebrations in early May.[37] When unknown gunmen fired on Belfast's 12 July parade, the powderkeg exploded. Three weeks later there were thirteen dead, dozens injured, and hundreds homeless. Midgley's own Dock constituency bore the brunt of the trouble, and his restrained, 'balanced' condemnation of events, possibly to avoid antagonizing his Protestant electors, alienated Catholics, who were the main victims of the unrest. Midgley's more outspoken defence of the Spanish Republic deepened the rift and cost him the Dock seat in 1938.[38]

The Spanish Civil War embarrassed sections of the Northern left. Beattie, with an eye on his union job and the Catholic component of his vote, kept a low profile. For others, it offered an ideal rallying point. Here at last was an issue on which they could hardly be accused of being anti-Protestant. Unionists took a non-interventionist view of Spain; naturally they had no sympathy with Spanish Catholic politics. For the first time since 1920, the political climate seemed less oppressive north of the border. Midgley warmed to this novelty and polemicized against clerical apologists for Franco. While the CP and the Socialist Party rallied to the *Irish Democrat*, Belfast Communist aims gradually swapped anti-partitionism for advocacy of a progressive opposition at Stormont. Spain, Munich, and concern at British appeasement of Hitler gave the anglo-centric left an agreeably non-nationalist agenda. Midgley beavered away at equating a 'commonwealth' outlook with internationalism, much to the irritation of his nationally minded colleagues.[39] The first formal challenge to the NILP's 'non-committal' stance on partition surfaced at the party's 1937 annual conference. It was defeated comfortably by a motion on 'internationalism', and Midgley consolidated his position in 1938 with a promise of financial assistance from the British Labour Party to fight the Westminster seats.[40] Sensitive to red scare tactics and gung-ho behind de Valera in the Economic War, the Labour Party also bridled at these developments. Executives of the two Labour parties met in 1936 to review an item in the NILP's annual report dealing with a united front with the CP. As Midgley was no less anti-communist than Norton, the problem wasn't insurmountable. The national question was not so easily dealt with. Though the Labour Party's 1936 constitution confirmed the NILP as its fraternal equivalent in the six counties, Norton ignored the NILP's annual conference in 1938 because of its attitude towards partition and links with British Labour. When informed that the conference had called for greater cross-border trade, Labour replied that political unity must precede any economic co-operation with the six counties. Against Norton's advice, Labour's annual conference voted heavily for renewed liaison in 1939, but when the NILP pledged support for the war, contact ceased for the duration.[41]

FORWARD WITH BRITAIN

Northern Ireland had a good war. There were teething problems, and a feeling that the region was not 'pulling its weight'. Certainly, the economy's full potential was not exploited under Craigavon and his hapless successor, J.M. Andrews; 60,000 workers had migrated to Britain by 1945.[42] But war production eventually boosted industrial employment by 20 per cent, virtually eliminating unemployment for the first and only time in 1944. Government subsidies kept prices in check, so that from 1939 to 1944 the cost of living rose by 29 per cent, whereas wages increased by 35 to 70 per cent, with lower-paid workers catching up on skilled grades. The gap in living standards with Britain narrowed. Income *per capita* stood at 71 per cent of the UK average in 1946.[43] Attitudes towards social services changed, notably after the publication of the Beveridge Report. London eased the mental adjustment by approving the principle of parity in social services between Northern Ireland and Britain.[44] At home, the greatest single tragedy of the war, the Belfast Blitz of 1941, created an evacuee problem which confronted middle-class people with the shocking conditions of working-class life.[45] Increased contact with London smartened up the slack Stormont administration. Research for post-war reconstruction revealed the extent of public health problems and the magnitude of housing neglect during the inter-war years, estimating the housing requirement at 100,000 new dwellings, or twice that if slums and overcrowding were to be elimated. In response, a Ministry of Health and Local Government was established in 1944.[46] Public opinion was liberalized also by the war agenda; at this level at least, it was possible to believe that local political values were converging with those of the wider world. Fortuitously, sectarian tensions were eased by the suspension of Orange parades for the duration and Catholic participation in the war effort, despite intermittent IRA action and the internment of hundreds of republicans.[47]

The war brought an immediate extension of state control over labour. Defence Regulation 55 allowed London to direct production, distribution and prices throughout the UK. Normal union trade practices were supended for the duration, strikes were made illegal, and disputes were to be referred to compulsory arbitration. A further imposition was introduced in 1942 with the Restrictions of Employment Order, which regulated the movement of workers between industries.[48] In contrast with the situation in Éire, trade unions co-operated quite happily with the new arrangements; their block vote also kept the NILP from adopting a policy of non-collaboration with Stormont on defence and campaigning against the Special Powers Act.[49] Eager to push for parity with British wage rates, union members were less compliant and a strong shop stewards movement evolved to fill the resultant leadership vacuum. Between 1941 and 1945, Northern Ireland recorded 523 strike days per 1,000 employees, compared with a UK average of 153.[50] The biggest wartime action began on 24 February 1944, when 1,200 shipyard engineers struck for a pay rise. By 24 March, the strike had spread to 20,000 men. When the five shop stewards leading the strike were imprisoned, dockers struck in sympathy. As the city near ground to a halt, Belfast trades council persuaded the five to accept bail. Employers then granted a wage increase and the jail sentences were lifted on appeal.[51] Union officialdom recovered its authority with the dismantling of wartime controls, and trade unions could reflect on a satisfactory record of membership growth; from about 114,000 in 1941 to 147,000 by 1945.[52] They were also able to check loyalist shop-floor opposition. The Ulster

Association of Loyalist Workers, founded in the shipyards in 1942, did not last long. More enduring was the Ulster Transport and Allied Operatives' Union. Formed among busworkers in dissent with the ATGWU, this union grew to 8,000 members after 1945. However, the 'Ulster' trade union idea did not spread further, and the union ultimately merged with the National Union of General and Municipal Workers.[53]

Membership expansion, the apparent debility of shop-floor loyalism, and the novel experience of collaboration with the state encouraged labour to create a regional trade union centre. Northern Ireland had made little input into Congress until the mid 1930s, when tensions between Irish and amalgamated unions spurred the latter to maximize their voting strength. Northern attendance at Congress grew rapidly after 1942 as union membership increased. Some timely criticism from Jack Beattie of the ITUC's silence on six-county affairs inspired the executive to appoint a special committee on the matter in 1943.[54] One year later, the executive announced the establishment of a sub-committee on Northern Ireland. From the outset, there was evident anxiety to keep the initiative under wraps. Not that Irish unions had any objections to separate machinery for the six counties; the fear was of rank and file loyalism. The Northern Ireland Committee (NIC), as it became known, was to have six members appointed by the executive, and to be advisory and consultative only. To forestall a debate on its significance, the executive presented the package to the 1944 congress as a *fait accompli*. In a rare display of unity at this time, both the ITGWU and the ATGWU opposed a motion that the NIC be elected. However the split in Congress instantly magnified the North's importance within the ITUC. With the CIU having no more than a toehold over the border, the NIC was now exclusively an ITUC concern. The executive soon agreed to raise its complement to thirteen, comprising the President, Vice-President, and Secretary of Congress, and ten nominees of an annual conference of Northern affiliates. While it remained technically a sub-committee 'empowered to act for the National Executive in matters peculiar to the Six County area', the NIC gradually assumed a *de facto* autonomy. Its democratic basis continued to be circumscribed; motions at its annual conference were devised by the NIC itself, and ratified by the National Executive, while the absence of a full-time staff restricted its capacity.

The war probed the deficiencies of the Unionist leadership. Craigavon's declining health had already reduced the cabinet to the same perfunctory role as the Stormont Commons. Morale sagged noticeably under the lack-lustre Andrews, who succeeded him in November 1940.[55] At the same time, Protestant opinion remained fervently pro-war; nationalists were tentative but acquiescent. In 1941, Midgley built upon his anti-fascist 'win the war' record, liberally side-swiping neutral Éire in the process, and returned to Stormont as MP for Willowfield in a by-election upset which trumpeted the depth of disgruntlement with the Andrews government.[56] In 1942, two Nationalist councillors on Belfast Corporation defected to the NILP and Jack Beattie re-joined the fold after eight years as an Independent MP. Midgley's mounting impatience for the party to declare openly for the constitutional position of Northern Ireland resuscitated old frictions with Beattie. When Beattie was elected party leader in December 1942, Midgley resigned, launched the Commonwealth Labour Party, and later entered the 'coalition' cabinet of Andrews' successor, Basil Brooke. The 'coalition', of which Midgley was the only non-Unionist minister, was a simulacrum of the Churchill administration, designed to cosmetize Stormont's image at Westminster. Surprisingly, Midgley carried few of his old comrades with him into Commonwealth Labour. Although the war was steadily creating a greater commonality of experience between the Northern and British left, and shaping the anglicized outlook so attractive to Midgley, many in the NILP now perceived him as self-centred and anti-Catholic.[57] Beattie too would soon quit the party, again edged out for collusion with the Nationalists. He then formed the Federation of Labour (Ireland), a loose assemblage committed to Irish unity and socialism. Coevally, Harry Diamond, an ex-Nationalist, founded the Socialist Republican Party.[58] None of this shuffling in the anti-partitionist undergrowth seemed significant at the time. The NILP continued to broaden its appeal, extending its branch network west of the Bann, and boosting the number of trade unions affiliated from eleven in 1941 to seventeen in 1945.[59]

The CP offers the most extraordinary example of the way in which the war conjured a vicarious political culture on the left. Having suffered arrests and suppression of its publications for opposition to the war after the Hitler-Stalin pact, the CP promptly turned enthusiastically pro-war when Germany invaded the Soviet

Union.[60] It also became more partitionist than the NILP, and in this respect matters were simplified by the dissolution of the party in Éire, which left the CP a Northern Ireland party for nearly thirty years. Throwing everything into their 'Second Front' campaign, Communists called on the NILP to enter a coalition government with the Unionists, denounced strikes in war industries, and applied, unsuccessfully, to affiliate to the NILP in 1943. Membership of the now respectable CP had mushroomed to 1,000, little less than the individual muster of the NILP.[61] Most of this support evaporated just as quickly, and the cold war brought cold times. The party stuck to its partitionist line until the early 1960s, when polemics from the London-based Connolly Association and the indefatigable Desmond Greaves induced a revision. One long-term legacy of the war years for Communists was the prominence they acquired in the trade union movement, notably on Belfast trades council and in the Amalgamated Engineering Union.

Socialists held high hopes of the first post-war elections. Figures for Belfast were impressive; the left aggregated nearly 45 per cent of votes cast.[62] Outside the city the NILP won an average 30 per cent of the poll in the seven constituencies it contested. These results translated into a disappointing two seats for the NILP, together with victories for Midgley, Beattie, and Diamond. The Westminster elections three weeks later more or less confirmed the left-wing vote in Belfast; elsewhere the NILP recorded a poor turnout in Antrim and Derry. Only West Belfast returned a left-wing MP, Jack Beattie. However, the NILP clocked up a good performance in the local elections in September, winning eight seats on Belfast Corporation, control of Newry and Warrenpoint urban councils, and increased representation elsewhere.[63] Ironically, in contests which the non-nationalist left fought on a 'Forward with British Labour' platform, convinced that the union would now be transformed into a conduit of progressive values, Diamond's breakthrough in the Falls division proved to be the real portent. After 1945, the catatonic Nationalist Party retired from Belfast, leaving the field to more dynamic and moderately radical personalities. Far from 'modernizing' the Protestant electorate, socialism became a means of rejuvenating nationalist politics in the city, paving the way eventually for the effective mobilization of Catholic voters across the six counties. Nor did post-war progress bring political change. More houses and new industries meant more patronage and more discrimination.

INDUSTRIAL UNITY

During the 1950s, the happiest decade in its brief and blood-stained history, the population of Northern Ireland increased from 1.37 million to 1.43 million. With some apprehension about granting a Labour government more control over its purse-strings, and talk of opting for dominion status instead, Stormont decided to follow accretions to the British welfare state 'step by step'. The greater peril, Unionists concluded, lay in sinking below Éire levels of public spending. Backed by a guaranteed British subvention, social services improved steadily. The annual rate of housing construction was doubled, enabling the target of 100,000 new dwellings to be met by 1965. The Education Act (1947) opened access to secondary and tertiary education. The Health Service Act (1948) placed health care on a par with Britain's national health service.[64] The cabinet also took the view that wage machinery for low-paid workers should be treated 'as part of the social security code', and extended the Wages Councils Act (1945) to Northern Ireland.[65]

Economic growth exceeded UK levels in the 1950s, and the number of insured workers rose from 438,000 to 450,000, but the gap with British income *per capita* had widened slightly by 1960, and the narrow manufacturing base presented recurring troubles.[66] As the immediate post-war consumer demand abated, the underlying problems of obsolescence or lack of competitiveness re-emerged in the traditional sectors. While Stormont created 3,000 new jobs each year through external investment in new industries, it failed to cope with the nearing crisis in the staples. Textile employment fell by 28 per cent over the decade, and employment in shipbuilding, repair, and marine engineering by 16 per cent.[67] With a continuing flight from the land, unemployment climbed to 6.8 per cent in 1955, and 9.3 per cent in 1959. Difficulties multiplied over the next five years. One-third of linen plants shut down between 1958 and 1964, with the loss of 27,000 jobs. In shipbuilding and allied sectors, 11,500 jobs were lost between 1960 and 1964.[68] The impact on the Protestant working class led to the NILP's most serious challenge to Unionist hegemony. Though confidently ahead of the Republic in living standards and social services, the electorate were beginning to expect parity with Britain, the more so as, unlike the inter-war years, Northern Ireland was no longer one of a number of depressed pockets of the UK; it was the only region suffering high unemployment. In parity lay an argument that would prove to be the regime's undoing.

Trade union membership continued to consolidate after 1945, reaching 200,000 by 1953 and 263,000 by 1970, when roughly 55 per cent of employees were unionized.[69] Strike activity declined in the 1945-51 period but still remained well above the UK average.[70] The composition of the movement was still predominantly male—80 per cent—manual, and manufacturing, though the proportion of insured women workers was double the pre-war figure at 20 per cent, and white collar unionism was growing with the health and education services. Reflecting the rapid strides of general unionism over the previous decade, the ATGWU made up 73,000 of the 1953 total. The sizeable craft sector included thirty unions with 52,000 members, the largest being the Amalgamated Engineering Union. Out of ninety-two unions in all, eighteen were local, with 27,000 members; for a variety of reasons—size, insularity, politics, or legal restrictions in the case of civil service associations—they took little interest in the wider movement, though some of the smallest societies were in effect part of bigger, amalgamated unions. A mere five unions, with 8,700 members, were Dublin based.[71] Inter-union relations remained fairly stable, apart from an instructive Derry shirt tale in 1952–53 which involved the Clothing Workers' Union, a local splinter from the National Union of Tailors and Garment Workers, merging with the ITGWU. Protestant women who had defected to the Clothing Workers' refused to join the ITGWU and reverted to the National Union.[72]

Against the background of political friction between the two Congresses and within the NILP, unions succeeded to a remarkable extent in fostering a strategic consensus around the NIC. The secret of that success was the overwhelming dominance of the amalgamateds in Northern Ireland, the hegemony of British labourist values among union activists, and the amalgamateds' desire to maintain a presence in Éire and keep loyalism at arm's length in the North. Thus, the heave against the ITUC in the south and Unionist requests for a six-county congress reinforced Northern commitment to the cross-border link. It was a politics with its own equilibrium none the less, and too much pressure from any quarter might have tipped the scales. The NIC's inaugural conference in November 1945 convened forty-one delegates from nineteen trade unions and Belfast trades council.[73] Three functions were adopted for its remit; to discuss industrial and economic questions, excluding politics, except in so far as it affected trade unionists; to promote trades councils; and to obtain a formal recognition from the government of its status as the 'representative organ of the trade unions operating in Northern Ireland'. Its immediate task, however, was to secure recognition from local branches of the trade union federations, the pillars of the hitherto disparate Northern movement, and in this it encountered surprisingly little resistance. Equally, it persuaded most unions to affiliate to the ITUC—90 per cent of members were in affiliation with the Congresses in 1953—the only active resistance coming from two overtly 'Ulster' societies, the Ulster Teachers' Union and the Ulster Transport and Allied Operatives'.[74] Further successes were scored in building up labour's profile beyond its traditional Belfast stomping ground. Despite difficulties in sustaining a presence outside Belfast and Derry, the number of trades councils in Northern Ireland rose from two in 1945 to eleven in 1955, including one in Ballymena which declined to affiliate to the NIC on the ground that it answered to a foreign congress.

The 'foreign congress' argument became the great stumbling block for the NIC in its attempts to nurse a working relationship with Stormont. The NIC's letter of introduction evidently had not commended itself to Prime Minister Brooke, who dismissed implicitly its similarly implicit request for recognition. Sensitive of Unionist mistrust of independent labour, the NIC opted to pursue recognition on an *ad hoc* basis. Early signals were mixed. Some queries were responded to, and contacts remained friendly, but in 1947 the Minister of Labour advised the NIC to create a separate Northern Ireland congress. By 1948, only the Health Ministry gave any indication of acknowledging the NIC's status. The crunch came in 1950 when the Minister of Labour, now Major Ivan Neill, rebuffed appeals for consultation on the Employment and Training Bill. Neill was happy to deal with UK trade unions, but not with a body whose headquarters were in a foreign country. The ITUC rallied the trade union federations to pledge non-co-operation with schemes set up under the Employment and Training Act, but Neill swung the cabinet behind him. By February 1951, the crux had

become one of general recognition. Again the ITUC sought to escalate trade union non-co-operation; this time the unions said no. Yet
despite their reluctance to confront the government, and Neill's
encouragement for a six-county TUC, affiliates stood squarely
behind the NIC in its selective boycott of the administration.
Perversely, the government tarnished its argument and infuriated
trade unions in its steadfast refusal to follow Westminster in
repealing the Trade Disputes and Trade Union Act (1927). The
imperative of cultivating efficient labour-state relations against a
background of rising unemployment and a dawning realization of
the need to modernize Northern Ireland's ageing industrial base
gradually isolated the government. The cabinet's obduracy was
highlighted in 1955 when it established an Industrial Development
Council—the Chandos Council—without consulting the NIC, and
the NIC kept up the pressure by convening a major conference on
the economy the following year. By the end of the decade, both the
Protestant Churches and the business community were urging a
compromise.

Congress unity moves in the Republic complicated the NIC's
position. However, Unionist hopes that the process of *rapprochement* with the nationally-minded CIU would provoke a Northern
breakaway never looked like being fulfilled. If still under-repre-
sented, Northern participation in the ITUC increased in the 1950s.
A Belfast-based president was elected in 1953, Northern business
featured more on the agenda of annual congresses, and the jealousies that plagued cross-border debate during the Emergency
yielded to a pointed amity. Labour leaders were keen to carry the
North with them into the new dispensation, as well they might be
since it accounted for 60 per cent of the ITUC affiliation.[75] In
February 1956 the newly inaugurated PUO briefed union officials,
the NIC, and the federations in Belfast. The NIC received a full-
time official in 1957, and the PUO later acceded to demands that
the ICTU constitution allow the NIC to be elected. Of course the
constitution's provisions for guaranteed Irish control of Congress
did not pass without criticism, notably from the Amalgamated
Engineering Union, and they reinforced Unionist antipathy to the
NIC, though Unionists did nothing practical to promote a Northern
Ireland TUC or stop the merger. The recognition problem persisted
until Brookeborough finally handed over to the reform-minded
Terence O'Neill in 1963. O'Neill's signals for a fresh start in labour-

state relations were reciprocated when the ICTU granted the NIC a formal autonomy. O'Neill then appointed NIC representatives to the new Northern Ireland Economic Council, a prestigious replacement for the embarrassingly ineffective Chandos Council. Four years later the statelet began its descent into turmoil, and the once ostracized NIC became courted as a privileged ally in the establishment's propaganda battle for the restoration of normality.

POLITICAL DIVISION

Jubilant at the election of a Labour government at Westminster, the NILP entered the post-war era in good heart. The Labour triumph encouraged it to extend the 'forward with Britain' line to emphasis on the anomalies of the Unionist state. In addition to its perennial concern with bread and butter issues, the party enlisted NIC support to solicit the British Home Secretary to repeal of the Special Powers Act, the Trade Unions and Trade Disputes Act, and the Franchise Act. Northern Ireland Labour's concern with civil rights reached a peak at the party's 1947 conference, which called for the disbandment of the B Specials.[76] The Attlee government, of course, upheld the 'Speaker's convention' that the use of powers devolved to Northern Ireland should not be discussed at Westminster. The limits of anglo-centrism were exposed too, in a rather different way, by the Friends of Ireland, a caucus of some thirty Labour MPs, formed in 1945 to raise six-county grievances and marshal Labour parties in all three jurisdictions behind a united Ireland policy.[77] Initially, the Friends attached some importance to the NILP. Speakers from the caucus visited Northern Ireland, and persuaded British Labour to assist the NILP in the County Down Westminster by-election in 1946. This rapport was soon overshadowed by an alliance between the Friends and the Anti-Partition League. Given the legacy of the war years, the widening gap in welfare provision and living standards between Northern Ireland and Éire, and the split in Congress, there could hardly have been a less propitious time to launch an anti-partition campaign, and Labourites in all jurisdictions were prone to the same counter-productive policies as the League. The Friends merely uncovered pro-Union sentiment in both the NILP and the British government, where some senior figures, notably Herbert Morrison, nursed bitter memories of Irish neutrality.

Once the association of the Friends with the League became more prominent, pro-Union elements in the NILP objected. They had their own bandwaggon already rolling.[78] Affiliated unions were particularly anxious to lock the North within the UK in view of anti-amalgamated feeling in Éire, though there were exceptions, and positions often depended on the proclivities of local officials. Anti-partitionists tried to halt the momentum. Under the chairmanship of Jack Macgougan, the NILP opened relations with the ITUC and activated the 'Waterford agreement', a joint machinery constructed between the NILP and the Labour Party in 1939. However, this was soon balanced by the revelation that the NILP was receiving financial aid from Britain, and by the secondment of a full-time British Labour Party organizer to Northern Ireland in mid 1948. For a time it seemed as if the centre might hold. The Irish government's proposed declaration of a republic was countered by Attlee's assurance 'that no change should be made in the constitutional status of Northern Ireland without Northern Ireland's full consent'. Those in the NILP who favoured the 'non-committal' *status quo* were relieved to receive a new political formula with the *imprimatur* of British Labour. But Attlee had encouraged partitionists in the belief that his party would look favourably on a merger with the NILP. They turned up the heat at the party conference in November. The ATGWU and the Union of Shop Distributive and Allied Workers proposed a motion hostile to the Friends of Ireland, which was passed by 183–96 votes. When the West Belfast branch convened a conference in protest, it was expelled forthwith. On 28 November, the executive tried to sidestep the nearing storm by approving an approach to the British Labour Party for affiliation as a regional council. London however declined to become embroiled. The debacle threatened to alienate the 'non-committals' as well as the anti-partitionists.

Events moved briskly in January. Early in the month the NILP unveiled plans for a new party structure involving closer ties with British Labour. Fortified with a cast-iron constitutional guarantee from Attlee, Brooke announced a general election on 21 January to be fought, naturally, on the constitution. On 24 January, the Irish Labour Party met dissident Northern labourites and agreed to embrace them in a 32-county structure. It had earlier warned the NILP that links with British Labour would force this eventuality.

Three days later the first meeting of the All-Party Anti-Partition Committee called for a church gate collection for anti-partition candidates, who included five Belfast labour men, in the six counties. The NILP then issued a pro-partition statement. The 'chapel gates' election was a bruising experience for Labourites of all hues. Beattie donned a steel helmet for his outdoor speeches and got 200 British Labour MPs to demand that the contest be postponed until the passions subsided. The result was a disaster for the NILP, despite a vigorous, unambiguously pro-Union campaign. The left at Stormont now comprised two anti-partitionists, Harry Diamond and Frank Hanna.

After the hustings, anti-partitionists forged ahead with the extension of the Labour Party, or the Irish Labour Party (IrLP) as the provincial Northern mind insisted on calling it, to the six counties.[79] Backing came chiefly from Diamond's Socialist Republican Party, ex-NILP branches grouped in the Irish Labour Association, other adherents from the NILP, and Beattie's following. Clearly, a sectarian geography mapped out the Labour split, but the IrLP attracted prominent Protestant activists and contested Protestant constituencies. Prospects looked deceptively good. The IrLP appeared to have a united and talented leadership. With Diamond, Hanna, and Beattie, it enjoyed the unique position of being represented in the Irish government, Stormont, and Westminster. At the base, it gained strongholds in west Belfast, Derry, south Armagh, and south Down. In the 1949 local elections, Labour swept all seven seats in the Falls and Smithfield wards of Belfast, and won control of Newry and Warrenpoint urban councils. Trade unions kept their distance however, despite the presence of many union officials in the IrLP, and some anti-partitionists declined to join the party out of deference to their unions. The ITUC took a detached stand on the schism from the outset. Pressure from southern delegates to snub the NILP for its partition policy was checked with an appeal for unity in the industrial field.[80] The Congress had no wish to fuel demands for a six-county TUC. Accordingly, it maintained links with both parties at national level, and a more *ad hoc* liaison through the NIC. Labour's wider goal of weaning support for Irish unity within the British movement failed disastrously. The Friends of Ireland divided in their response to the Ireland Bill, which passed through the Westminster Commons with much less opposition from Labour MPs than anyone expected.

Internal cracks appeared in the IrLP in 1951. The old Nationalist Party may have been dead in Belfast, but in the conservative 1950s Catholics were not quite ready for socialism. Diamond objected to IrLP criticism of Catholic influence on the Republic's laws and later took his followers into the Republican Labour Party in 1953. Hanna decamped to form a more explicitly Catholic Independent Labour group. The sectarian dimension was given an added twist by the fact that the leading lights of the IrLP, Beattie and Macgougan, were both Protestant. Hanna's group swept the IrLP out of Belfast Corporation in 1958; an election which saw the breakthrough of another faction, 'Dock Irish Labour', led by Gerry Fitt. A headquarters enquiry into this reverse never managed to cross the border. Thereafter, IrLP organization dwindled to 'lingering limbs' in Newry and Warrenpoint. Labour tried, in vain, to revitalize these branches in 1972, and then accepted the demise of its Northern section a year later.[81]

The NILP pledged itself formally to uphold the Union with Britain in April 1949. The block votes of the unions mustered 20,000 for the resolution; 700 votes were cast against.[82] As the anti-partitionists had already decamped, the major immediate repercussion was a hostile reaction within the ATGWU, which was reputed to have an even balance of Catholic and Protestant members. To end the controversy, the union disaffiliated. This still left the NILP with some twenty-two union affiliates and about 17,000 corporate members.[83] While this support was of doubtful value electorally, it gave the party a badly needed internal weight. Slowly but surely, the partitionist line took its toll on the size, calibre, and courage of the NILP. The British Labour Party withdrew its agent in 1952, offering instead an annual subvention of £300 for three years. With about 300 members, the party still found itself in difficulties. After another disappointment in the 1953 Stormont elections, the party chose to place greater emphasis on its loyalty to the constitution.[84] Not that an impartial observer could seriously doubt its existing loyalty. In London the NILP sponsored an Ulster Labour Group to counter the 'misleading and dishonest propaganda of the Anti-Partition League'. The group's president, David Bleakley, favoured the six-county TUC option, and many of his colleagues were uncomfortable about the provisions of the ICTU constitution. Indeed, the NILP became as fond of disparaging the 'backward' Republic as the Unionist Party.[85] Unionism was arraigned for incompetence rather than sectarianism. The party no longer contested nationalist constituencies, and canvassers were advised to support the B Specials and the Special Powers Act; 'guarded criticism' of discrimination in housing and employment, and gerrymandering was permissable only in response to 'pointed questions'.[86] Inevitably, it came to be perceived as Protestant, though Catholics were said to form some 30 per cent of individual membership.[87]

The crescendo of Protestant job losses at the turn of the decade finally paid dividends for the NILP. In 1958 the party won four Stormont seats, and held them with bigger majorities in 1962. Thus emboldened, sections in the party challenged its silence on sectarianism. Warning signals from MPs like Bleakley and Billy Boyd were shown to be informed, if none the less self-interested, in 1964 when a wrangle over opening Belfast's park swings on Sunday divided the party between sabbatarians and liberals. Yet O'Neillite Unionism also stole Labour's clothes, and compelled pursuit of the liberal agenda. In 1966, the party joined with the NIC to underwrite a 'Joint Memorandum on Citizen's Rights in Northern Ireland'.[88] In 1968, the NILP, the Republican Labour Party, and the Labour Party formed another cross-border Council of Labour. Two years later the NILP again applied for a merger with the British Labour Party. The response from London, and Dublin, was almost exactly the same as in 1949.[89] History was coming full circle, too late.

Conclusion

James Connolly once said that capitalism was the most foreign thing in Ireland. In truth, since Connolly's time, labour has never been exactly national either.

It had been different before the 1890s. Within six years of the decriminalization of trade unions in 1824, labour politics in southern Ireland became determined by the need to protect native industry from foreign competition. The craft elite of the working class were badly hit by free trade with Britain's developing manufacture after 1826, and theirs was the premier call for Repeal of the Union. In labour's first engagement with parliamentary politics, they supported Daniel O'Connell, not because the rising sun of cultural nationalism obscured their real interests, but because they realized that the constitutional question was a labour question. One could not long defend wages, conditions, or employment levels in a declining economy; one could not reverse decline without tariff protection; one could not have tariffs without self-government. Whatever the deficiencies of successive national movements, whatever the prospects under a native regime might be, and workers were less naive about both than historians have given them credit for, trade unionists regarded economic sovereignty as absolutely essential to the survival of their livelihoods and their unions. Popular sovereignty too was impossible without self-determination. Nationalism was not therefore a thing apart to be quashed or shaped into a socialist mould, but the defining framework of Irish politics, both radical and conservative, and a prerequisite of democracy and economic recovery.

The alliance with the Repeal agitation in the 1830s set the pattern for labour politics over the next fifty years. Workers supported the leading national movement of the day, be it constitutional or republican, though trade unions remained wary of formal association with revolutionists. It was a strategy that, of its nature, militated against making class division the central question in politics and ingrained in labour bodies a tendency to look to the national elite for leadership. But it can hardly explain the weakness of forces for socialism or the marginalization of labour issues in the late nineteenth century; the reasons for these must be sought in de-industrialization. And de-industrialization left labour with little option but to prioritize the demand for self-government. One could scarcely speak credibly of a socialist future when capitalist colonization was not making the working class, but unmaking it. Irish labour was therefore exceptional in nineteenth-century Europe in two respects. First, it faced overwhelmingly a problem of de-industrialization, long before most other countries had begun to industrialize. Secondly, though labour's place in the national movement remained subordinate, self-determination was as much a labour issue as a middle-class one. Indeed, a nagging fear of the Dublin craft unions in the 1830s was that O'Connell would accept something short of Repeal. In Ireland, nationalism provided a rallying point for trade unions and a platform for grievances. Invariably, it politicized labour; occasionally, as in 1848 and 1916–23, it pushed workers to the far left.

With the growing coherence of interest group politics in the 1880s, the growth of trades councils, the extension of the franchise, and the stimulus of new unionism, the possibility of building a Lab-Nat parliamentary lobby became real. However, just when it seemed that labour might finally swap its diminishing share-hold in the national movement for a junior partnership, countervailing forces were to steer it in a completely different direction. Industrial and demographic decline had now reached the point where most Irish trade unions saw no future for themselves as independent societies. After decades of rearguard action against the encroachment of British trade unionism, they gave up the ghost. By 1900, labour broadly regarded itself as a part of the British movement, adopting British principles of industrial and political strategy uncritically. Paradoxically, the splinter from the British TUC deepened this anglicization. The ITUC was the last of four attempts to establish a congress between 1889 and 1894. Each of the previous three had envisaged a more political entity, in line with the vintage strategy of using the national movement as the channel of labour goals. Dublin trades council directed a decisive breach with this tradition by seeking to copy the British TUC. The outcome was a nice, neat trade union forum, but one which narrowed the definition of labour from the working class to members of nice, neat trade unions, and which focused on industrial organization, where labour was weak, rather than politics, where it had some leverage. Political influence, if required, was to emanate from the ITUC's mythical industrial strength, and pursue industrial grievances only. Anything to do with the national question was no longer legitimate terrain. Because English, Scottish, and Welsh nationalism were seen as hostile to the cohesion of the emerging British labour movement, so the ITUC blandly assumed that the same reasoning must hold true for Ireland too. From here on, labour would see nationalism as a problem, not an opportunity. The result was not a seedling socialism, but depoliticization. Whilst farmers, town tenants, and agricultural workers all pursued social interests through the Home Rule party, the urban working class opted out.

It was not unusual that labour should have been influenced by its nearest, and most successful counterpart. The years from 1889 to 1923 were formative in the history of labour movements worldwide. The German Social Democratic Party offered a model for kindred parties in Scandinavia. French ideas helped to shape Italian and Spanish socialism. Canadian workers looked to the United States. British craftsmen built the most powerful trade unionism in the world after 1850, and exported it to most of the white English-speaking countires. But the vast gulf in political culture, economy, and employment structure between a highly advanced country and the undeveloping region on its western periphery makes it impossible to understand how anyone could have thought of applying the British model to Ireland without an immersion in mental colonization.

New unionism was the first of three great waves of agitation that revolutionized labour between 1889 and 1923. If new unionism reinforced Irish dependency on British labour, Larkinism, from 1907 to 1913, challenged that relation, and syndicalism, from 1917 to 1923, sealed the making of the modern Irish labour movement. Larkin came to Ireland a convinced opponent of dividing unions along national lines. Within two years he had concluded that British-based unions could not build a bargaining power for the mass of Irish workers. The formation of the ITGWU marked the beginning of a long and painful decolonization that, combined with

Connolly's industrial unionism, modernized the movement and made it more relevant to native conditions.

The colonial legacy invariably acted to frustrate the modernization process. The legacy survived most obviously in the sectionalist pattern of trade union organization, which the amalgamateds defended tooth and nail, opposing Congress efforts to introduce industrial unionism in 1919 and 1939. And on the latter occasion the proposal generated so much friction that industrial unionism was never raised again as a serious option. It survived too in a pervasive anglicized outlook. Strategically, for example, unions continued to place greatest emphasis on industrial strength, and pursue a bargaining power through wage militancy in free collective bargaining in a voluntary system of industrial relations. If they had a political agenda, that was to be implemented by a Labour government. This *laissez faire* approach was all very well for a strong trade union movement in a strong economy, with a strong political wing. Yet, none of these conditions applied in Ireland before 1946. And clinging to a simulacrum of British labour ideology left the ITUC ill-equipped to cope with the trajectory of Fianna Fáil legislative intervention to develop a native manufacturing base after 1932.

The heightening tensions within Congress over attitudes towards labour-state relations induced a crisis of trade union ideology, culminating in the 1945 split. Superficially, the split was one between left-wing internationalists and right-wing nationalists. Structurally, it revealed a division between the better off unions who wished to preserve the *status quo*, and their weaker colleagues who were willing to accept a change in labour-state relations in the hope of augmenting their membership and bargaining power. That the former should subscribe, nominally at least, to a radical outlook and the latter identify with more conservative political forces, illustrates the degree to which orthodoxy had become disabling rather than enabling. The mistaken basis of that ideology is evident too from the fact that legislative intervention in industrial relations actually strengthened the movement. After all the huffing and puffing against the Trade Union Act (1941), the Act led to a modest wartime increase in union membership, and contributed to the fabulous and forgotten post-war expansion underpinned by the Industrial Relations Act (1946), the establishment of the Labour Court, and the wage rounds. Now for the first time, it became possible for all workers unable to win a bargaining power through wage militancy alone to become organized. The recruitment of over 100,000 additional trade unionists between 1945 and 1950 indicates the size of the constituency which the *laissez faire* approach had been incapable of reaching.

The CIU's efforts to construct an indigenous trade unionism failed miserably. Connolly and Larkin, arguably William O'Brien too, had seen that nationalism could be an enabling ideology, but never an end in itself. The nationalism espoused by the CIU as an antidote to mental colonization was no substitute for it. Indeed, the CIU's duplication of the ITUC merely reinforced anglicization. Rather than pioneer new models itself, the CIU awaited the growing involvement of labour with the nation-state to generate the need for a purely Irish congress. Of course the state was not the nation, and the appointment of workers to state boards, developments in the law, and the pay rounds created a tempo for a unified centre. Once membership expansion decelerated sharply after 1951, the CIU had faint hopes of becoming that centre. In 1953, as in 1936, government intervention prompted reform, this time with the happier outcome of Congress unity in 1959.

Labour politics equally betrayed a provincial deference to British ideas. With the emergence of an Irish labour movement, Congress modified its position of neutrality on the national question to one of acceptance of the prevailing consensus. But, as the history of the CIU would later demonstrate so clearly, nationalism is not the same as decolonization. If Labour was willing, when necessary, to be as green as its rivals, it never shook off the sense that constitutional questions were foreign territory, something to be kept on the backburner. This attitude was far more effective in subordinating Labour to the conservative parties than a direct engagement with nationalism, as it invariably left the party tagging along behind the agenda of others. However, the crucial consequence of anglicization was the alienation of Labour ideology from native reality. The post-1922 Labour Party failed completely to grasp the centrality of political and economic dependency on Britain to Irish politics. The dominant party cleavage between Fianna Fáil and Cumann na nGaedheal/ Fine Gael was understood as a continuation of Civil War politics rather than an expression too of conflicting social interests over dependency. Unable to make sense of Irish political culture, Labour waited for nationalism to run its course, hoping that modernization would eventually replicate British class politics in Ireland, oblivious to the fact that the Irish party system bore comparison with many advanced third world countries, or that the British system was itself exceptional in inter-war Europe in the purely social basis of its cleavages. Another reflex of anglo-centrism was Labour's self-image as 'the child of the unions'. The upshot of this delusion was a passive attitude towards trade unionism. The party never sought to map out a policy for Congress or clarify the dilemmas that confronted it in the middle decades of the century. It was also achingly unimaginative in tactics and thinking, less than effective in defending its natural constituency, and illiterate in political theory.

One might construct a counterfactual view of history in which the Lab-Nat tendency promoted by Michael Davitt in the 1890s matured within the Home Rule party, broke into independent opposition during the conscription crisis, led the national swing to the left in 1918, and went on to greater glory in the new state. Even as a late-comer, so late indeed that it has almost been seen as a gate-crasher, Labour still had its chances in the early Saorstát. Once Fianna Fáil entered Dáil Éireann, its fate was sealed. Given the employment structure and the prevailing hostility to socialism in a highly conformist society, the obstacles to a strictly class based leftism, however innocuous, were too formidable. Communists and social republicans, who made the dependency question more central to their politics, and, if anything, overstated the importance of nationalism, were spectacularly unsuccessful in sustaining a vibrant revolutionary movement, precisely because it was revolutionary.

What has been said so far refers to the south, reflecting the southern domination of the labour movement. Distinctive in its politics, economy, industrial relations, and social culture, the industrial north was ever at odds with the dynamic of southern trade unionism. In organizational terms however, the differences can be exaggerated. The rise of the factory system of textile production, Ulster's first industrial revolution, smashed the old craft unions in the trade, and textiles gradually became women's work. Textile employees in the late nineteenth century, no less than Ulster's agricultural, transport, and general operatives, shared the same problems as the bulk of the southern workforce, being mainly unskilled, low-paid, and too awkward for British labour to organize. Up to 1914, the textile, and many other northern, unions were small, native, and weak, and they looked to Congress for assistance. There is no reason to doubt that Ulster would have been incorporated into the ascendant Irish labour movement but for two factors. First,

Ulster's second industrial revolution reproduced an approximation of British industrial relations in shipbuilding and engineering. For reasons of exclusivity, politics, and the British orientation of their employment culture, the sturdy craft unions which emerged in these sectors never played a significant role in Irish trade unionism up to the 1940s. In consequence, Ulster remained marginal, despite the high profile of delegates from the small northern unions and Belfast trades council in the pre-Larkinite ITUC. The all-Ireland format of Congress contained a potential for synergy, but it never amounted to a real unity of north and south. Though 'unity' was sometimes given as the reason for Congress detachment from the national movement, the excuse was paper thin. With the maturation of a genuine labour movement after 1909, Congress decisions took scant regard of northern loyalist susceptibilities. Secondly, the growth of British, rather than Dublin-based, unions in Ulster during World War I underwrote the partition of labour. The maintenance of cross-border unity at Congress level was no substitute for an integrated all-Ireland trade unionism.

If British unions were never attuned to the economic and political realities of southern Ireland, they were even less fitted to tackle the Rubik's cube of divided Ulster. The self-protective myth that the secular model of trade union organization transcended the divisions of the northern working class was a conceit. It served to camouflage sectarian discrimination, excuse the Protestant working class from confronting the reactionary content of its own politics, and patronize and circumscribe the wishes of Protestant workers. The result is that trade unionism in Northern Ireland is based on a pretence; it offers neither unity or democracy. If the amalgamateds put a premium on secular class unity, and they invariably justified prevarication, inaction, or sheer duplicity on this ground, they ought to have followed the precedents of the British TUC and Labour Party and withdrawn from Ireland, thereby compelling the Protestant working class to choose between 'Ulster' unions or the more solid Dublin alternatives. If their priority was democracy, and there was certainly an argument that Protestant workers should not be railroaded into Irish unions, then they should have made provision for confessional structures in Northern Ireland to allow social and political consciousness to develop freely among the rank and file. Yet such was the hegemony of British labourism in Northern Ireland that no one doubted that Ulster workers should conform to the British model, not the other way round, and the amalgamateds were quite unconscious of being part of the colonial burden.

Political labour found its metropolitan, secular assumptions more indecently confounded by the northern conundrum. No political party could successfully avoid the constitutional question; Catholics never tolerated anglo-centrism in politics to the degree that they did in trade unionism; and labour ideology, as distinct from industrial organization, could not digest the sectarian and supremacist character of Unionism. There was of course a secular case for the Union, and groups like William Walker's ILP, Harry Midgley's Commonwealth Labour Party, and the post-1949 NILP made it with some ephemeral effect. But if labour was drawn naturally towards accepting the jurisdictional status quo and defining itself within a UK context, Unionist aggression periodically reversed the trend. It is not surprising that up to the 1920s the (mainly Protestant) left shared an aversion to partition, pleading instead the advantages of Irish or UK unity, or that the NILP's attempt to pursue an intermediate path should eventually be subverted by the irresistable tug of anglo-centrism meeting the immoveable bedrock of anti-Unionism. For anti-partitionists the IrLP promised a refreshing escape into the joys of untrammelled unambiguity and national unity. They soon hit unexpected snags. Belfast Catholics were shifting from conservative nationalism, but not from ghetto politics, and they were not entirely ready to accept a secular, Dublin based Labour Party. Moreover, thinking on both sides of the border remained incorrigibly naive or vapid on the task involved in building a party capable of bridging divergent mentalities in two jurisdictions and two economies.

One of southern Ireland's oddities is the contrast between a relatively strong trade union movement and a weak political left. Here, the unions have solved their problems better than the socialists. The disastrous strategic errors of the 1890s have gradually been corrected. Indeed the history of southern trade unionism in the twentieth century has been one of slow revision of the colonial legacy. Unions have also shown some imagination in coping, however belatedly, with the challenges of partition, inter-union conflict, and state intervention in industrial relations. Operating for the most part in conditions of chronic unemployment, and a fragile economy, they have fared surprisingly well. In the nature of things, trade unions must face facts or go under. Socialists, on the other hand, never have to confront reality in the same way. In Northern

Ireland too, trade union success seems to stand in spectacular contrast with socialist failure. But here, the comparison is deceptive. Northern unions have bought a highly conditional shopfloor unity at the expense of democracy and principle, while Northern Ireland politics is distorted twice over, by the confessional divide and the region's acute dependency on state spending. So the parties competing for the Catholic vote call themselves socialist; and the parties competing for the Protestant vote align with the right. And on social and economic issues, dependency makes Keynesians of them all.

References

Prologue (pp.1–5)
1. On the guilds see J.J. Webb, *The Guilds of Dublin* (Dublin 1929); Sean Daly, *Cork, A City in Crisis: a history of labour conflict and social misery, 1870–1872, Vol. 1* (Cork 1978), 253–81; and Seamus Pender, 'The Guilds of Waterford, 1650–1700, parts I–V', *Journal of the Cork Historical and Archaeological Society*, 58–62 (1953–57).
2. Eighteenth-century labour is still in the realm of proto-history, but see John W. Boyle, *The Irish Labor Movement in the Nineteenth Century* (Washington, D.C. 1989), 7–25; Andrew Boyd, *The Rise of the Irish Trade Unions* (Tralee 1985), 11–30; Fergus A. D'Arcy and Ken Hannigan, eds, *Workers in Union* (Dublin 1988), 2–3; M.G. Doyle, 'The Development of Industrial Organization amongst Skilled Artisans in Ireland, 1780–1838' (M.Phil, Southampton 1973); John Swift, *History of the Dublin Bakers and Others* (Dublin 1948); and Daly, 253–81.
3. Boyle, 16.
4. Henry Patterson, 'Industrial Labour and the Labour Movement, 1820–1914', in Liam Kennedy and Philip Ollerenshaw, eds, *An Economic History of Ulster, 1820–1939* (Manchester 1985), 173.
5. Daly, 264.
6. Emmet O'Connor, *A Labour History of Waterford* (Waterford 1989), 11–21.
7. George Cornewall Lewis, *Local Disturbances in Ireland* (London 1836), a classic on the topic. See also M.R. Beames, *Peasants and Power: the Whiteboy movements and their control in pre-Famine Ireland* (Brighton 1983).
8. Paul E.W. Roberts, 'Caravats and Shanavests: Whiteboyism and faction fighting in east Munster, 1802–11', in Samuel Clark and James S. Donnelly Jr, *Irish Peasants: Violence and Political Unrest, 1780–1914* (Dublin 1983), 66.

Chapter 1 (pp.6–28)
1. For events in Britain see Henry Pelling, *A History of British Trade Unionism* (London 1971).
2. For an overview of economic developments see L.M. Cullen, *An Economic History of Ireland since 1660* (London 1987).

3. Aspects of northern industrialization are discussed in Liam Kennedy and Philip Ollerenshaw (eds), *An Economic history of Ulster, 1820–1939* (Manchester 1985).

4. Robert Kane, *The Industrial Resources of Ireland* (Shannon 1971, first ed. Dublin, 1844), pp.391–427 discusses trade unionism and wage rates as deterrents to capital investment.

5. For Dublin craft rates and bread prices see Fergus A. D'Arcy, 'Skilled Tradesmen in Dublin, 1800–50; A Study of Their Opinions, Activities, and Organizations' (MA, UCD, 1968), pp.168–76, appendix VII, pp. xliii–li. For other wage rates see the *Third Report from the Commissioners for inquiry into the Condition of the Poorer Classes in Ireland* (BPP 1836), xxx, 100–104; *First Report from the Select Committee to inquire into the state of the law regarding Artisans and Machinery* (BPP 1824), v, 189–90. For conditions of agricultural labourers on the eve of the Famine see John W. Boyle, 'A marginal figure: the Irish rural laborer', in Samuel Clark and James S. Donnelly Jr. (eds), *Irish Peasants: Violence and Political Unrest, 1870–1914* (Dublin 1983), pp.311–38.

6. Except where stated, accounts following of Dublin craft unionism are based on D'Arcy (1968).

7. Anthony D. Buckley, 'On the club; Friendly societies in Ireland', *Irish Economic and Social History*, 14 (1987), 39–58.

8. John W. Boyle, *The Irish Labor Movement in the Nineteenth Century* (Washington D.C., 1988), pp.30–31.

9. See J.J. Webb, *The Guilds of Dublin* (Dublin 1929).

10. For details of trade unionism in Cork at this time see Sean Daly, *Cork, A City in Crisis: A History of Labour Conlict and Social Misery, 1870–1872*. Volume One (Cork 1978), pp.253–314; for dates of the Union of Trades see p.21, p.280.

11. Fergus A. D'Arcy and Ken Hannigan, *Workers in Union* (Dublin 1988), p.3.

12. Boyle (1988), pp.39–41. John Doherty (1799–1854), was born in Buncrana, Co. Donegal and emigrated to Manchester; elected secretary of the Manchester Spinners' Union in 1828, and of the Society for the Enforcement of the Factory Act in 1830; founded the *Conciliator, or Cotton Spinners' Weekly Journal*, the *Voice of the People*, and the *Poor Man's Advocate*; again secretary of the Manchester Spinners, 1834–36, after the failure of attempts to build a national labour organization; retired from public life in 1838. For the response in Belfast see Mel Doyle, 'Belfast and Tolpuddle: attempts at strengthening a trade union presence, 1833–34', *Saothar*, 2 (1974), 2–12.

13. The quotations cited are from the evidence of James Fagan, timber merchant, in the *Report of the Select Committee on Combinations of Workmen* (BPP 1837–38), viii, 388.

14. *Report of the Select Committee on Combinations of Workmen* (BPP 1837–38), viii, 336, 506–11.
15. See reprint of article in the *Waterford Mirror*, 2 April 1842.
16. George Cornewall Lewis, *Local Disturbances in Ireland* (London 1836). For a general account of Whiteboy and Ribbon activity see Donal McCartney, *The Dawning of Democracy; Ireland, 1800–1870* (Dublin, 1987), pp.63–109. For a study of Rockism see James S. Donnelly Jr, 'Pastorini and Captain Rock: millenarianism and sectarianism in the Rockite movement of 1821–4', in Clark and Donnelly (eds), pp.102–39.
17. Accounts following of craft unionism in Dublin are based on D'Arcy (1968).
18. Quoted in the *Dublin Evening Mail*, 27 April 1825. See also D'Arcy (1968), p.23.
19. *Waterford Mirror*, 4 March 1826.
20. Quoted in D'Arcy (1968), pp.29–30.
21. Boyle (1988), pp.26–27; Henry Patterson, 'Industrial labour and the labour movement, 1820–1914', in Kennedy and Ollerenshaw, pp.158–83.
22. Maura Murphy, 'The working classes of nineteenth-century Cork', *Journal of the Cork Historical and Archaeological Society* (1980), 28; Andy Bielenberg, 'Bandon weavers and the industrial revolution', *Labour History News*, 3 (1987).
23. Gearóid Ó Túathaigh, *Ireland Before the Famine, 1798–1848* (Dublin 1972), pp.118–19; Cullen, pp.108–9.
24. See F.A. D'Arcy, 'The murder of Thomas Hanlon; an episode in nineteenth-century Dublin labour history', *Dublin Historical Record*, 4 (1971), 89–100.
25. Boyle (1988), pp.37–38. For a report of the general turnout at Clonmel see the *Waterford Mirror*, 6 October 1828.
26. For a concise account of the tithe question see Ó Túathaigh, pp.173–82.
27. Quoted in K. Theodore Hoppen, *Ireland Since 1800: Conflict and Conformity* (London 1989), p.19.
28. Belfast *Newsletter*, 4 February 1834. For conflict in 1834–35 see Boyle (1988), pp.38–41. For Belfast see also Doyle. Kerr's pamphlet cited below is reprinted in Andrew Boyd, *The Rise of the Irish Trade Unions* (Tralee 1985), pp.122–40.
29. See D'Arcy (1968), pp.79–91.
30. For trade unionism in the 1840s see D'Arcy (1968), pp.92–166; Boyle (1988), pp.47–53.
31. Quoted in D'Arcy (1968), pp.122–23.
32. Quoted in D'Arcy (1968), p.125.
33. For Dublin craft societies and Repeal see F.A. D'Arcy, 'The artisans of Dublin and Daniel O'Connell, 1830–47', *Irish Historical Studies*, 66 (1970), 221–43; 'The National Trades' Political Union and Daniel

O'Connell, 1830–1848', *Eire-Ireland*, XVII, 3 (1982), 7–16; and Boyle (1988), pp.41–47. For Dublin Protestant attitudes see Jacqueline Hill, 'The protestant response to repeal; the case of the Dublin working class', in F.S.L. Lyons and R.A.J. Hawkins (eds), *Ireland Under the Union: Varieties of Tension* (Oxford 1980), pp.35–68; and Jacqueline Hill, 'Artisans, sectarianism, and politics in Dublin, 1829–48', *Saothar*, 7 (1981), 12–27.

34. For the economic views of Repealers see Richard Davis, *The Young Ireland Movement* (Dublin 1987), pp.185–200.

35. Rachel O'Higgins, 'Irish trade unions and politics, 1830–50', *Historical Journal*, 4 (1961), 208–17.

36. O'Higgins, 213. See also Brian Inglis, *The Freedom of the Press in Ireland* (1952), pp.204–5.

37. Quoted in D'Arcy (1970), 221.

38. See the *First Report from the Select Committee on Combinations of Workmen: minutes of Evidence* (BPP 1837–38); *Second Report on Combinations of Workmen* (BPP 1837–38).

39. For Owenism in Ireland see J.F.C. Harrison, *Robert Owen and the Owenites in Britain and America* (London 1969), pp.25, 29–30, 170–71.

40. William Thomson (1775–1833), socialist, feminist, atheist, and vegetarian; started a co-operative on his estate at Rosscarbery; wrote *An Inquiry into the Principles of the Distribution of Wealth Most Conducive to Human Happiness* (1824), *Practical Considerations for the Speedy and Economic Establishment of Communities on the Principle of Co-operation* (1825), and *An Appeal of One Half of the Human Race, Women, against the Pretentions of the Other Half, Men, to Retain them in Political, and thence in Civil and Domestic Slavery* (1825); influenced by Bentham and Ricardo, critical of Owen's theories.

41. See Rachel O'Higgins, 'Ireland and Chartism: a Study of the Influence of Irishmen and the Irish Question on the Chartist Movement' (Ph.D. TCD 1959), pp.92–93.

42. Contemporary Owenites left three first-hand accounts of Ralahine: E.T. Craig, *The Irish Land and Labour Question, Illustrated in the History of Ralahine and Co-operative Farming* (London 1882); William Pare, *Co-operative Agriculture: A Solution to the Land Question as Exemplified in the History of the Ralahine Cooperative Association* . . . (London 1870); John Finch, 'Ralahine; or Human Improvement and Human Happiness', *New Moral World*, 31 March to 29 September 1838.

43. James 'Bronterre' O'Brien (1804–64); born in Longford; wrote on Repeal and working-class issues for Carpenter's Political Letters, 1831; edited the *Poor Man's Guardian*, 1832; founded *Bronterre's National Reformer*, 1837; condemned O'Connor's 'dictatorial' leadership of Chartism and clashed with him over Irish and labour policies; advocated

Babeufian schemes for land nationalization; after 1848 he survived as an adult education teacher in London and died in poverty. Feargus O'Connor (1794–1855); born in Connorville, Cork. After quarrelling with O'Connell, he founded the *Marylebone Radical Association*, 1835, and the *Northern Star*, 1837, becoming leader of Chartism and MP for Nottingham from 1847 until committed to an asylum in 1852. His main political interests in the 1840s were Ireland and land reform.

44. Patrick O'Higgins (1790–1854), born in Ballymagrahan, Co. Down; apprenticed to a woollen draper and later a woollen merchant in Dublin; expelled from National Trades Political Union for condemning the Whig Coercion Act; became involved with Chartism in 1840; usually sided with O'Connorites; wrote the tract *Landlord and Tenant* (1845); sceptical of Confederates at first but approved of Confederate-Chartist alliance in 1848. Did not re-enter politics after the Rising, though supported Fullam's Irish Democratic Association. For Chartism in Ireland see O'Higgins (1959); Bernard Reaney, 'Irish Chartists in Britain and Ireland; rescuing the rank and file', *Saothar*, 10 (1984), 94–103; and Takashi Koseki, 'Patrick O'Higgins and Irish Chartism', *Hosei University Ireland-Japan Papers*, 2 (Hosei, n.d.).

45. See Hill (1980) (1981); Hoppen, p.20; Reaney, 98.

46. For rural crime figures see Charles Townshend, *Political Violence in Ireland: Government and Resistance Since 1848* (Oxford 1983), p.24.

47. O'Higgins (1961), 216.

48. For relations between labour, Confederates, and Chartists see O'Higgins (1959) (1961), Reaney, Koseki, and John Saville, *1848; The British State and the Chartist Movement* (Cambridge 1987).

49. Georgina Flynn, 'The Young Ireland movement in Waterford', *Decies*, 19 (1982), pp.53–60.

50. For the Dublin trades' protest against Queen Victoria see the *Freeman's Journal*, 27 July 1849. For the rising see Michael Cavanagh (ed), *Memoirs of General Thomas Francis Meagher* (Worcester, Mass. 1892), p.283.

51. O'Higgins (1959), p.160; D'Arcy (1968), appendix XII, pp.lix–lxi; Reaney.

Chapter 2 (pp.29–45)

1. The undevelopment thesis is argued *a fortiori* in Raymond Crotty, *Ireland in Crisis; A Study in Capitalist Colonial Underdevelopment* (Dingle 1986). For a discussion of income levels see Kieran A. Kennedy, Thomas Giblin, and Deirdre McHugh, *The Economic Development of Ireland in the Twentieth Century* (London 1988), pp.12–25.

2. See Mary E. Daly, *Social and Economic History of Ireland since 1800* (Dublin 1981), and *Dublin, The Deposed Capital; A Social and Economic History, 1860–1939* (Cork 1984), for a closer look.

3. See Liam Kennedy and Philip Ollerenshaw (eds), *An Economic History of Ulster, 1820–1914* (Manchester 1985).

4. Allen Hutt, *British Trade Unionism: A Short History* (London 1975), pp.27–28.

5. J. Dunsmore Clarkson, *Labour and Nationalism in Ireland* (New York 1925), pp.165–66.

6. The bakers' agitation was noted in some detail in Karl Marx, *Capital, Volume 1* (Lawrence and Wishart 1974 ed), p.241. See also Andrew Boyd, *The Rise of the Irish Trade Unions* (Tralee 1985), pp.55–58; John W. Boyle, *The Irish Labor Movement in the Nineteenth Century* (Washington, D.C. 1988), p.55; Emmet O'Connor, *A Labour History of Waterford* (Waterford 1989), p.76.

7. Boyle (1988), pp.104–5; O'Connor, p.76.

8. Boyle (1988), pp.54–61.

9. *Irish People*, 13–27 August, 19 November 1864. For connections between Ireland and the British Congress see Boyle (1988), pp.65–72, 127–43.

10. The Cork unrest is detailed in Sean Daly, *Cork, A City in Crisis: A History of Labour Conflict and Social Misery, 1870–72*, Volume 1 (Cork 1978).

11. Boyle (1988), pp.67–71.

12. O'Connor, p.79; Boyle (1988), pp.339–41; Henry Patterson, *Class Conflict and Sectarianism: The Protestant Working Class and the Belfast Labour Movement, 1868–1920* (Belfast 1980), p.25; *Trade Union Information*, 5, 28 (October 1951), p.9; *Waterford Mail*, 24 September to 24 October 1877.

13. Jim Cooke, *Technical Education and the Foundation of the Dublin United Trades' Council* (Dublin 1987), p.5; Seamus Cody, John O'Dowd, and Peter Rigney, *The Parliament of Labour: 100 Years of Dublin Council of Trade Unions* (Dublin 1986).

14. See L.A. Clarkson, 'Population change and urbanization, 1821–1911', in Kennedy and Ollerenshaw, pp.137–54; Michael Farrell, *Northern Ireland: The Orange State* (London 1976), p.18; L.M. Cullen, *An Economic History of Ireland since 1660* (London 1987), pp.16–62; James Henderson, *A Record Year in My Existence as Lord Mayor of Belfast in 1898* (Belfast 1898).

15. For industrial trends in Ulster see Philip Ollerenshaw, 'Industry, 1820–1914', in Kennedy and Ollerenshaw, pp.62–102. For the impact on labour see Henry Patterson, 'Industrial labour and the labour movement, 1820–1914', in Kennedy and Ollerenshaw, pp.158–80.

16. Eithne McLaughlin, 'Women and work in Derry City; a survey', *Saothar*, 14 (1989), pp.35–45.

17. BPP, *Report Upon Conditions of Work in Flax and Linen Mills* (1893–94), C.7287.XVII.

18. BPP, *Factory Inspectors' Reports for 1865–66* (1866), 3622.XXIV.
19. BPP, *Factory Inspectors' Reports for 1865–66* (1866), 3622.XXIV.
20. Emily Boyle, 'The linen strike of 1872', *Saothar*, 2 (1974), pp.12–22; for trade union organization and membership figures see Boyle (1988), pp.98–99.
21. W.E. Coe, *The Engineering Industry of the North of Ireland* (Belfast 1969), pp.178–82.
22. BPP, *Royal Commission on Labour: Third Report* (1893–94), C.6894. XXXII.
23. Austen Morgan, 'Politics, the labour movement, and the working class in Belfast, 1905–23' (Ph.D, QUB 1978), 54–55.
24. Quoted in Patterson (1985), p.176.
25. See Patterson (1985), p.178; Ronnie Munck, 'The formation of the working class in Belfast, 1788–1881', *Saothar*, 11 (1986), 84; Christopher Norton, 'Unionist Politics, the Belfast Shipyards, and the Labour Movement in the inter-war period' (D.Phil, University of Ulster, Jordanstown 1987), pp.3–8.
26. Boyle (1988), pp.72–74; Patterson (1980), pp.1–12.
27. Patterson (1980), pp.25–27.
28. Joseph Lee, *The Modernization of Irish Society, 1848–1918* (Dublin 1973), pp.2–3.
29. See David Fitzpatrick, 'The disappearance of the Irish agricultural labourer, 1841–1912', *Irish Economic and Social History*, 7 (1980), pp.66–92.
30. The most comprehensive account of labourers' conditions, organization, and politics, is John W. Boyle, 'A marginal figure; the Irish rural laborer', in Samuel Clark and James S. Donnelly Jnr (eds), *Irish Peasants: Violence and Political Unrest, 1780–1914* (Dublin 1983).
31. Boyle (1983), pp.316–17.
32. BPP, *Reports From poor-law inspectors on the wages of agricultural labourers in Ireland* (1870), C.35.XIV.1.
33. Pamela L.R. Horn, 'The National Agricultural Labourers' Union in Ireland, 1873–9', *Irish Historical Studies*, 17, no. 67 (1971), pp.340–52. See also Daly (1978), pp.109–37.
34. Boyle (1983), p.325, p.332; Dan Bradley, *Farm Labourers: Irish Struggle, 1900–1976* (Belfast 1988), p.25.
35. *Waterford News*, 17–24 October 1884.
36. Boyle (1983), pp.332–33. See also Elizabeth R. Hooker, *Readjustments of Agricultural Tenure in Ireland* (Chapel Hill 1938).
37. Boyle (1988), pp.61–65.
38. On Fenianism, Cork, and the First International see Sean Daly, *Ireland and the First International* (Cork 1984). On the International see also Boyle (1988), pp.75–91.

216   *References*

39. Friedrich Engels to Karl Marx, 9 December 1869 in R. Dixon (ed), *Marx and Engels on Ireland* (Moscow 1971), p.283.
40. Boyle (1983), p.332.
41. For the extension of British new model unions to Ireland see Boyle (1988), pp.92–99, and Boyd (1985), pp.51–58.

Chapter 3 (pp.46–66)
1. John W. Boyle, *The Irish Labor Movement in the Nineteenth Century* (Washington D.C. 1988), p.105; for the official history of the United Corporation Workmen see Sean Redmond, *The Irish Municipal Employees' Trade Union, 1883–1983* (Dublin 1983).
2. For official strike statistics for this period see the Board of Trade, *Reports on Strikes and Lock Outs* (BPP 1889, C.6176; 1890, C.6476; 1891, C.6890; 1892, C.7403; 1893, C.7566; 1894, C.7901; 1895, C.8231; 1896, C.8643; 1897, C.9012; 1898, C.9437; 1899, Cd.316; 1900, Cd.689); PROL, Ministry for Labour reports on strikes and lockouts, 1901–6, LAB 34/1–6.
3. The following account of new unionism in transport is based on official records; Boyle (1988), pp.99–103, pp.106–9; and C. Desmond Greaves, *The Irish Transport and General Workers' Union; The Formative Years, 1909–1923* (Dublin 1982), pp.4–7. The official histories of the main societies concerned are A. Marsh and V. Ryan, The Seamen; *A History of the National Union of Seamen, 1887–1987* (Oxford 1989); Eric Taplin, *The Dockers' Union, A History of the National Union of Dock Labourers, 1889–1922* (Leicester 1986); Philip S. Bagwell, *The Railwaymen; The History of the National Union of Railwaymen* (London 1963). For the collapse of the NUDL in Belfast in 1892–1893 see also John Gray, *City in Revolt; James Larkin and the Belfast Dock Strike of 1907* (Belfast 1985), pp.24–25. The National Amalgamated Sailors' and Firemens' Union collapsed in 1894 and was replaced with the National Sailors' and Firemens' Union.
4. See Joseph J. Leckey, 'The railway servants' strike in Co. Cork, 1898', *Saothar*, 2 (1976), pp.39–45.
5. Boyle (1988), pp.105–7; see also Henry Pelling, 'The Knights of Labour in Britain, 1880–1901', *History Review*, IX (1956, no. 2); Shane McAteer, 'The "New Unionism" in Derry, 1889–1892; a demonstration of its inclusive nature', *Saothar*, 16 (1991).
6. Boyle (1988), pp.109–14; Greaves (1982), pp.4–7. For some detail of NUGGL activity in Dublin see Dermot Keogh, *The Rise of the Irish Working Class; the Dublin trade union movement and the labour leadership, 1890–1914* (Belfast 1982), pp.93–104.
7. Based on Board of Trade, *Reports on Strikes and Lock Outs* (BPP 1891), C.6890.

8. Boyle (1988), pp.105, 109–17. For NAUL activities in Belfast see also Henry Patterson, *Class Conflict and Sectarianism; the Protestant Working Class and the Belfast Labour Movement, 1868–1920* (Belfast 1980), pp.30–35.

9. Board of Trade, *Report on Trades Unions, 1896* (BPP 1897), C.8644, XCIX.275; Patterson (1980), pp.37–38.

10. Board of Trade, *Reports on Strikes and Lock Outs* (BPP 1889, C.6176; 1890, C.6476; 1891, C.6890; 1892, C.7403; 1893, C.7566; 1894, C.7901; 1895, C.8231; 1896, C.8643; 1897, C.9012; 1898, C.9437); Board of Trade, *Report on Trade Unions, 1896* (BPP 1897), C.8644, XCIX.275.

11. For Derry see McAteer; for Belfast see Boyle (1988), p.124; Patterson (1980), pp.30–31.

12. PROL, RIC Intelligence notes, CO 903/2, 1887–92. For auto-biographical comments on rural labour organization at this time see Daniel D. Sheehan, *Ireland Since Parnell* (London 1921), pp. 168–86.

13. National Archives, RIC District Inspectors' Crime Special reports on secret societies, DICS/3, 1891–94.

14. J. A. Venn, *The Foundations of Agricultural Economics* (Cambridge 1933), p.231; John W. Boyle, 'A marginal figure: the Irish rural laborer', in Samuel Clark and James S. Donnelly, Jr (eds), *Irish Peasants: Violence and Political Unrest, 1780–1914* (Dublin 1983), p.334.

15. Dan Bradley, *Farm Labourers: Irish Struggle, 1900–1976* (Belfast 1988), pp.24–31.

16. Board of Trade, *Reports on Strikes and Lock Outs, 1892, 1896– 97, 1900* (BPP 1894, 1897–97, 1901), C.7403, LXXXI.1; C.8643, LXXXIV.239; C.9012, LXXXVIII.423; Cd.689, LXXIII.591.

17. Austen Morgan, 'Politics, the labour movement, and the working class in Belfast, 1905–23' (Ph.D. QUB 1978), 54–55.

18. Patterson, pp.23–24, 30–37; see also W.E. Coe, *The Engineering Industry of the North of Ireland* (Belfast 1969), p.91, pp.178–86.

19. For details of trades council membership and foundation dates see Boyle (1988), p.339.

20. See Seamus Cody, John O'Dowd, Peter Rigney, *The Parliament of Labour, 100 Years of the Dublin Council of Trade Unions* (Dublin 1986), pp.30–35; Boyle (1988), pp.155–57.

21. Boyle (1988), pp.132–35; Fergus A. D'Arcy and Ken Hannigan (eds), *Workers in Union* (Dublin 1988), pp.106–110.

22. Boyle (1988), pp.135–36.

23. Boyle (1988), pp.137–40. The son of a '48 man, William Field was prominent in the Nationalist Registration Association, the temperence movement, the Fisherman's Society, and the Dublin Victuallers, which he founded. Elected as an 'Independent Nationalist and Labour candidate' in 1892. Field regularly attended Dublin Mayday meetings

and the ITUC, which, with Dublin trades council, he acted for at Westminster. As a cattle-dealer, he took an interest too in rural labour. Field wrote two plays and was a popular singer. See J.F. Reid, *The Irish Party's Work Epitomised; A Biography of William Field, MP* (Dublin 1918).

24. For details on the formation of Congress see Boyle (1988), pp.127–40.
25. NLI, ITUC, *Report*, 1894.
26. Quoted in Boyle (1988), p.151, fn.32.
27. David Bleakely, 'Trade union beginnings in Belfast and district, with special reference to the period 1881–1900 and to the work of the Belfast and District Trades Council during that period' (MA, QUB 1955), pp.78–82.
28. NLI, ITUC, *Reports*, 1895, 1896, 1902; on ITUC organization and finance see J.D. Clarkson, *Labour and Nationalism in Ireland* (New York 1925), pp. 190–95. For individual union membership see the Board of Trade, *Abstracts of Labour Statistics*, 1902–4, 1905–6 (BPP 1905, 1907), Cd.2491, LXXVI.139; Cd.3690, LXXX.515.
29. NLI, ITUC, *Reports*, 1894–1901.
30. Board of trade, *Reports on Trades Union*, 1896, 1901 (BPP, 1897, 1902), C.8644, XCIX.275; Cd.1348, XCVII.377.
31. See Boyle (1988), pp.224–32, 234–36, 239–43.
32. Cody, O'Dowd, Rigney, pp.32–33.
33. Boyle (1988), pp.278–80, 339. William Walker (1870–1918), the son of a boilermaker, was apprenticed as a joiner in the shipyards and later represented the Amalgamated Society of Carpenters and Joiners on Belfast trades council. During the new unionist period he took a leading role in the organization of platers' helpers and female mill hands, and in the ILP. A full-time officer of his union after 1901, president of Belfast trades council in 1902 and of the ITUC in 1904, Walker became Ireland's best-known trade unionist before Larkin; a statute which lent some credibilitiy to his attempt to reconcile Unionism and Labourism. Shortly after his famous dispute with Connolly over the national question, he left the labour movement for an administrative post under the new National Insurance scheme. His influence had been long on the wane.
34. For Dublin and Belfast see Boyle (1988), pp.251–55, 278–88; Cody, O'Dowd, Rigney, pp.30–46. See also Maura Murphy, 'Fenianism, Parnellism, and the Cork trades, 1860–90', *Saothar*, 5 (1979), 33 Emmet O'Connor, *A Labour History of Waterford* (Waterford 1989), pp.107–9. For the Limerick reference see C. Desmond Greaves, *The Life and Times of James Connolly* (London 1961), p.90.
35. Bradley, pp.26–31; Boyle (1983), p.333.
36. For details of socialist activity during these years see Boyle (1988), pp.173–215. Among the extensive literature on Connolly the

standard biography is Greaves (1961). Samuel Levenson, *James Connolly: A Biography* (London 1973) adopts a more personal focus.

37. A comprehensive account of Belfast working-class politics and William Walker's role is found in Boyle (1988), pp.272–327. See also Patterson, pp.42–61.

Chapter 4 (pp.67–93)

1. The outstanding biography of Larkin is Emmet Larkin, *James Larkin, 1876–1947; Irish Labour Leader* (London 1965). C. Desmond Greaves, *The Irish Transport and General Workers' Union; The Formative Years* (Dublin 1982), p.9 corrects the date and place of Larkin's birth.

2. John Gray, *City in Revolt; James Larkin and the Belfast Dock Strike of 1907* (Belfast 1985) is a very readable study of Larkinism in Belfast.

3. PROL, Ministry of Labour reports on strikes and lockouts, LAB 34/6–7, 34/24–25.

4. Greaves (1982) provides a concise account of Larkin's career and ITGWU activities. A broader, but episodic, treatment of Dublin events at this time is found in Dermot Keogh, *The Rise of the Irish Working Class; The Dublin Trade Union Movement and Labour Leadership* (Belfast 1982).

5. PROL, LAB 34/8, 34/26.

6. This explanation is accepted by Greaves (1982), p.20, and Keogh (1982), pp.135–36.

7. The most detailed account of early Congress politics remains J.D. Clarkson, *Labour and Nationalism in Ireland* (New York 1925); see pp.228–31, and Greaves (1982), pp.44–50.

8. See Seamus Cody, John O'Dowd, and Peter Rigney, *The Parliament of Labour; 100 Years of Dublin Council of Trade Unions* (Dublin 1986), pp.52–94; Henry Patterson, *Class Conflict and Sectarianism; The Protestant Working Class and the Belfast Labour Movement, 1868–1920* (Belfast 1980), pp.62–91; for Cork see Larkin, p.77, Greaves (1982), p.42; Emmet O'Connor, *A Labour History of Waterford* (Waterford 1989), pp.119–21. Official statistics of trades councils are found in Board of Trade, *Seventeenth Report on Trades Unions, 1908–10* (BPP), Cd.6109, XLVII.655.

9. NLI, William O'Brien Ms. 15674(1); for Connolly's career see C. Desmond Greaves, *The Life and Times of James Connolly* (London 1961), pp.185–212.

10. Brendan Mark Browne, 'Trade Boards in Northern Ireland, 1909–45' (Ph.D, QUB 1989), pp.45–56, 340.

11. Henry Pelling, *A History of British Trade Unionism* (London 1974), pp.128–33; a detailed account of unrest is found in Board of Trade, *Report on Strikes and Lockouts in the United Kingdom* (BPP, 1912),

Cd.6472, XLVII.43. For the impact on Ireland see Greaves (1982), pp.59–75; Larkin, pp.89–94.

12. See Bob Holton, *British Syndicalism, 1900–1914* (London 1976).

13. PROL, LAB 34/11, 34/29.

14. For the Wexford town dispute see Michael Enright, *Men of Iron; Wexford Foundry Disputes 1890 & 1911* (Wexford 1987).

15. Based on PROL, LAB 34/11, 34/29.

16. Board of Trade, *Seventeenth Report on Trades Unions, 1908–10* (BPP), Cd.6109, XLVII.655; Board of Trade, *Sixteenth Abstract of Labour Statistics of the United Kingdom, 1912* (BPP, 1914), Cd.7131, LXXX.301.

17. Greaves (1982), p.70.

18. PROL, LAB 34/29.

19. For the dimensions of these disputes see PROL, LAB 34/29–31.

20. Greaves (1982), p.59; O'Connor, p.126.

21. Greaves (1982), pp.64–66; for provincial reaction to the rail strike see, for example, O'Connor, pp.122–23.

22. For a detailed study of Dublin labour see Peter Murray, 'Electoral politics and the Dublin working class before the First World War', *Saothar*, 6 (1980), 8–22. For the wider picture see Arthur Mitchell, *Labour in Irish Politics, 1890–1930; The Irish Labour Movement in an Age of Revolution* (Dublin 1974), pp.27–30, 52–53, 63–64.

23. See Cork Workers' Club, *The Connolly-Walker Controversy; On Socialist Unity in Ireland* (Historical Reprints, No.9). For contrasting views of Connolly's work in Belfast and response to the problem of partition see Greaves (1961), pp.213–45; Kieran Allen, *The Politics of James Connolly* (London 1990), pp.100–122; and Austen Morgan, *Labour and Partition; the Belfast Working Class, 1905–23* (London 1991), pp.145–78.

24. Greaves (1961), pp.224–28; Allen, pp.106–9, 123–25.

25. Patterson, p.81; Morgan, pp.126–39.

26. On the formation of the party see Mitchell, pp.36–40.

27. PROL, LAB 34/31.

28. PROL, LAB 34/31; Greaves (1982), pp.86–93; for Waterford see O'Connor, pp.124–25.

29. We await a biography but for sketches of Murphy's character see Keogh (1982), pp.13–19, and Dermot Keogh, 'William Martin Murphy and the origins of the 1913 lock-out', *Saothar*, 4 (1976), 15–34.

30. There is still no definitive history of the lockout. The official ITGWU account is Greaves (1982), pp.92–121. On Larkin see Larkin, pp.113–58. Keogh (1982), pp.178–244 is strong on the role of the Catholic Church. Cathal O'Shannon (ed.), *Fifty Years of Liberty Hall* (Dublin 1959) includes an assessment by William O'Brien, secretary of the Lock-out Committee in 1913. For contemporary views see also Donal Nevin (ed),

1913: Jim Larkin and the Dublin Lock-out (Dublin, 1964); and the employers' perspective in Arnold Wright, *Disturbed Dublin; The Story of the Great Strike of 1913–13* (London 1914). The social setting is outlined in *Curriculum Development Unit, Dublin 1913; A Divided City* (Dublin 1978); and the social background examined in Mary E. Daly, *Dublin, The Deposed Capital; A Social and Economic History, 1860–1914* (Cork 1985). The main labour printed primary sources are ITUCLP, *Annual Report*, 1914; ITGWU, *Annual Report*, 1918; British TUC, Reports, 1913, 1915. For the report of the government enquiry see *Dublin Disturbances Commission, Official Report on Riots, 30 August to 1 September 1913 and Minutes of Evidence of Enquiry* (BPP 1914), Cd.7269, XVIII.513–990; see also *Board of Trade, Report on Strikes and Lockouts in the United Kingdom in 1913* (BPP 1914), Cd.7658, XXXVI.489.

31. Wright, p.153, p.105.
32. See W.P. Ryan, *The Labour Revolt and Larkinism; The Later Irish Pioneers and the Co-operative Commonwealth* (London 1913).
33. Quoted in Holton, p.188.
34. Larkin, pp.167–69; *Daily Herald*, 3–4 February 1914.
35. For contrasting approaches to this phase of Connolly's life see Greaves (1961), pp.274–347; Allen, pp.120–60; and David Howell, *A Lost Left; Three Studies in Socialism and Nationalism* (Manchester 1986).
36. Eight delegates were unrecorded. Twenty delegates from Ulster and four from Britain attended the Congress. See Mitchell, p.45.
37. For personal accounts of the ICA see P. Ó Cathasaigh [Sean O'Casey], *The Story of the Irish Citizen Army* (Dublin 1919, reprinted London 1980); Frank Robbins, *Under the Starry Plough: Recollections of the Irish Citizen Army* (Dublin 1977). White left the ICA in May to work as a organizer for the Irish Volunteers. In 1916 he led a strike of Welsh miners in an effort to save Connolly's life. See James Robert White, *Misfit: An Autobiography* (London 1930).
38. Greaves (1982), pp.128–38.
39. For Labour electoral activity in Dublin in 1915 see Mitchell, pp.63–67.
40. O'Casey's claim of 1,000 ICA members in Dublin city and county in mid 1914 (Ó Cathasaigh, p.31) is fanciful. The ICA had 340 names on the books in 1915 and mobilized 200 members during Easter Week. See Greaves (1982), p.166. The estimate of ex-ITGWU men with the British army is in J.W. Boyle, 'Irish labor and the rising', *Eire-Ireland, 3* (1967), 128.
41. David Fitzpatrick, 'Strikes in Ireland, 1914–21', *Saothar*, 6 (1980), 36; Board of Trade, *Fourteenth Abstract of Labour Statistics of the United Kingdom, 1908–9* (BPP 1911), Cd.5458, CX.307; Board of Trade, *Report on Strikes and Lock Outs for 1912*, (BPP 1913), Cd.7089, XLVIII.363; Greaves (1961), p.299.

42. Greaves (1982), pp.150–56. For attitudes to the loan of ICA arms to pickets and Connolly's difficulties see Robbins, pp.31–33.
43. For the events surrounding Easter Week see Dorothy Macardle, *The Irish Republic* (London 1968), pp.133–78.
44. Greaves (1961), pp.323–34; Greaves (1982), pp.163–64.
45. Mitchell, pp.70–71; Allen, pp.153–55.
46. Mitchell, pp.71–77. When challenged on the question, the ITGWU President, Tom Foran, declared to congress that his union 'was proud of the actions taken by the Irish Citizen Army', but did not seek to have the report amended.

Chapter 5 (pp.94–116)

1. See L.M. Cullen, *An Economic History of Ireland Since 1660* (London 1987), pp.171–72; David Johnson, *The Interwar Economy in Ireland* (Dublin 1985), pp.3–5.
2. NLI, ITUCLP and ILPTUC, *Annual Reports*, 1916–20.
3. The following account of the wages movement is based on Emmet O'Connor, *Syndicalism in Ireland, 1917–23* (Cork 1988), pp.20–53.
4. For strike statistics during these years see PROL, Ministry of Labour annual reports on strikes and lockouts 1914–21, LAB 34/14–20, 34/32–39. See also David Fitzpatrick, 'Strikes in Ireland, 1914–21', *Saothar*, 6 (1980), pp.26–39, for its fine statistical analysis.
5. See Brendan Mark Browne, 'Trade Boards in Northern Ireland, 1909–45' (Ph.D, QUB 1989), pp.146–57, 340.
6. A further 8,000 or so Irish worked in munitions in Britain. See Imperial War Museum, London, French MSS, memorandum from Sir Thomas Stafford and Sir Frank Brooke to the Viceroy's advisory council, 20 November 1918, 75/46/12; Fitzpatrick (1980), pp.29–34.
7. Philip Bagwell, *The Railwaymen; The History of the National Union of Railwaymen* (London 1963), pp.356–57.
8. For ITGWU activities see especially C. Desmond Greaves, *The Irish Transport and General Workers' Union: The Formative Years* (Dublin 1982).
9. The most detailed account of Labour involvement in the anti-conscription campaign is J. Anthony Gaughan, *Thomas Johnson* (Dublin 1980), pp.86–122.
10. For the impact of growth on trade union organization and policy see O'Connor, pp.60–69. The most vigorous expression of rank and file syndicalism is found in *New Way*, published by industrial unionists in the NUR from 1917 to 1919. The *Voice of Labour* and the *Watchword of Labour* reflected Liberty Hall's flirtation with syndicalism.
11. Soviets are discussed in O'Connor, pp.51–53. See also D.R. O'Connor Lysaght, 'The Munster soviet creameries', *Saotharlann Staire Eireann*, 1 (1981), 36–39.

12. Northern events and the contrast with the south are discussed in O'Connor, pp.168–79. For a more detailed treatment, from a different perspective, see Henry Patterson, *Class Conflict and Sectarianism: The Protestant Working Class and the Belfast Labour Movement, 1868–1920* (Belfast 1980), pp.92–142.

13. Gaughan is a detailed, if apolitical, biography of Johnson. For O'Brien see *Forth the Banners Go; Reminiscences of William O'Brien as Told to Edward MacLysaght* (Dublin 1969), which does not venture beyond 1923 and D.R. O'Connor Lysaght, 'The rake's progress of a syndicalist; the political career of William O'Brien, Irish Labour leader', *Saothar, 9* (1983), 48–62.

14. Daly, an old lieutenant of Larkin's, had hoped to succeed Connolly in the ITGWU but found himself squeezed out by O'Brien, who regarded him as untrustworthy. Daly later allied with Larkin's sister Delia, then at odds with the Irish Women Workers' Union, and tried to build a power-base in the movement among 'Larkinites'. When Daly was elected secretary of Dublin trades council in 1919, the ITGWU disaffiliated and secured Congress recognition for the rival Dublin Workers' Council. Daly hit back in a weekly paper *Red Hand*. Larkin, from New York, asked both sides to patch up their differences, and the split had relatively little effect. See Arthur Mitchell, *Labour in Irish Politics, 1890–1930: The Irish Labour Movement in an Age of Revolution* (Dublin 1974), pp.93–94. For Congress policy at this time see O'Connor, pp.60–69.

15. Mitchell, p.92. Labour-republican relations are discussed in O'Connor, pp.83–95. Brian Farrell, *The Founding of Dail Eireann: Parliament and Nation Building* (Dublin 1971), pp.34–42 considers Labour's decision to abstain from the 1918 general election in detail.

16. Austen Morgan, *Labour and Partition; The Belfast Working Class, 1905–23* (London 1991), pp.254–57.

17. See O'Connor, pp.60–69.

18. NA, Dail Eireann MSS, DE 2/27, 2/52, 2/111, 2/333–34. Etchingham had been a leading trade unionist in Wexford.

19. Liam Cahill, *Forgotten Revolution: Limerick Soviet, 1919, A Threat to British Power in Ireland* (Dublin 1990); Charles Townshend, 'The Irish railway strike of 1920; industrial action and civil resistance in the struggle for independence', *Irish Historical Studies*, XXI, 83 (1979), 212–82.

20. Mitchell, pp.122–29.

21. For the food control crisis see Gaughan, pp.179–84; for the political prisoners strike see Mitchell, pp.119–20.

22. Mitchell, pp.144–53.

23. Gaughan, p.88. Northern events are discussed more fully below.

24. Except where stated the following account is based on O'Connor, pp.96–164.

25. *Voice of Labour*, 17 December 1921, 7–14 January 1922; Charles McCarthy, 'Labour and the 1922 general election', *Saothar*, 7 (1981), 115–21.
26. R.J. Connolly, 'Our party', in the *Workers' Republic*, 27 October 1923. For Communist politics at this time see Mike Milotte, *Communism in Modern Ireland: The Pursuit of the Workers' Republic since 1916* (Dublin 1984), pp.36–69.
27. Milotte, p.66.
28. Mitchell, p.186.

Chapter 6 (pp.117–136)
1. For Congress affiliation figures see Charles McCarthy, *Trade Unions in Ireland 1894–1960* (Dublin 1977), p.635.
2. For the evolution of the Saorstát economy see James Meenan, *The Irish Economy Since 1922* (Liverpool 1971); Kieran A. Kennedy, Thomas Giblin, and Deirdre McHugh, *The Economic Development of Ireland in the Twentieth Century* (London 1988), pp.34–40. The figure for graziers is cited in Raymond Crotty, *Farming Collapse: National Opportunity* (Dublin 1990), p.5.
3. David Johnson, *The Inter-war Economy in Ireland* (Dublin 1985), pp.39, 43; Finbarr Joseph O'Shea, 'Government and Trade Unions in Ireland, 1939–46; the Formulation of Labour Legislation' (MA, UCC 1988), pp.14–15.
4. Statistics for industrial conflict are found in the *Irish Free State Statistical Abstract*, 1931. The disputes with Larkin and the WUI are dealt with in Emmet Larkin, *James Larkin; Irish Labour Leader, 1876–1947* (London 1965), pp. 275–93; Arthur Mitchell, *Labour in Irish Politics, 1890–1930; The Irish Labour Movement in an Age of Revolution* (Dublin 1974), pp.230–35.
5. See D.R. O'Connor Lysaght, 'The rake's progress of a syndicalist; the political career of William O'Brien, Irish labour leader', *Saothar*, 9 (1983), 48–62.
6. C. Desmond Greaves, *The Irish Transport and General Workers' Union; The Formative Years, 1909–23* (Dublin 1982), p.321.
7. McCarthy, pp.110–111 remarks briefly on the declining relevance of trades councils; for Congress efforts at re-organization see J. Anthony Gaughan, *Thomas Johnson* (Dublin 1980), pp.363–64.
8. Cathal O'Shannon (ed). *Fifty Years of Liberty Hall* (Dublin 1959), p.83; Mitchell, pp.196–97.
9. For Labour politics in the 1920s see Mitchell, pp.192ff; on Johnson see Gaughan, pp.212ff.
10. J. Bowyer Bell, *The Secret Army; A History of the IRA, 1916–1970* (London 1972), p.76.

11. Quoted in Mitchell, p.245.
12. Mitchell, p.201.
13. For Labour protests on unemployment see NLI, ILPTUC, *Unemployment 1922–24: The Record of the Government's Failure* (Dublin 1924), MS IR 304 P18.
14. For communist/republican politics at this time see Sean Nolan (ed), *Communist Party of Ireland; Outline History* (Dublin n.d.), pp.7–31; Mike Milotte, *Communism in Modern Ireland; The Pursuit of the Workers' Republic since 1916* (Dublin 1984), pp.70–101; E. Rumpf and A.C. Hepburn, *Nationalism and Socialism in Twentieth-Century Ireland* (Liverpool 1977), pp.91–96.
15. Henry Patterson, *The Politics of Illusion; Republicanism and Socialism in Modern Ireland* (London 1989), p.36.
16. Gaughan, pp.295–325; Mitchell, pp.274–78; Milotte, pp.88–92.
17. For the Labour Party at this time see Enda McKay, 'Changing with the tide; the Irish Labour Party, 1927–33', *Saothar*, 11 (1986), 27–38; Mitchell, pp.278–81. T.J. O'Connell is best remembered for co-founding the Educational Building Society and writing *100 Years of Progress: The Story of the Irish National Teachers' Organization, 1868–1968* (Dublin 1969). For a biographical note see Gaughan, p.477.
18. An account by Tom Johnson of the party's 'first internal crisis' is quoted in Gaughan, pp.471–74. Johnson was not impressed with O'Connell's leadership.
19. Patterson, p.32.

20. Emmet O'Connor, *Syndicalism in Ireland* (Cork 1988), pp.93, 152–53; C. Desmond Greaves, *Liam Mellows and the Irish Revolution* (London 1971).
21. For a critique of O'Donnell's career and of left republican politics at this time see Richard English, 'Peadar O'Donnell; socialism and the republic, 1925–37', *Saothar*, 14 (1989), pp.47–58.
22. Milotte, pp.96–181 discusses the career of contemporary Marxist groups.
23. Patterson, p.46; Milotte, p.100.
24. Milotte, pp.106–10; Bell, pp.111–13.
25. See Eoin O'Leary, 'The Irish National Teachers' Organisation and the marriage bar for women national teachers, 1933–58', *Saothar*, 12 (1987), pp.47–52.
26. Recent interest in Gralton has inspired two pamphlets: Pat Feeley, *The Gralton Affair* (Dublin 1986), and Des Guckian, *Deported: Jimmy Gralton, 1886–1945* (Carrick-on-Shannon 1988). See also Luke Gibbons, 'Labour and local history; the case of Jim Gralton, 1886–1945', *Saothar*, 14 (1989), 85–94.

27. The standard history is Maurice Manning, *The Blueshirts* (Dublin 1971).

28. Milotte, pp.102–21, 141–57.

29. For an account of the conference see *Republican Congress*, 13 October 1934; Milotte, pp.150–57; Sean Cronin, *Frank Ryan, The Search for the Republic* (Dublin 1980), pp.56–58; and Macdara Doyle, 'The Republican Congress (A Study in Irish Radicalism)' (MA, UCD 1988).

30. Gaughan, pp.339–63 offers the most detailed account to date of the Labour Party from 1932 to 1934 and reveals the depth of support within the party for Fianna Fáil during these years. See pp.477–78 for a biographical note on Norton.

31. Emmet O'Connor, *A Labour History of Waterford* (Waterford 1989), p.214.

32. McCarthy, p.112–13.

33. Brian Girvin, 'Protectionism, Economic Development, and Independent Ireland, 1922–60' (Ph.D, UCC 1986), pp.148–56.

34. As K. Theodore Hoppen, *Ireland Since 1800; Conflict and Conformity* (London 1989), p.211 has noted, 'Irish historians (for reasons of social background, ideology, and academic fashion)' have been unsympathetic to Fianna Fáil's policies in the 1930s. Recent economic studies have emphasised the underlying achievements. See Brian Girvin, *Between Two Worlds; Politics and Economy in Independent Ireland* (Dublin 1989), pp.88–130; and Kennedy, Giblin, and McHugh, pp.40–49. M.E. Daly, 'The employment gains from industrial protection in the Irish Free State during the 1930s; a note', *Irish Economic and Social History*, 15 (1988), 71–75 examines the debate on employment creation in detail and upholds the Soviet comparison. For improvements in labour law see R.J.P. Mortished, 'The Industrial Relations Act, 1946', *Journal of the Statistical and Social Inquiry Society of Ireland*, 17 (1946–47), 670–90; *Trade Union Information*, 1, 3 (July 1949), p.7; and Dan Bradley, *Farm Labourers: Irish Struggle* (Belfast 1988), pp.93–111.

35. Johnson, pp.40–41.

36. *Irish Free State Statistical Abstract*, 1931–36; O'Connell, pp.482–84.

37. John Curry, *The Irish Social Services* (Dublin 1980), pp.24–25, p.31.

38. Census, 1926, 1936; *Irish Free State Statistical Abstract*, 1936.

39. McCarthy, p.621a.

40. Gaughan, pp.357–61. For Dublin trades council and fascism in the 1930s see also Seamus Cody, John O'Dowd, and Peter Rigney, *The Parliament of Labour; 100 Years of the Dublin Council of Trade Unions* (Dublin 1986), pp.167–70.

41. Gaughan, pp.361–63; Milotte, pp.158–78.

42. For examples of Labour support for the Christian Front see Michael Gallagher, *The Irish Labour Party in Transition, 1957–82* (Dublin 1982),

p.14; O'Connor (1989), p.241. On support for the Spanish government see Michael O'Riordan, *Connolly Column; the Story of the Irishmen Who Fought in the Ranks of the International Brigades in the National-Revolutionary War of the Spanish People, 1936–1939* (Dublin 1979).

43. The controversy over the party constitution and Norton's intervention on Spain is discussed in Gallagher, pp.13–14.

44. Cornelius O'Leary, *Irish Elections, 1918–1977; Parties, Voters, and Proportional Representation* (Dublin 1979), p.29, p.102.

45. Milotte, pp.159–62; for strike statistics see the *Irish Free State Statistical Abstract, 1931–39*.

46. McCarthy, p.121. Except where stated, the following is based on McCarthy's detailed account, pp.118–68, though the interpretation differs.

47. O'Shea, p.39.

48. Government attitudes and ITGWU complaints are discussed in Girvin (1989), pp.124–25, and McCarthy, pp.182–83.

49. NLI, ITUC, *Report of the Trade Union Conference, 1939, with Terms of Reference and Memoranda of the Commission of Enquiry* (Dublin 1940).

Chapter 7 (pp.137–154)

1. 'War makes the chronic acute', Senator James Douglas, Seanad Éireann Debates, 24 (1940), 14 March, col.1004.

2. *Statistical Abstract of Ireland*, 1939–44.

3. For details of the congress see NLI, ITUC, *Annual Report*, 1939.

4. Charles McCarthy, *Trade Unions in Ireland, 1894–1960* (Dublin 1977), p.194.

5. For an impression of Emergency life see Bernard Share, *The Emergency: Neutral Ireland, 1939–45* (Dublin 1978); strike statistics are in the *Statistical Abstract of Ireland*, 1939–45; for aggregate trade union membership see W.K. Roche and Joe Larragy, 'The trend of unionization in the Irish Republic' in UCD, *Industrial Relations in Ireland; Contemporary Issues and Developments* (Dublin 1987); on the economic impact see James F. Meenan, *The Irish Economy Since 1922* (Liverpool 1970), pp.33–36; L.M. Cullen, *An Economic History of Ireland Since 1660* (London 1987), p.181; on wages see NLI, ITGWU, *Annual Report*, 1942; Dan Bradley, *Farm Labourers: Irish Struggle, 1900–1976* (Belfast 1988), p.109–10; on health, see J.J. Lee, *Ireland, 1912–1985; Politics and Society* (Cambridge 1989), p.314.

6. Finbarr Joseph O'Shea, 'Government and Trade Unions in Ireland, 1939–46; the Formulation of Labour Legislation' (MA, UCC 1988), pp.28–35.

7. Bradley, pp.110–11.

8. Share, p.91.

9. NLI, ITGWU, *Annual Report*, 1942.
10. Bradley, pp.74–92. Dunne later sat as a Labour TD from 1948 to 1956, and 1965 until his death six days after the 1969 general election.
11. A trade union view of the strike is found in Sean Redmond, *The Irish Municipal Employees' Trade Union, 1883–1983* (Dublin 1983), pp.104–7. The most thorough account of the framing of the Trade Union Act (1941) is O'Shea, pp.36–80; see also McCarthy, pp.181–206; and Fergus D'Arcy and Ken Hannigan, *Workers in Union* (Dublin 1988); pp.200–2.
12. For the reaction to the bill see O'Shea, pp.81–123; McCarthy, pp.207–43; Seamus Cody, John O'Dowd, and Peter Rigney, *The Parliament of Labour; 100 Years of Dublin Council of Trade Unions* (Dublin 1986), pp.171–77.
13. Dublin Council of Action circular, quoted in McCarthy, p.209.
14. Commission on Vocational Organisation, *Report* (Dublin, 1944). In reality, de Valera hoped to fob off the vocational lobby in appointing the Commission, and the government gave its report a hostile reception. Ministers and civil servants opposed its demands for greater consultation with social organizations and a diffusion of decision making powers. The CIU later endorsed the report, but with its industrial aspects in mind; some CIU leaders suspected its general thrust as proto-fascist. Whilst vocationalism continued to be championed by Catholic action groups into the 1950s, the public saw it as a relic of the 1930s, out of tune with post-war ideas. See Joseph Lee, 'Aspects of corporatist thought in Ireland; The Commission on Vocational Organisation, 1939–43', in Art Cosgrove and Donal McCartney (eds), *Studies in Irish History* (Dublin 1979), pp.324–46; J.H. Whyte, *Church and State in Modern Ireland, 1923–79* (Dublin 1980), pp.96–119; McCarthy, pp.116–17, 379–82.
15. ee McCarthy, pp.186–89.
16. For an account of *An Cor Deántais* see Share, p.92; J.P. Duggan, *A History of the Irish Army* (Dublin 1991), pp.229, 30, pp.289–90. It was disbanded in 1948.
17. Other unions loaned lesser sums. *An Comhaltas Cána* for example offered £500. See John Campbell, *A Loosely Shackled Fellowship; the History of* Comhaltas Cána (Dublin 1989), p.55.
18. Lee (1979), p.332.
19. ITGWU, *Annual Report*, 1942; McCarthy, p.197, pp.260–61.
20. McCarthy, pp.207–20.
21. McCarthy, pp.230–42.
22. O'Shea, pp.138; McCarthy, pp.237–38.
23. Lee (1989), pp.277–86, p.314; Lemass's evolving labour policy is discussed in Brian Girvin, *Between Two Worlds; Politics and Economy in Independent Ireland* (Dublin 1989), pp.137–57; O'Shea, pp.124–92;

Most. Rev. J. Dignan, *Social Security. Outlines of a Scheme for National Health Insurance* (Sligo 1945). Dignan was Bishop of Clonfert and chairman of the National Health Insurance Society.

24. McCarthy, pp.245–49.
25. McCarthy, pp.238–43, pp.250–51.
26. For electoral details see Michael Gallagher, *Political Parties in the Republic of Ireland* (Manchester 1985), pp.75–76, pp.109–10.
27. McCarthy, pp.253–59 and J. Anthony Gaughan, *Thomas Johnson* (Dublin 1980), pp.376–81 are detailed on the Larkin-O'Brien friction; for the Communist connections see Mike Milotte, *Communism in Modern Ireland; The Pursuit of the Workers' Republic since 1916* (Dublin 1984), pp.183–200.
28. McCarthy, pp.260–61, pp.274–75.
29. McCarthy, p.260, p.273.
30. McCarthy, pp.261–67; NLI, ITUC, *Annual Report*, 1939.
31. McCarthy, pp.272–77.
32. McCarthy, p.277.
33. For example the Bakers included Northern Ireland members; the Women Workers nursed an old fear of being assimilated into the ITGWU; and the WUI secured admittance to the ITUC shortly after the split. There were also influential 'internationalists' in each of those unions; respectively, John Swift, Louie Bennett, and Larkin. On the other hand, the Federation of Rural Workers joined the ITUC like its parent, the WUI, though the secretary, Sean Dunne, was a staunch republican. For a list of affiliations to both Congresses see McCarthy, pp.615–21.
34. The Irish National Teachers' Organization, for example, had initiated the deletion of the Workers' Republic clause in the Labour Party constitution. See Michael Gallagher, *The Irish Labour Party in Transition, 1957–82* (Manchester 1982), p.13.
35. Examples of membership indifference and lack of consultation with members are given in Ken Hannigan, 'British based unions in Ireland; building workers and the split in Congress', *Saothar*, 7 (1981), pp.40–49; Terence Gerard Cradden, 'Trade Unionism and Socialism in Northern Ireland, 1939–53' (Ph.D, QUB 1988), p.353.

Chapter 8 (pp.155–172)
1. For economic developments during these years see Kieran A. Kennedy, Thomas Giblin, and Deirdre McHugh, *The Economic Development of Ireland in the Twentieth Century* (London 1988), pp.55–65.
2. For the background to the Industrial Relations Act see Finbarr Joseph O'Shea, 'Government and Trade Unions in Ireland, 1939–46; the Formulation of Labour Legislation (MA, UCC 1988), pp.147–92. The

Act itself is disected in R.J.P. Mortished, 'The Industrial Relations Act, 1946', *Journal of the Statistical and Social Inquiry Society of Ireland*, 17 (1946–47), pp.670–90.

3. The national pay rounds are discussed in Charles McCarthy, *Trade Unions in Ireland, 1894–1960* (Dublin 1977), pp.539– 40, pp.633–34; Donal Nevin (ed). *Trade Unions and Change in Irish Society* (Cork, 1980), pp.160–67; and Brian J. Hillery, 'An overview of the Irish industrial relations system', in UCD, *Industrial Relations in Ireland* (Dublin 1987), 1–12.

4. I am obliged to Donal Nevin for these details.

5. For strike statistics see the *Statistical Abstract of Ireland*, 1946–59.

6. McCarthy, pp.540–43. Mortished had formerly been secretary of the ILPTUC. He served with the International Labour Organization from 1930 until 1946. He died in 1957.

7. McCarthy, p.302, pp.622–23, p.635.

8. Emmet O'Connor, *A Labour History of Waterford* (Waterford 1989), pp.275–76.

9. The manifesto and accompanying commentary are found in Fergus A. D'Arcy and Ken Hannigan, *Workers in Union* (Dublin 1988), pp.207–12.

10. For communist politics see Mike Milotte, *Communism in Modern Ireland; The Pursuit of the Workers' Republic Since 1916* (Dublin 1984), pp.216–38.

11. J.H. Whyte, *Church and State in Modern Ireland, 1923–79* (Dublin 1980), pp.166–67; O'Connor, p.288.

12. See Ruaidhri Roberts, *The Story of the People's College* (Dublin 1986), pp.1–17; Whyte, pp.161–62.

13. A detailed account of Congress politics is found in McCarthy, pp.360–412.

14. Seamus Cody, John O'Dowd, and Peter Rigney, *The Parliament of Labour: 100 Years of Dublin Council of Trade Unions* (Dublin 1986), pp.190–93.

15. J.J. Lee, Ireland, *1912–1985; Politics and Society* (Cambridge, 1989), p.289.

16. For an account of Lemass's legislative proposals and discussions with the Congresses see McCarthy, pp.378–84, pp.546–49; Paul Bew and Henry Patterson, *Sean Lemass and the Making of Modern Ireland, 1945–66* (Dublin 1982), p.46–47.

17. Hynes's scheme is discussed in McCarthy, pp.379–82, pp.631– 32.

18. Lee, pp.297–98; For a brief history of Clann na Poblachta see Michael Gallagher, *Political Parties in the Republic of Ireland* (Manchester 1985), pp.110–14. For details on party strengths and general election results during these years see Galllagher, pp.156–60.

19. McCarthy, pp.386–88.

20. Lee, pp.303–6; Kennedy, Giblin, and McHugh, pp.55–56. For improvements in housing provision see Lee, p.309; *Statistical Abstract of Ireland, 1946–51.*

21. For an account of the 'Mother and Child' controversy see Whyte, pp.196–302. See also Browne's autobiography *Against The Tide* (Dublin 1986). Norton's attitude to trade union intervention is referred to in Terence Gerard Cradden, 'Trade Unionism and Socialism in Northern Ireland, 1939–1953' (Ph.D, QUB 1988), p.593.

22. Cradden, p.555. The impact of events in Northern Ireland is discussed below.

23. McCarthy, pp.395–412.

24. See for example Cody, O'Dowd, Rigney, p.199; and O'Connor, pp.280–81, p.284.

25. Cody, O'Dowd, Rigney, pp. 199–202. For an account of unemployed protests in Dublin during the 1950s see Evanne Kilmurray, *Fight, Starve, or Emigrate* (Dublin 1988). On Communist involvement see Milotte, p.228.

26. Cody, O'Dowd, Rigney, pp.197–98.

27. McCarthy, pp.403–4.

28. McCarthy, pp.426–47.

29. Michael Gallagher, *The Irish Labour Party in Transition, 1957–82* (Manchester 1982), pp.29–30; Provisional United Trade Union Organization, *A Trade Union Approach; Planning Full Employment* (Dublin n.d. [1956]).

30. McCarthy, pp.437–75.

31. Cited in McCarthy, p.460.

32. Gallagher (1982), p.63, p.75.

33. Gallagher (1982), p.37–38.

34. The 1913 Club was a discussion circle committed to the ideals of independence and social justice. Two of its associates, Deputies Noel Browne and Jack McQuillan, founded the National Progressive Democrats, which was dissolved in 1963 when Browne joined the Labour Party. See Gallagher (1982), p.34.

35. Gallagher (1982), pp.40–41.

Chapter 9 (pp.173–199)

1. K.S. Isles and Norman Cuthbert, *An Economic Survey of Northern Ireland* (Belfast 1957), p.65.

2. D.W. Bleakley, 'The Northern Ireland trade union movement', *Journal of the Statistical and Social Inquiry Society of Ireland* (1954), p.162.

3. J. Boyd H. Black, 'Industrial relations', in R.I.D. Harris, C.W. Jefferson, and J.E. Spencer (eds), *The Northern Ireland Economy; A Comparative Study in the Economic Development of a Peripheral Region* (London 1990), p.211.

4. *Annual Report of the Ministry of Labour for Northern Ireland for the Year 1922* (Belfast), p.18; *Report of the Ministry of Labour for Northern Ireland for the Years 1923–24* (Belfast), pp.34–35.

5. D.S. Johnson, 'The Northern Ireland economy, 1914–39', in Liam Kennedy and Philip Ollerenshaw (eds), *An Economic History of Ulster, 1820–1939* (Manchester 1985), pp.184–223.

6. W. Black, 'Industrial change in the twentieth century', in J.C. Beckett and R.E. Glasscock (eds), *Belfast; The Origins and Growth of An Industrial City* (London 1967), pp.157–168; Johnson, pp.192–93.

7. Patrick Buckland, *A History of Northern Ireland* (Dublin 1981), p.74; Johnson, pp.201–2; Isles and Cuthbert, p.457.

8. To date, studies of labour in Ulster have concentrated on Belfast, but see Jim Quinn, 'Labouring on the margins; trade union activity in Enniskillen, 1917–23', *Saothar*, 15 (1990), pp.57–64. For events in Belfast and the workplace expulsions see Henry Patterson, *Class Conflict and Sectarianism; The Protestant Working Class and the Belfast Labour Movement, 1868–1920* (Belfast, 1980), pp.115–42; Austen Morgan, *Labour and Partition; The Belfast Working Class, 1905–23* (London 1991), pp.250–312; Christopher Norton, 'Unionist Politics, the Belfast Shipyards, and the Labour Movement in the Inter-war period' (D.Phil, University of Ulster, Jordanstown 1987).

9. D.S. Johnson, 'The Belfast Boycott, 1920–22', in J.M. Goldstrom and L.A. Clarkson (eds), *Irish Population, Economy, and Society; Essays in Honour of the Late K.H. Connell* (Oxford 1981), pp.287–307.

10. Morgan, pp.260–62.

11. E. Rumpf and A.C. Hepburn, *Nationalism and Socialism in Twentieth century Ireland* (Liverpool 1977), p.179; Emmet O'Connor; *Syndicalism in Ireland, 1917–23* (Cork 1988), pp.178–79. For a closer look at the Ulster Unionist Labour Association see Maurice Goldring, *Belfast; From Loyalty to Rebellion* (Belfast 1991). The Ulster Workers' Trade Union operated mainly outside Belfast before the expulsions. Its entry into the shipyards was resisted effectively by other unions, who regarded it as 'yellow'. See Norton, pp.46–47. For cross-border union links see Terry Cradden, 'The left in Northern Ireland and the national question; the 'democratic alternative' in the 1940s', *Saothar*, 16 (1991).

12. Morgan, p.283; O'Connor, pp.100–101.

13. Boyd Black, 'Against the trend; trade union growth in Northern Ireland', *Industrial Relations Journal*, 17, 1 (1986), pp.71–80; Bleakley, p.158, cites a figure of 56,000 members in UK registered unions in Northern Ireland in 1933. To this must be added about 4,000 members of Dublin based unions; Isles and Cuthbert, pp.211–21, p.613.

14. Philip S. Bagwell, *The Railwaymen; The History of the National Union of Railwaymen* (London 1963), pp.523–27; Mike Milotte, *Communism*

in Modern Ireland; The Pursuit of the Workers' Republic since 1916
(Dublin 1984), pp.138–39;

15. *Ulster Year Book, 1938* (Belfast), p.163 cites a figure of 75,345 members
of UK unions. To this must be added members of Eire based unions.
Terence Gerard Cradden, 'Trade Unionism and Socialism in Northern
Ireland, 1939–53' (Ph.D, QUB 1988), p.201 cites a figure of 300,000
workers.

16. Buckland, p.81.

17. Rumpf and Hepburn, pp.177–79; Browne, p.227.

18. Edna Donnelly, 'The struggle for Whitleyism in the Northern
Ireland civil service', *Saothar*, 10 (1984), pp.12–18.

19. Browne, pp.221–97; Sabine Wichert, *Northern Ireland Since 1945*
(London 1991), p.22; Isles and Cuthbert, p.61.

20. Charles McCarthy, *Trade Unions in Ireland, 1894–1960* (Dublin 1977),
p.80–81. There was some spontaneous 'blacking' by dockers in
Northern Ireland during the British general strike of 1926. See Milotte,
p.124.

21. Graham Walker, 'The Northern Ireland Labour Party in the 1920s',
Saothar, 10 (1984), pp.19–29. Originally the 'Labour Party (Northern
Ireland)', the more familiar name came into widespread use in the late
1920s and was later adopted formally. To avoid confusion and minimize the acronymic alphabet soup, it will be used here throughout.

22. Walker (1928); For nationalist politics see Michael Farrell, *Northern
Ireland; The Orange State* (London, 1990), pp.98–120.

23. Rumpf and Hepburn, p.196; John Fitzsimons Harbinson, 'A History
of the Northern Ireland Labour Party, 1891–1949' (M.Sc.Econ, QUB
1966), p.295; Cradden, p.441.

24. Harbinson, p.49, p.55; Graham Walker, *The Politics of Frustration;
Harry Midgley and the failure of Labour in Northern Ireland*
(Manchester 1985), pp.86–87; Arthur Mitchell, *Labour in Irish Politics,
1890–1930; the Irish Labour Movement in an Age of Revolution* (Dublin
1974), p.221.

25. Harbinson, p.264.

26. Rumpf and Hepburn, pp.198–200. McMullen and Beattie had been
expelled from Harland and Wolff in the sectarian disturbances of
1912. For Midgley's career see Walker (1985).

27. McCarthy, p.69.

28. Michael Gallagher, *The Irish Labour Party in Transition, 1957–82*
(Manchester 1982), pp.131–32; Harbinson, p.54.

29. Milotte, p.126.

30. Walker (1985), p.60; Cradden, p.104.

31. Milotte, pp.125–28.

32. Milotte, p.135.

33. The following account of the outdoor relief strike is based on Milotte, pp.128–32; Walker (1985), pp.61–67; and Paddy Devlin, *Yes We Have No Bananas; Outdoor Relief in Belfast, 1920–39* (Belfast 1981), pp.116–45.

34. Milotte, pp.132–38; Walker (1985), pp.63–66.

35. Milotte, pp.150–57; Sean Cronin, *Frank Ryan, The Search for the Republic* (Dublin 1980), pp.56–58; and Macdara Doyle, 'The Republican Congress (A Study in Irish Radicalism)' (MA, UCD 1988).

36. Milotte, p.162–66.

37. Milotte, pp.162–66; Walker (1985), pp.75–76; Devlin, p.144.

38. For Midgley's attitude to the riots and Spain see Walker (1985), pp.76–110. Others take a less apologetic view of Midgley. See for example the view of contemporaries in Devlin, p.143; and 'Letting Labour lead; Jack Macgougan and the pursuit of unity, 1913–58', *Saothar*, 14 (1989), p.114.

39. Milotte, pp.169–81; Cronin, p.104; Walker (1985), pp.101–18.

40. Harbinson, pp.84–86; Walker (1985), p.115.

41. Harbinson, p.105; Gallagher, pp.131–32.

42. Walker (1985), p.121. The official history of the period is John W. Blake, *Northern Ireland in the Second World War* (Belfast 1956). See also Robert Fisk, *In Time of War; Ireland, Ulster, and the Price of Neutrality, 1939–45* (London 1985).

43. McCarthy, pp.260–61; Isles and Cuthbert, pp.213–16, p.457.

44. Buckland, p.83; Wichert, p.41.

45. See Brian Barton, *The Blitz: Belfast and the War Years* (Belfast 1989).

46. Wichert, p.41, pp.47–49.

47. For republican politics see Farrell, pp.150–76.

48. McCarthy, pp.260–61; Wichert, p.39.

49. Walker (1985), p.122.

50. Boyd Black (1990), p.218.

51. Milotte, p.205; Harbinson, pp.165–68.

52. Bleakley, p.158; 5,000 has been added to Bleakley's figures to cover members of Eire based unions.

53. Cradden, p.154, p.208; Bleakley, p.160. In one instance unions boycotted a National Insurance Court of Referees because an Ulster Transport and Allied Operatives' Union member sat on the bench. See Cradden, p.433.

54. McCarthy, pp.261–64, pp.316–17.

55. Buckland, pp.81–83.

56. For the 'Midgley affair' and the NILP at this time see Harbinson, pp.105–31. Walker (1985), pp.123ff. discusses Midgley's path to eventual membership of the Unionist Party.

57. 'Jack Macgougan', *Saothar*, 14 (1989), p.115.

58. Cradden, p.165; Harbinson, p.179; Farrell, p.178, p.377n.
59. Cradden, p.158.
60. For the CP in the war years and after see Milotte, pp.200ff.
61. Milotte, p.209; Cradden, p.159.
62. For contrasting interpretations of the results see Rumpf and Hepburn, p.201; Cradden, pp.165–85.
63. Cradden, pp.441–42.
64. Wichert, pp.43–54; Buckland, p.85.
65. Browne, p.299.
66. Wichert, p.62.
67. Wichert, pp.58–60.
68. Buckland, p.94.
69. Bleakely, p.158; McCarthy, p.597; Buckland, p.95.
70. Boyd Black (1990), p.220.
71. Bleakley, pp.158–64; Isles and Cuthbert, pp.211–12.
72. Eithne McLaughlin, 'Women and work in Derry city; a survey', *Saothar*, 14 (1989), p.39.
73. For the NIC and its relations with Stormont see McCarthy, pp.320–49; Cradden, pp.423–89; and Andrew Boyd, *Have the Trade Unions Failed the North?* (Cork 1984), for a more sceptical view.
74. Bleakley, p.163; Cradden, p.432.
75. Bleakley, p.163.
76. Cradden, pp.439–43.
77. See Bob Purdie, 'The Friends of Ireland; British Labour and Irish nationalism, 1945–49', in Tom Gallagher and James O'Connell (eds), *Contemporary Irish Studies* (Manchester 1983), pp.81–94.
78. 'Jack Macgougan', *Saothar*, 14 (1989), p.117. For the events that led to the NILP schism see also Harbinson, pp.190–235, and Cradden, pp.510–42.
79. See Cradden, pp.536–38, pp.603–5; Gallagher, pp.133–35; 'Jack Macgougan', *Saothar, 14* (1989), pp.119–24.
80. McCarthy, p.328.
81. Farrell, pp.223–24; Rumpf and Hepburn, pp.191–92; Gallagher, pp.133–35.
82. Harbinson, pp.220–35.
83. Bleakley, pp.163–67.
84. Cradden, pp.606–8.
85. Andrew Boyd, *Northern Ireland; Who is to Blame?* (Cork 1984), pp.86–92; Bleakley, p.168.
86. Cradden, p.667.
87. Harbinson, p.280.
88. Rumpf and Hepburn, p.206; Cradden, pp.668–69.
89. Gallagher, p.134.

Select Bibliography

CONTENTS

A. Labour reports
B. State papers
C. Books, articles, and pamphlets
D. Dissertations

A. LABOUR REPORTS

British Trade Union Congress, *Reports*, 1913, 1915
Irish Labour Party and Trade Union Congress, *Reports*, 1919–20
——, *Unemployment 1922–24: The Record of the Government's Failure* (1924)
Irish Trade Union Congress, *Reports*, 1894–1902, 1939
——, *Report of the Trade Union Conference, 1939, with Terms of Reference and Memoranda of the Commission of Enquiry* (1940)
Irish Trade Union Congress and Labour Party, *Reports*, 1914–18
Irish Transport and General Workers' Union, *Annual Reports*, 1918, 1942
Provisional United Trade Union Organization, *A Trade Union Approach; Planning Full Employment* (n.d. [1956])

B. STATE PAPERS

1. Irish
Census, 1926, 1936
Dáil Éireann MSS, DE 2/27, 2/52, 2/111, 2/333–34
Irish Free State Statistical Abstract, 1931–37

Royal Irish Constabulary, District Inspectors' Crime Special reports
on secret societies, DICS/3, 1891–94
Seanad Éireann *Debates*, 24 (1940), 14 March
Statistical Abstract of Ireland, 1938–59

2. Northern Ireland

*Annual Report of the Ministry of Labour for Northern Ireland for the
Year 1922*
*Report of the Ministry of Labour for Northern Ireland for the Years
1923–24*
Ulster Year Book, 1938

3. British parliamentary papers

*First Report from the Select Committee to inquire into the state of the
law regarding Artizans and Machinery* (1824, V)
*Third Report from the Commissioners for inquiry into the Condition of
the Poorer Classes in Ireland* (1836, XXX)
Report of the Select Committee on Combinations of Workmen (1837–38,
VIII)
*First Report from the Select Committee on Combinations of Workmen:
minutes of Evidence* (1837–38)
Second Report on Combinations of Workmen (1837–38)
Factory Inspectors' Reports for 1865–66 (1866, 3622, XXIV)
*Reports from poor-law inspectors on the wages of agricultural labourers in
Ireland* (1870, C.35, XIV)
Royal Commission on Labour: Third Report (1893–94, C.6894, XXXII)
Report Upon Conditions of Work in Flax and Linen Mills (1893–94,
C.7287, XVII)
Board of Trade, *Reports on Strikes and Lock Outs* (1889, C.6176; 1890,
C.6476; 1891, C.6890; 1892, C.7403; 1893, C.7566; 1894, C.7901;
1895, C.8231; 1896, C.8643; 1897, C.9012; 1898, C.9437; 1899,
Cd.316; 1900, Cd.689; 1912, Cd.6472; 1913, Cd.7658, XXXVI)
——, *Reports on Trades Unions* (1896, C.8644, XCIX; 1901, Cd.1348,
XCVII; 1908–10, Cd.6109, XLVII)
——, *Abstracts of Labour Statistics* (1902–4, Cd.2491, LXXVI; 1905–6,
Cd.3690, LXXX; 1908–9, Cd.5458, CX; 1912, Cd.7131, LXXX)
*Dublin Disturbances Commission, Official Report on Riots, 30 August to
1 September 1913 and Minutes of Evidence of Enquiry* (1914,
Cd.7269, XVIII)

4. *Manuscript material in the Public Record Office, London*
Ministry of Labour reports on strikes and lockouts, 1901–21, LAB 34/1–20, 34/24–39
Royal Irish Constabulary, Intelligence notes, CO 903/2, 1887–92

C. BOOKS, ARTICLES, AND PAMPHLETS

1. Labour

Allen, Kieran, *The Politics of James Connolly* (London 1990)

Bagwell, Philip S., *The Railwaymen; The History of the National Union of Railwaymen* (London 1963)

Bielenberg, Andy, 'Bandon weavers and the industrial revolution', *Labour History News*, 3 (1987)

Black, Boyd, 'Against the trend; trade union growth in Northern Ireland', *Industrial Relations Journal*, 17, 1 (1986)

——, 'Industrial relations', in R.I.D. Harris, C.W. Jefferson, and J.E. Spencer (eds), *The Northern Ireland Economy; A Comparative Study in the Economic Development of a Peripheral Region* (London 1990)

Bleakley, D.W., 'The Northern Ireland trade union movement', *Journal of the Statistical and Social Inquiry Society of Ireland* (1954)

Boyd, Andrew, *Have the Trade Unions Failed the North?* (Cork 1984)

——, *The Rise of the Irish Trade Unions* (Tralee 1985)

Boyle, Emily, 'The linen strike of 1872', *Saothar*, 2 (1974)

Boyle, John W., 'Irish labor and the rising', *Éire-Ireland*, 3 (1967)

——, 'A marginal figure; the Irish rural laborer', in Samuel Clark and James S. Donnelly Jr (eds), *Irish Peasants: Violence and Political Unrest, 1870-1914* (Dublin 1983)

——, *The Irish Labor Movement in the Nineteenth Century* (Washington D.C. 1988)

Bradley, Dan, *Farm Labourers: Irish Struggle, 1900–1976* (Belfast 1988)

Browne, Noel, *Against The Tide* (Dublin 1986)

Cahill, Liam, *Forgotten Revolution: Limerick Soviet, 1919, A Threat to British Power in Ireland* (Dublin 1990)

Campbell, John, *A Loosely Shackled Fellowship; the History of Comhaltas Cana* (Dublin 1989)

Cavanagh, Michael (ed), *Memoirs of General Thomas Francis Meagher* (Worcester, Mass. 1892)

Cody, Seamus, John O Dowd, and Peter Rigney, *The Parliament of Labour: 100 Years of Dublin Council of Trade Unions* (Dublin 1986)

Clarkson, J. Dunsmore, *Labour and Nationalism in Ireland* (New York 1925)

Cooke, Jim, *Technical Education and the Foundation of the Dublin United Trades' Council* (Dublin 1987)

Cork Workers' Club, *The Connolly-Walker Controversy; On Socialist Unity in Ireland* (Historical Reprints, No.9)

Cradden, Terry, 'The left in Northern Ireland and the national question: the 'democratic alternative ' in the 1940s', *Saothar*, 16 (1991)

Craig, E.T., *The Irish Land and Labour Question, Illustrated in the History of Ralahine and Co-operative Farming* (London 1882)

Cronin, Sean *Frank Ryan, The Search for the Republic* (Dublin 1980)

Daly, Sean, *Cork: A City in Crisis. A History of Labour Conlict and Social Misery, 1870–1872.* Volume One (Cork 1978)

——, *Ireland and the First International* (Cork 1984)

D'Arcy, Fergus A., 'The Artisans of Dublin and Daniel O'Connell, 1830–47', *Irish Historical Studies*, 66 (1970)

——, 'The murder of Thomas Hanlon; an episode in nineteenth century Dublin labour history', *Dublin Historical Record*, 4 (1971)

——, 'The National Trades' Political Union and Daniel O'Connell, 1830–1848', *Éire-Ireland*, XVII, 3 (1982)

—— and Ken Hannigan, *Workers in Union; Documents and Commentaries on the History of Irish Labour* (Dublin, 1988)

Dixon, R. (ed), *Marx and Engels on Ireland* (Moscow 1971)

Donnelly, Edna, 'The struggle for Whitleyism in the Northern Ireland civil service', *Saothar*, 10 (1984)

Doyle, Mel, 'Belfast and Tolpuddle: attempts at strengthening a trade union presence, 1833–34', *Saothar*, 2 (1974)

Enright, Michael, *Men of Iron; Wexford Foundry Disputes 1890 & 1911* (Wexford 1987)

English, Richard, 'Peadar O Donnell; socialism and the republic, 1925–37', *Saothar*, 14 (1989)

Feeley, Pat, *The Gralton Affair* (Dublin 1986)

Finch, John, 'Ralahine; or human improvement and human happiness', *New Moral World*, 31 March to 29 September 1838

Fitzpatrick, David, 'Strikes in Ireland, 1914–21', *Saothar*, 6 (1980)

——, 'The disappearance of the Irish agricultural labourer, 1841–1912', *Irish Economic and Social History*, 7 (1980)

Gallagher, Michael, *The Irish Labour Party in Transition, 1957–82* (Dublin 1982)

Gaughan, J. Anthony, *Thomas Johnson* (Dublin 1980)

Gibbons, Luke, 'Labour and local history; the case of Jim Gralton, 1886–1945', *Saothar*, 14 (1989)

Gray, John, *City in Revolt; James Larkin and the Belfast Dock Strike of 1907* (Belfast 1985)

Greaves, C. Desmond, *The Life and Times of James Connolly* (London 1961)

——, *Liam Mellows and the Irish Revolution* (London 1971)

——, *The Irish Transport and General Workers' Union; The Formative Years* (Dublin 1982)

Guckian, Des, *Deported: Jimmy Gralton, 1886–1945* (Carrick on Shannon 1988)

Hannigan, Ken, 'British based unions in Ireland; building workers and the split in Congress', *Saothar*, 7 (1981)

Hill, Jacqueline, 'The protestant response to repeal; the case of the Dublin working class', in F.S.L. Lyons and R.A.J. Hawkins (eds), *Ireland Under the Union; Varieties of Tension* (Oxford 1980)

——, 'Artisans, sectarianism, and politics in Dublin, 1829–48', *Saothar*, 7 (1981)

Hillery, Brian, J., 'An overview of the Irish industrial relations system', in UCD, *Industrial Relations in Ireland* (Dublin 1987)

Holton, Bob, *British Syndicalism, 1900–1914* (London 1976)

Horn, Pamela L.R., 'The National Agricultural Labourers' Union in Ireland, 1873–9', *Irish Historical Studies*, 17, no.67 (1971)

Howell, David, *A Lost Left; Three Studies in Socialism and Nationalism* (Manchester 1986)

Hutt, Allen, *British Trade Unionism: A Short History* (London 1975)

Keogh, Dermot, 'William Martin Murphy and the origins of the 1913 lock-out', *Saothar*, 4 (1976)

——, *The Rise of the Irish Working Class; the Dublin trade union movement and the labour leadership, 1890–1914* (Belfast 1982)

Kilmurray, Evanne, *Fight, Starve, or Emigrate* (Dublin 1988)

Koseki, Takashi, 'Patrick O Higgins and Irish Chartism', *Hosei University Ireland-Japan Papers*, 2 (Hosei, n.d.)

Larkin, Emmet, *James Larkin, 1876–1947; Irish Labour Leader* (London 1965)

Leckey, Joseph J., 'The railway servants' strike in Co. Cork, 1898', *Saothar*, 2 (1976)

'Letting Labour lead; Jack Macgougan and the pursuit of unity, 1913–58', *Saothar*, 14 (1989)

Levenson, Samuel, *James Connolly: A Biography* (London 1973)

McAteer, Shane, 'The 'New Unionism' in Derry, 1889–1892; a demonstration of its inclusive nature', *Saothar*, 16 (1991)

McCarthy, Charles, *Trade Unions in Ireland 1894–1960* (Dublin 1977)

——, 'Labour and the 1922 general election', *Saothar*, 7 (1981)

McKay, Enda, 'Changing with the tide; the Irish Labour Party, 1927–33', *Saothar*, 11 (1986), 27–38

McLaughlin, Eithne, 'Women and work in Derry City; a survey', *Saothar*, 14 (1989)

Marsh A. and V. Ryan, *The Seamen; A History of the National Union of Seamen, 1887–1987* (Oxford, 1989)

Marx, Karl, *Capital, Volume 1* (London 1974 ed)

Milotte, Mike, *Communism in Modern Ireland: The Pursuit of the Workers' Republic since 1916* (Dublin 1984)

Mitchell, Arthur, *Labour in Irish Politics, 1890–1930; The Irish Labour Movement in an Age of Revolution* (Dublin 1974)

Morgan, Austen, *Labour and Partition; The Belfast Working Class, 1905–23* (London 1991)

Mortished, R.J.P., 'The Industrial Relations Act, 1946', *Journal of the Statistical and Social Inquiry Society of Ireland*, 17 (1946–47)

Munck, Ronnie, 'The formation of the working class in Belfast, 1788–1881', *Saothar*, 11 (1986)

Murphy, Maura, 'Fenianism, Parnellism, and the Cork trades, 1860–90', *Saothar*, 5 (1979)

——, 'The working classes of nineteenth century Cork', *Journal of the Cork Historical and Archaeological Society* (1980)

Murray, Peter, 'Electoral politics and the Dublin working class before the First World War', *Saothar*, 6 (1980)

Nevin, Donal (ed), *1913: Jim Larkin and the Dublin Lock-out* (Dublin 1964)

—— (e.d), *Trade Unions and Change in Irish Society* (Cork 1980)

Nolan, Sean (ed), *Communist Party of Ireland; Outline History* (Dublin, n.d.),

O'Brien, William, *Forth the Banners Go; Reminiscences of William O'Brien as Told to Edward MacLysaght* (Dublin 1969)

Ó Cathasaigh, P. [Sean O'Casey], *The Story of the Irish Citizen Army* (Dublin 1919, reprinted London 1980)

O'Connell, T.J., *100 Years of Progress: The Story of the Irish National Teachers' Organization, 1868–1968* (Dublin 1969)

O'Connor, Emmet, *Syndicalism in Ireland, 1917–23* (Cork 1988)

——, *A Labour History of Waterford* (Waterford 1989)

O'Connor Lysaght, D.R., 'The Munster soviet creameries', *Saotharlann Staire Éireann*, 1 (1981)

O'Connor Lysaght, D.R., 'The rake's progress of a syndicalist; the political career of William O Brien, Irish Labour leader', *Saothar*, 9 (1983)

O'Higgins, Rachel, 'Irish trade unions and politics, 1830–50', *Historical Journal*, 4 (1961)

O'Leary, Eoin, 'The Irish National Teachers' Organisation and the marriage bar for women national teachers, 1933–58', *Saothar*, 12 (1987)

O'Shannon, Cathal (ed), *Fifty Years of Liberty Hall* (Dublin 1959)

O'Riordan, Michael, *Connolly Column; the Story of the Irishmen Who Fought in the Ranks of the International Brigades in the National-Revolutionary War of the Spanish People, 1936–1939* (Dublin 1979)

Pare, William, *Cooperative Agriculture: A Solution to the Land Question as Exemplified in the History of the Ralahine Cooperative Association . . .* (London 1870)

Patterson, Henry, *Class Conflict and Sectarianism: The Protestant Working Class and the Belfast Labour Movement, 1868–1920* (Belfast 1980)

——, 'Industrial labour and the labour movement, 1820–1914', in Liam Kennedy and Philip Ollerenshaw (eds), *An Economic History of Ulster, 1820–1939* (Manchester 1985)

——, *The Politics of Illusion; Republicanism and Socialism in Modern Ireland* (London 1989)

Pelling, Henry, 'The Knights of Labour in Britain, 1880–1901', *History Review*, IX (1956, no.2)

——, *A History of British Trade Unionism* (London 1971)

Pender, Seamus, 'The guilds of Waterford, 1650–1700, parts I-V', *Journal of the Cork Historical and Archaeological Society*, 58–62 (1953–57)

Purdie, Bob, 'The Friends of Ireland; British Labour and Irish nationalism, 1945–49', in Tom Gallagher and James O Connell (eds), *Contemporary Irish Studies* (Manchester 1983)

Quinn, Jim, 'Labouring on the margins; trade union activity in Enniskillen, 1917–23', *Saothar*, 15 (1990)

Reaney, Bernard, 'Irish Chartists in Britain and Ireland; rescuing the rank and file', *Saothar*, 10 (1984)

Redmond, Sean, *The Irish Municipal Employees' Trade Union, 1883–1983* (Dublin 1983)

Reid, J.F., *The Irish Party's Work Epitomised; A Biography of William Field, MP* (Dublin 1918)

Robbins, Frank, *Under the Starry Plough: Recollections of the Irish Citizen Army* (Dublin 1977)

Roberts, Paul E.W., 'Caravats and Shanavests; Whiteboyism and faction fighting in east Munster, 1802–11', in Samuel Clark and James S. Donnelly Jr, *Irish Peasants; Violence and Political Unrest, 1780–1914* (Dublin 1983)

Roberts, Ruaidhri, *The Story of the People's College* (Dublin 1986)

Roche, W.K. and Joe Larragy, 'The trend of unionization in the Irish Republic' in UCD, *Industrial Relations in Ireland; Contemporary Issues and Developments* (Dublin 1987)

Rumpf, E. and A.C. Hepburn, *Nationalism and Socialism in Twentieth Century Ireland* (Liverpool 1977)

Ryan, W.P., *The Labour Revolt and Larkinism; The Later Irish Pioneers and the Co-operative Commonwealth* (London 1913)

Saville, John, *1848; The British State and the Chartist Movement* (Cambridge 1987)

Swift, John, *History of the Dublin Bakers and Others* (Dublin 1948)

Taplin, Eric, *The Dockers' Union, A History of the National Union of Dock Labourers, 1889–1922* (Leicester 1986)

Townshend, Charles, 'The Irish railway strike of 1920; industrial action and civil resistance in the struggle for independence', *Irish Historical Studies*, XXI, 83 (1979)

Walker, Graham, 'The Northern Ireland Labour Party in the 1920s', *Saothar*, 10 (1984)

——, *The Politics of Frustration; Harry Midgley and the failure of Labour in Northern Ireland* (Manchester 1985)

Webb, J.J., *The Guilds of Dublin* (Dublin 1929)

White, James Robert, *Misfit: An Autobiography* (London 1930)

Wright, Arnold, *Disturbed Dublin; The Story of the Great Strike of 1913–13* (London 1914)

2. General

Barton, Brian, *The Blitz: Belfast and the War Years* (Belfast, 1989)

Beames, M.R., *Peasants and Power; The Whiteboy Movements and their Control in Pre-Famine Ireland* (Brighton 1983)

Bell, J. Bowyer, *The Secret Army; A History of the IRA, 1916–1970* (London 1972)

Bew, Paul and Henry Patterson, *Sean Lemass and the Making of Modern Ireland, 1945–66* (Dublin 1982)

Black, W., 'Industrial change in the twentieth century', in J.C. Beckett and R.E. Glasscock (eds), *Belfast; The Origins and Growth of An Industrial City* (London 1967)

Blake, John W., *Northern Ireland in the Second World War* (Belfast 1956)

Boyd, Andrew, *Northern Ireland; Who is to Blame?* (Cork 1984)

Buckland, Patrick, *A History of Northern Ireland* (Dublin 1981)

Buckley, Anthony D., 'On the club; Friendly societies in Ireland', *Irish Economic and Social History*, 14 (1987)

Clarkson, L.A., 'Population change and urbanization, 1821–1911', in Liam Kennedy and Philip Ollerenshaw, *An Economic History of Ulster, 1820–1939* (Manchester 1985)

Coe, W.E., *The Engineering Industry of the North of Ireland* (Belfast 1969)

Commission on Vocational Organisation, *Report* (Dublin 1944)

Crotty, Raymond, *Ireland in Crisis; A Study in Capitalist Colonial Underdevelopment* (Dingle 1986)

——, *Farming Collapse: National Opportunity* (Dublin 1990)

Cullen, L.M., *An Economic History of Ireland since 1660* (London 1987)

Curriculum Development Unit, *Dublin, 1913; A Divided City* (Dublin 1978)

Curry, John, *The Irish Social Services* (Dublin 1980)

Daly, Mary E., *Social and Economic History of Ireland since 1800* (Dublin 1981)

——, *Dublin, The Deposed Capital; A Social and Economic History, 1860–1914* (Cork 1984)

——, 'The employment gains from industrial protection in the Irish Free State during the 1930s; a note', *Irish Economic and Social History*, 15 (1988)

Davis, Richard, *The Young Ireland Movement* (Dublin 1987)

Devlin, Paddy, *Yes We Have No Bananas; Outdoor Relief in Belfast, 1920–39* (Belfast 1981)

Dignan, Most Rev. J., *Social Security. Outlines of a Scheme for National Health Insurance* (Sligo 1945).

Donnelly, James S. Jr, 'Pastorini and Captain Rock: millenarianism and sectarianism in the Rockite movement of 1821–4', in Samuel Clark and James S. Donnelly Jr (eds), *Irish Peasants: Violence and Political Unrest, 1870–1914* (Dublin 1983)

Duggan, J.P., *A History of the Irish Army* (Dublin 1991)

Farrell, Brian, *The Founding of Dáil Éireann: Parliament and Nation Building* (Dublin 1971)

Farrell, Michael, *Northern Ireland: The Orange State* (London 1980)

Fisk, Robert, *In Time of War; Ireland, Ulster, and the Price of Neutrality, 1939–45* (London 1985)

Flynn, Georgina, 'The Young Ireland movement in Waterford', *Decies*, 19 (1982)

Gallagher, Michael, *Political Parties in the Republic of Ireland* (Manchester 1985)

Girvin, Brian, *Between Two Worlds; Politics and Economy in Independent Ireland* (Dublin 1989)

Goldring, Maurice, *Belfast; From Loyalty to Rebellion* (Belfast 1990)

Harrison, J.F.C., *Robert Owen and the Owenites in Britain and America* (London 1969)

Henderson, James, *A Record Year in My Existence as Lord Mayor of Belfast in 1898* (Belfast 1898)

Hooker, Elizabeth, R., *Readjustments of Agricultural Tenure in Ireland* (Chapel Hill 1938)

Hoppen, K. Theodore, *Ireland Since 1800: Conflict and Conformity* (London 1989)

Inglis, Brian, *The Freedom of the Press in Ireland*, London (1952)

Isles, K.S. and Norman Cuthbert, *An Economic Survey of Northern Ireland* (Belfast 1957)

Johnson, D.S., 'The Belfast Boycott, 1920–22', in J.M. Goldstrom and L.A. Clarkson (eds), *Irish Population, Economy, and Society; Essays in Honour of the Late K.H. Connell* (Oxford 1981)

——, D.S., *The Interwar Economy in Ireland* (Dublin 1985)

——, 'The Northern Ireland economy, 1914–39', in Liam Kennedy and Philip Ollerenshaw (eds), *An Economic History of Ulster, 1820–1939* (Manchester 1985)

Kane, Robert, *The Industrial Resources of Ireland* (Shannon 1971, first ed. Dublin, 1844)

Kennedy, Kieran A., Thomas Giblin, and Deirdre McHugh, *The Economic Development of Ireland in the Twentieth Century* (London 1988)

Kennedy, Liam and Philip Ollerenshaw (eds), *An Economic history of Ulster, 1820–1939* (Manchester 1985)

Lee, Joseph J., *The Modernization of Irish Society, 1848–1918* (Dublin 1973)

——, 'Aspects of corporatist thought in Ireland; The Commission on Vocational Organisation, 1939–43', in Art Cosgrove and Donal McCartney (eds), *Studies in Irish History* (Dublin 1979)

——, *Ireland, 1912–1985; Politics and Society* (Cambridge 1989)

Lewis, George Cornewall, *Local Disturbances in Ireland* (London 1836)

Macardle, Dorothy, *The Irish Republic* (London 1968)

McCartney, Donal, *The Dawning of Democracy; Ireland, 1800–1870* (Dublin 1987)

Manning, Maurice, *The Blueshirts* (Dublin 1971)

Meenan, James, *The Irish Economy Since 1922* (Liverpool 1971)

O'Leary, Cornelius, *Irish Elections, 1918–1977; Parties, Voters, and Proportional Representation* (Dublin 1979)

Ollerenshaw, Philip, 'Industry, 1820–1914', in Liam Kennedy and Philip Ollerenshaw, *An Economic History of Ulster, 1820–1939* (Manchester 1985)

Ó Tuathaigh, Gearóid, *Ireland Before the Famine, 1798–1848* (Dublin 1972)

Share, Bernard, *The Emergency: Neutral Ireland, 1939–45* (Dublin 1978)

Sheehan, Daniel D., *Ireland Since Parnell* (London 1921)

Townshend, Charles, *Political Violence in Ireland: Government and Resistance Since 1848* (Oxford 1983)

Venn, J.A., *The Foundations of Agricultural Economics* (Cambridge 1933)

Whyte, J.H., *Church and State in Modern Ireland, 1923–79* (Dublin 1980)

Wichert, Sabine, *Northern Ireland Since 1945* (London, 1991)

D. DISSERTATIONS

Bleakely, David, 'Trade Union beginnings in Belfast and district, with special reference to the period 1881–1900 and to the work of the Belfast and District Trades Council during that period' (MA, QUB 1955)

Browne, Brendan Mark, 'Trade Boards in Northern Ireland, 1909–45' (Ph.D, QUB 1989)

Cradden, Terence Gerard, 'Trade Unionism and Socialism in Northern Ireland, 1939–53' (Ph.D, QUB 1988)

D'Arcy, Fergus A., 'Skilled Tradesmen in Dublin, 1800–50; A Study of Their Opinions, Activities, and Organizations' (MA, UCD 1968)

Doyle, Macdara, 'The Republican Congress (A Study in Irish Radicalism)' (MA, UCD 1988)

Doyle, M.G, 'The Development of Industrial Organizations amongst Skilled Artisans in Ireland, 1780–1838' (M.Phil, Southampton 1973)

Harbinson, John Fitzsimons, 'A History of the Northern Ireland Labour Party, 1891–1949' (M.Sc.Econ, QUB 1966)

Norton, Christopher, 'Unionist Politics, the Belfast Shipyards, and the Labour Movement in the Inter-war period' (D.Phil, University of Ulster, Jordanstown 1987)

O'Higgins, Rachel, 'Ireland and Chartism: a Study of the Influence of Irishmen and the Irish Question on the Chartist Movement' (Ph.D, TCD, 1959)

O'Shea, Finbarr Joseph, 'Government and Trade Unions in Ireland, 1939–46; the Formulation of Labour Legislation' (MA, UCC 1988)

Index